AN AUTOBIOGRAPHY VOLUME I

THE SKY IS NO LIMIT

PER WIMMER

Published by
LID Publishing
An imprint of LID Business Media Ltd.
LABS House, 15-19 Bloomsbury Way,
London, WC1A 2TH, UK

info@lidpublishing.com
www.lidpublishing.com

A member of:

businesspublishersroundtable.com

Printed by Gutenberg Press, Malta
ISBN: 978-1-911687-28-3
ISBN: 978-1-911687-29-0 (ebook)

Cover and page design: Caroline Li

AN AUTOBIOGRAPHY VOLUME I

THE SKY IS NO LIMIT

PER WIMMER

MADRID | MEXICO CITY | LONDON
BUENOS AIRES | BOGOTA | SHANGHAI

THE SKY IS NO LIMIT

LEE WERNER

CONTENTS

FOREWORD

When I first stepped on the Moon in July 1969 together with Neil Armstrong and looked back upon our beautiful Earth, it was the culmination of many years of determination and efforts. The view was uniquely beautiful and – even today – the image stands as clear in my mind as if it was yesterday. With people around the world watching the first Moon landing, we knew that this was a historic milestone in the quest of mankind to conquer space.

Now, we are at the beginning of a new revolution within space exploration: the opening of space to purely private, non-governmental initiatives in space. Few can probably appreciate the full implications ahead, just as we couldn't during the Apollo program. Yet, with all the creativity, entrepreneurship and competitiveness that private enterprise brings along, space is likely to experience a strongly renewed interest.

My good friend, Per Wimmer, space pioneer, space enthusiast, financier and philanthropist is one of the persons at the forefront of this development. Having bought his first – of several – trips to space in 2000 as one of the first ever and having joined my charity, ShareSpace Foundation, as the first founding member, he clearly shares my deeply felt passion for space and space development, as well as the important educational and motivational aspects through his motivational speaking at schools.

I am following the developments of Wimmer Space with great interest and only wish Per all the best of luck on his many trips to space whilst thanking him for the important charity work and his inspiration to the younger generation that we both acknowledge is so important for the future.

Ad astra,

Commander Buzz Aldrin
Apollo 11 Astronaut
First Mission to the Moon

INTRODUCTION

I was sitting in the cockpit of a Russian MiG-25 fighter jet on the runway at Zhukovsky airbase near Moscow. Zhukovsky had been an important aircraft test centre during the Cold War. I was wearing my jet fighter suit, which was hooked up to tubes that pumped in air to put pressure on my legs, keeping blood in the upper part of the body and helping prevent me from blacking out when I experienced the high G-forces produced by the jet's acceleration.

I had been helped into my suit back in the airbase's Gromov Flight Research Institute by two Russian ladies who worked there. They were very serious, like all the Russians on the base, and rather formidable, but it's always nice to have a little assistance. Then I was taken to a simulator of a MiG-25 cockpit and shown the controls. The instructors were especially keen to draw my attention to two red handles located below the seat, between my legs. "If anything goes wrong," they said, "you pull the handles, the cockpit canopy flies open, and you are ejected at high speed into the air. A parachute is deployed, which, in principle, will bring you safely back to Earth." It was only so reassuring.

When the MiG-25 entered service in 1970, it was the fastest jet fighter in the world, specifically designed to intercept a new range of supersonic American bombers. It could fly up to 80,000 ft and had a top speed of Mach 3, which surprised and worried the

American military, who thought they had been gaining a strategic advantage with the development of their new range of supersonic nuclear bombers. The MiG-25 was capable of flying as fast, but higher than the most advanced bomber prototype the Americans had in development at the time. And I was about to fly up to the very edge of space in one of these amazing aircraft.

We walked out onto the runway. It was a freezing cold day in the middle of winter, but the flight suit kept me warm. I climbed into the cockpit of the waiting jet, and the ground staff carried out a final safety check to make sure all my systems were plugged in and functioning properly. Then they closed the cockpit canopy. We taxied onto the main runway and waited for permission to take off.

Suddenly, the jet engine roared into life: we were off!

The acceleration on the ground was startling. I was pushed hard back into my seat. Almost immediately, we were airborne. With the afterburners providing additional thrust, we were climbing incredibly quickly – and the G-forces were increasing. A MiG fighter can produce G-forces of up to 9 G; on my flight into space, I might experience forces of around 6 G. This flight was a part of my astronaut preparation and experiencing G-forces and learning how to deal with them was a key part of the training. I tensed my muscles and did the breathing exercises I had been taught and managed to stay conscious – just.

We climbed toward the edge of space. The speeds involved are hard to comprehend. Mach 3 is around 2,200 mph – about 37 miles every minute. After 10 minutes of flight, we could reach Helsinki to the north, Nizhny Novgorod on the Volga River to the east, or Belarus to the west. And of course, at supersonic speeds, everything is silent: the sound of your engines can't catch up with you. Once we reached our incredible cruising altitude, everything was silent and peaceful. The G-force of acceleration had ended; there was no real sense of the tremendous speed we were travelling at. The Earth below looked like the view from space, with coastlines and major features clearly visible. The sky at the horizon was a beautiful blue, but above us it began to show the blackness of space. It was an amazing experience. It gives you a new perspective of our astonishing planet.

My flights in the MiG-25 were part of the training for my coming trip into space.

I bought my first ticket to space in 2000, from the Space Adventures Company. I had made some useful money when I was working with the investment bank Goldman Sachs, which had decided, after many years of debate, to move from being a private company owned by its partners to becoming a public company listed on the US stock market. Goldman Sachs had been my first job after graduating from Harvard University with a master's degree in Public Administration – my fourth master's degree. The Goldman Sachs Initial Public Offering (IPO) in 1999 was one of the largest financial services offerings in US history. I was executive director of the European Equities Division at the time, having joined Goldman Sachs in 1998 straight from Harvard as an associate and been quickly promoted, so I had been given some shares and options. Top partners made a fortune, literally, when the company went public, but even my shares were worth a useful amount. I decided to celebrate by doing something I had always dreamed of, which was just becoming a possibility for the first time in history – to travel into space as a private individual, rather than an as an astronaut in a government space programme.

At the time, Space Adventures was the only company offering private flights into space. They had been launched by a man called Eric Anderson, who had developed some very good relationships with Roscosmos, the Russian space agency. He struck a deal with them to allow private astronauts to fly into space onboard Russia's workhorse Soyuz spacecraft and dock with the International Space Station (ISS) in its permanent low Earth orbit, spending nearly eight days on board the station.

The first private astronaut to fly with Space Adventures was to be Dennis Tito, the American billionaire. Dennis used to be a scientist at NASA's Jet Propulsion Laboratory, but then made his fortune when he founded Wilshire Associates, an investment management firm that used the mathematical techniques Dennis had used as a rocket engineer to analyse financial markets. The field is known as 'quantitative analysis' – you may have heard of people in finance called 'quants,' who are basically scary mathematical geniuses who know how this stuff works. Dennis was a pioneer in the field.

Like me, Dennis had also got the 'space bug.' It is said he paid $20 million for his 2001 ticket to the ISS (I believe he got a decent discount, but this was never discussed publicly) – but, like I said, Dennis is reckoned to be a billionaire today. Back then, at the time of the space flight, he was probably only worth around $300 million; you know, not a billionaire yet, but with a few dollars in the bank!

Twenty million dollars was too much for my bank balance. I had signed up for Space Adventure's new project: more affordable 'suborbital' trips that take you beyond Earth's atmosphere for a brief spell in space, a breathtaking view of the Earth and the experience of weightlessness. They planned to use a spaceplane being developed by Russia, called the Cosmopolis XXI or C-21. The spaceplane would be taken up to over 80,000 ft by a launch aircraft originally designed for high-altitude reconnaissance and would then be released from the mothership to blast its way on up into space under its own power.

In October 2004, Space Adventures had invited me to the Mojave Air and Space Port to witness the launch of what was, in effect, a competitor to their planned C-21 spaceplane: a spacecraft called SpaceShipOne that had been developed by a company called Scaled Composites, with backing from Microsoft cofounder Paul Allen. The venture hoped to be able to claim the Ansari X Prize: a newly created prize for the first reusable commercial crewed spaceship to fly into space twice within two weeks. The rest is history: SpaceShipOne completed its second flight into space successfully on October 4 2004 – the 47th anniversary of the launch of Sputnik 1, the world's first artificial satellite – and claimed the $10 million prize. Developing the spacecraft was rumoured to have cost Paul Allen $25 million, but at least he got some of his money back! To top off that historic day, Sir Richard Branson, founder of the Virgin Group, announced the launch of a new venture, Virgin Galactic, which would be offering flights into space on SpaceShipTwo, a new spaceplane to be used for space tourism, based on the design of the now-prize-winning SpaceShipOne. The spacecraft would be built by a new entity, The Spaceship Company, founded by Branson's Virgin Galactic and Burt Rutan of Scaled Composites – Rutan was the rocket genius who had designed SpaceShipOne and its mothership, WhiteKnightOne.

My name was getting to be well known in the private space industry as being the first European to buy a private ticket to space. One day, soon after I had witnessed SpaceShipOne's epoch-making flight at Mojave, two of Richard Branson's early employees with Virgin Galactic, commercial director Stephen Attenborough and head of astronaut relations David Clark, called me and asked if I would like to meet them for a drink and chat, and I said I would be delighted. We met at the Coq D'Argent, a bar/restaurant in the heart of the city of London. There, they told me that because of my background and profile in the private space area, I was the ideal 'ambassador' to become a founding astronaut with Virgin Galactic. I thanked them for the drinks and the kind invitation and told them I would think very seriously about it. One thing was certain, this was absolutely the early days of private space travel. This was like the early days of commercial air travel, back in the 1920s. Who knew if private space flight would actually become a reality? I fervently hoped and believed that it would, but Space Adventures' C-21/M-55X suborbital flights were still a gleam in Eric Anderson's eye; they weren't a reality. At the time, I saw the Virgin Galactic ticket as a kind of insurance policy in case Space Adventures didn't work out. And if I ended up going into space not once but twice, I wasn't going to complain. Within a few days, I got back to Stephen and David and accepted their offer.

Then fate took another turn and I ended up buying a third ticket into space! A small company called XCOR had set up at the Mojave Air and Space Port. XCOR basically built rocket engines. Really cool rocket engines. They designed and built the first-ever privately built rocket-powered airplane, the EZ-Rocket. The EZ-Rocket used XCOR's rocket engine to replace the propeller in a light aircraft called the Rutan Long-EZ, designed by – guess who? – Burt Rutan. XCOR developed another rocketplane called the Rocket Racer that was designed to take part in the Rocket Racing League, a madcap idea for racing rocketplanes on a virtual racetrack in the air that someone dubbed 'NASCAR with rockets' (NASCAR is America's National Association for Stock Car Auto Racing). The idea was backed by Peter Diamandis, founder of the X Prize, and was intended to drive innovation and inspire a new generation of flight enthusiasts. Sadly, the Rocket Racing League never became a reality – but XCOR's Rocket Racer rocketplane was very real. (Diamandis' X Prize Foundation was later sponsored by the Iranian-born telecoms entrepreneurs, Hamid and Anousheh Ansari, and became known as the Ansari X Prize.)

Then XCOR had the idea of developing a rocketplane with the capability of making suborbital spaceflights: the Lynx rocketplane, about the size of a typical light aircraft and able to carry one passenger or a payload. As with the guys from Virgin Galactic, I got a call from the XCOR team 'out of the blue.' It went along similar lines, but with an added twist. Obviously, everyone knew I worked in finance as well as being a space enthusiast, so the XCOR call was more along these lines: "Per, hi! We know you're passionately committed to the idea of private space exploration, so we'd like to talk to you about two things. Number one, would you like to buy a ticket to space on board our beautiful Lynx rocketplane and, number two, would you like to invest in XCOR because we need a bit more money to be able to make the whole project happen?" The man in charge of XCOR was Jeff Greason, who is a great guy and a very clever engineer. And they were right; I really was passionate about going into space, and I wanted to help XCOR succeed if I could, so I ended up not only becoming XCOR's number-one astronaut but also putting some meaningful equity into the project.

One of the nice things about XCOR was that it was run on a shoestring because it was always short of cash, and it was very good at keeping costs low. One day, I took my mum and my sister to see the XCOR site in Mojave. We were on a trip to the US, and we visited Virgin Galactic and Scaled Composites and also XCOR because I was excited to show them the space projects I was so closely involved with. My mum is very straightforward and not overawed by anything much, and we went to visit the XCOR hangar, which had maybe 20 or 30 people working there. And they are brilliant at what they do, but it wasn't exactly NASA – or even

Scaled Composites – in terms of scope and size; it was a pretty small operation run by real enthusiasts. And my mum said, "Well, it was very nice to visit the bike shop!" She meant that the XCOR operations struck her as being like a small bicycle factory – something she knew all about, since my dad had started his career working in a bicycle repair shop in Denmark before joining the car dealership that he would eventually own. And she did have a point! There was one excellent example: the Virgin Galactic team had a couple of engineers working on the design of the astronauts' seats in their spacecraft, making sure they could be adjusted every which way and were perfectly ergonomically designed and so on and so forth. XCOR went out and bought a few racing car seats and put them in the Lynx: "There you go – seats!" It was a whole different approach.

Back in 2001, when I got to fly to the edge of space in the Russian MiG-25 as part of the Space Adventures training programme, I was invited to join their team to witness Dennis Tito's historic launch into space to join the ISS and become the first private astronaut. I had flown into Moscow with the other trainee private astronauts, and we boarded a private jet that would take us to Baikonur Cosmodrome, the base for the space programme of the USSR. Baikonur is in Kazakhstan, but after the collapse of the Soviet Union, the spaceport continued to be rented by the Russian Federation. A group from the State Duma (the lower house of Russia's Federal Assembly) travelled from Moscow with us on the jet – all house members with some connection to Roscosmos, the Russian space agency. Part of the package was some pretty impressive security. The head of our security detail was a guy called Sergei, and we soon learned that Sergei seemed to have a lot of influence. If we had any kind of problem with bureaucracy or whatever, we would say, "Sergei, we have a problem ..." and Sergei would say "No problem!" And then, as if by magic, it wasn't a problem any more. We don't know how he did it, but we got the distinct impression that Sergei was not someone local officials wanted to say "no" to.

The city of Baikonur, where we were staying, has about 40,000 inhabitants, and all of them basically serve the spaceport in one way or another. We stayed at the only hotel in town: the Hotel Sputnik – but of course! Sputnik was the world's first artificial satellite, launched from Baikonur on 4 October 1957, which is why 4 October is a big 'space day' even now. Yuri Gagarin, the first human to travel into outer space and orbit the Earth (on 12 April 1961) stayed at the Hotel Sputnik, and now we were staying there too. I know I am a bit of a space fanatic, but it was very exciting. On a personal and corporate note, 4 October is a big day for me too. I try to launch new ventures on precisely that day – my first company, Wimmer Financial, was launched on 4 October 2007, exactly 50 years after the launch of Sputnik.

The next day we went to witness the launch of Soyuz TM-32, with Dennis on board. Astonishingly, we were allowed onto the launchpad itself, something that would be completely unthinkable with NASA. We stood with Dennis's family literally at the foot of the rocket and waved as Dennis climbed the stairs. He couldn't touch us because he was in quarantine, but we were right there to wish him luck … and then we had to get off the launchpad sharpish before the countdown started!

I did find Russia pretty 'wild' in those days – in many ways. Back in Moscow, we were staying at the Marriott Hotel and there were guys with Kalashnikov machine guns standing outside a room just down the corridor from us, guarding whoever was staying there. I don't know about you, but I had never been to a Marriott Hotel before where there were people with machine guns in the corridor. Everything was a bit rough and ready – maybe not like the old Soviet days, but it still had a bit of a Wild West feel to it.

The next day, we boarded the coach for the one-and-a-half-hour trip to Zhukovsky airbase, where I was to take my flight in the MiG-25. That really was like something out of the old Soviet Union – a Cold War airbase that had been a major aircraft testing site. It was also where they tested the Buran spaceplane, a kind of Russian Space Shuttle that made one unmanned flight. The programme petered out after the collapse of the Soviet Union, and the spacecraft itself was accidentally destroyed when the hangar it was stored in collapsed.

We certainly didn't get the red-carpet treatment in Zhukovsky, no matter who we were or thought we were! We needed a medical exam before we were allowed to fly, and the Russian doctor treated us like I assume he treats every rookie Russian pilot: no smiles, no nonsense and absolutely no favours. Luckily, I passed – but if you didn't pass, you didn't fly. He wasn't interested in the fact that we were private, commercial flyers. I remember the paint was peeling off the buildings outside and the whole thing felt like we had stepped back in time and were getting this amazing, privileged access to an old Cold War airbase – a throwback to the days when new aircraft and spacecraft were being rapidly developed in an attempt to get a strategic advantage over the enemy, and brave young pilots were putting their lives at risk to try out these experimental new flying machines. We felt that we were pioneers, too, in our own small way, because we were the first cadre of private astronauts. It was exhilarating, but also quite humbling.

After my amazing flight in the MiG-25, we switched to Aero L-39 Albatros jet trainers, built in Czechoslovakia. The L-39 is less powerful than the MiG-25, but it is incredibly manoeuvrable. We did all kinds of acrobatics. At one point the pilot told me in broken English to take the controls: "You take stick! Stick! Roll! Roll!" So I grabbed the stick and managed to do a kind of roll. It's pretty amazing to find yourself flying upside down but still flying! When the pilot pulled some more extreme aerobatics, it did make me feel pretty queasy, though I managed not to throw up. We did a 'Split S' – a half-roll and a half-loop that leaves you flying at more or less the same speed in exactly the opposite direction; a manoeuvre used to 'disengage from combat;' a euphemism for "let's get the hell out of here!" Then we did a range of other loops, rolls and spins. It was incredible.

With part of my space training completed, I returned to London and to my career in finance. My journey to space would take more twists and turns, and I would become very close to Richard Branson and the Virgin Galactic team as they worked on the development of SpaceShipTwo and pursued their dream of giving private individuals their own life-changing opportunity of a trip into space.

There would be many challenges, breakthroughs and disasters to face in the years to come. With all such entrepreneurial ventures, there are holdups and technical problems; cashflow is sporadic or non-existent and companies struggle to stay afloat; test vehicles crash or explode; brave technicians and test pilots are injured and even killed. This was the dawn of a new era. Dedicated teams were trying to make exciting new things happen, but many of them would inevitably fail. It's a tough road, but that's just how it is when you are breaking radically new ground – it is only by trying to achieve something new and innovative that we discover, through trial and error, what works and what doesn't. Along the way, a lot of companies go bust and lose a lot of money – but the ones that succeed stand to make a fortune. It was the same with the dot.com revolution – something I was heavily involved with in my days at Goldman Sachs.

Space Adventures continued to be very successful with their programme, taking private astronauts to the ISS via Russia's Soyuz programme, but the Russians never did manage to develop the C-21 spaceplane for their planned suborbital operation.

XCOR ran into financial troubles and finally filed for bankruptcy in 2017. I had been very involved in the enterprise, not just financially, but also flying out to Los Angeles as their 'Astronaut Number One' to help with PR when they announced deals with travel agencies or distribution agencies and so on. I genuinely wished them well, and not just because I hoped to fly to space with them.

That left me with a ticket to space with Virgin Galactic. I am eternally grateful that I decided to buy several tickets to space as that 'insurance policy' – there are no certainties on this new frontier.

My own journey through life continued at what felt like breakneck speed. A meeting in a London pub with the manager of an Australian oil and gas company would lead to a life-changing trip to Australia. I would successfully broker a $10 million deal for my Australian contact and forge many more new relationships that would in time pave the way for the launch of my own investment bank, Wimmer Financial, on what would turn out to be the eve of the greatest financial crash of modern times: the collapse of Lehman Brothers and the beginning of the Great Recession. With the very survival of my new company hanging in the balance, I would take part in a record-breaking skydive over Mount Everest. I would later be one of the 'Secret Millionaires' featured in a hugely popular TV programme and go undercover as a social worker in a deprived area of my homeland, Denmark, revealing at the end of the programme which social ventures I felt could benefit most from my support.

I would launch other companies: Wimmer Family Office, to manage the wealth of high-net-worth individuals, and I would acquire part of quant hedge fund later to be rebranded as Wimmer Horizon. I did my fair share of partying with the rich and famous in Monaco, St Tropez and St Barts. I would attend glamorous social events, party on world-famous yachts and visit Richard Branson and his family on Necker Island, Richard's idyllic private island in the Caribbean. I would be awarded a prestigious fellowship by the New York Explorers club. And somewhere in the middle of all that, I would fall truly in love for the first time in my life.

It's been an amazing journey. I feel as if I have lived three lives already.

I hope you will join me as I revisit the rollercoaster road of my life – but hang on to your hat; it's going to be quite a ride!

A WORLD
WAITING TO BE
DISCOVERED

The house where I was born still stands on the tree-lined street of Slotsalléen, in the medieval market town of Slagelse, a community then of only around 22,000 people in the Southwest of Zealand, Denmark's largest island. Our house, Slotsalléen 11, was a handsome, detached villa, set back from the road. I realize now that the villa was an impressive family home, expressing something of my parent's ambitions for themselves and their family. When I was growing up, of course, it was simply 'home.'

My father, Leif, was one of eight children. For much of his childhood, there was barely enough food on the table. His own father, my grandfather, Osvald, who died when I was just one year old, worked as a driver for a DIY chain and his wife, Kristine, my paternal grandmother, worked as a cleaner at the local liquor distillery. The older children lent a hand in any way they could to help the family get by, and then wasted no time in getting out into the world to earn a living.

My mother's upbringing was more comfortable in comparison. Her name is Lis, so my parents were Leif and Lis! She grew up on a farm in Stillinge, just outside Slagelse. It was a traditional household of its time: my grandfather worked on the farm while my grandmother worked mainly in the kitchen. I spent some wonderful holidays on the farm when I was a child, looking after the animals and learning how to drive a tractor. I spent a lot of quality time with my grandparents. Like my father, my mother is also very energetic and active. They were both brought up with a similar approach to hard work that put a premium on commitment and diligence.

My father worked first as a mechanic in a bicycle repair shop and then, when the business became a car dealership and workshop, he learned new skills, eventually becoming head of the spare parts division and then head of sales. The owner of the dealership was Per Martin Olsen, and their primary brand was Opel, which was part of General Motors. When Olsen died, his widow took over, but was never fully committed to the business. As the company's fortunes went rapidly downhill, my father made the brave decision to buy the business. He approached my maternal grandparents for help with the funding, but they declined, nervous of investing in a business they had no familiarity with. He managed to raise the money from the bank and went ahead, with the full support of my mother. Once the deal was done, he never looked back. He set out to bring about a complete turnaround of the company, and within a few years he had succeeded; his determination and his high business and ethical standards made for happy customers and appreciative suppliers, and the dealership became one of the most successful GM dealerships in Denmark.

Mum and Dad had married in June 1965 and, in August 1968, they had their first child, a baby boy. Me! Dad's commitment to the business meant long hours at work, but he still managed to be an active and attentive father. His entrepreneurial spirit and energy are a constant source of inspiration to me.

At the age of three, before I was old enough to go to kindergarten, my mother arranged for me to be looked after by a couple with two older children, so that she could start work part-time. She got a job working as a secretary at Andersvænge, a school for adults with disabilities, where she was to stay for 30 years, earning a medal for her loyalty from the Queen of Denmark, Margrethe II. Being looked after by the Madsen family was a positive experience for me from the outset. The couple had two children, Helle and Torben, both a little older than me, and I became very attached to Preben, the father, and 'Mor Mads,' as his wife was affectionately known as, the family name being Madsen. The family played a key part in my upbringing; I felt surrounded by caring adults I could rely on 100%. I kept in touch with Helle and Torben for years after.

According to my mother, my time at kindergarten was not always so smooth! Perhaps I was beginning to show signs of a more independent attitude and was becoming a little more opinionated, but I have no bad memories of Rosenkilde, as the kindergarten was called. It was quite close to my mother's work – a consideration that became even more important when my sister, Dorte, joined the world when I was five years old. We were a tight-knit family. Dorte and I received an unending supply of support, love and encouragement as we set out to explore the world.

That exploration began in earnest when I started school, an experience that would shape my life for years to come. Østre Skole was in an old building dating back to 1898, and it too was only a short distance from our home. In the mornings, either my mother or Mor Mads would walk me there. It was an ordinary Danish 'folkeskole,' publicly funded and open to everybody. There were pupils from a wide variety of social backgrounds and the children showed up on that first day with very different levels of both preparation and expectation. I can't remember what my own expectations were, but there was an underlying understanding in our family that education was an opportunity one should make the most of. Later, my father would give me small amounts of money when I came home with good grades and reports. Although he took some adult classes in later life to develop his business skills, he had finished his own schooling at the first opportunity, like his siblings, to start earning a living, and he thought of education very much as a privilege to be cherished.

I don't know to what extent his views influenced my own at that young age, but I do know that I fell in love with school from the very beginning. The teachers were kind and I felt comfortable socially – but above all, I loved the feeling of the world opening up and becoming accessible to me. Everything was new and exciting. Of course, I liked some subjects more than others, but the experience of school and the business of learning simply suited me very well indeed. I just had this strong inner desire to explore.

As soon as we progressed to producing written assignments and presentations, I wanted to excel. I was ambitious and felt a strong sense of pride whenever my work was singled out for praise or for its quality. This has stayed with me since my first years at Østre Skole and helps explain why I chose to spend so much time in education and went to great lengths to take my education to the highest level possible. Unlike most of my classmates, I positively enjoyed homework, with the same feeling of gaining a new and deeper understandings of the world, almost regardless of the subject. I came to enjoy sports as well and was brought up to throw myself wholeheartedly into everything I did. As a family, we were a competitive bunch with plenty of energy, so I guess those three family traits – wanting to excel; enjoying study and practice; and being competitive – explain a lot about why I drove myself to succeed. When I look back, I recognize myself in that seven-year-old boy first entering Østre Skole in August 1975, thrilled to find the whole world out there waiting to be discovered and hungry to learn everything about it.

Østre Skole closed when I reached 5th grade in 1981, and all the students were transferred to Antvorskov Skole. This meant that I had to turn left rather than right when I exited our front garden in the mornings, but the distance to the new school was just as short, and I simply transferred my enthusiasm and love for learning and achievement to the new school. Then something happened that made everything even more fun – Lars Jørgensen came to our school and joined my class. We immediately became friends and fierce competitors. Lars had the same enthusiasm, dedication and curiosity as I did. His father, Jens, was an academic and became headmaster of Slagelse Gymnasium, which Lars and I would both later attend. Jens also became our handball coach.

Lars and I would always try to beat each other's test scores and grades. We sat next to each other at the back of the class, keen to display our knowledge and assert our opinions at all times. It was a great thing for me to no longer be the only kid who really liked school. When another new classmate, Marie-Louise, joined the school, we immediately formed our own little band of schoolwork enthusiasts. She brought a more questioning and rebellious approach, which made school even more fun and rewarding for me. Lars is a close personal friend to this day, and Marie-Louise recently reached out to me, having followed me in the Danish media for years. In 2021, we finally met up again for the first time since we left folkeskole. There was a great atmosphere, both in the classroom and during recess. We would wind each other up, as children do, but in our class, there was never any real bullying or seriously bad behaviour.

I am aware that ever since graduating from high school I have been working and moving in highly competitive circles, often among the very best people in their field. I think of competition as a very positive force. Although it is a basic element of human nature, there is immense variation, with some people having too little in the way of competitive spirit and others having way too much, to the point where it jeopardizes their ability to interact constructively with others. But, harnessed in the right way, the competitive spirit is a force that can take you far. For me, growing up in elementary school, I would say that I was just as motivated by learning for its own sake as by my (very real) desire to be the best in my class.

Sport was an obvious area where my competitive spirit came to the fore; it played a big role in my childhood and helped shape me as a person. At 11 years old, I began playing badminton in the Slagelse Badminton Club. I liked the sport immediately. It has been the sport that I have pursued most consistently and at which I've reached the highest level. I started playing at my father's suggestion, but soon the whole family joined in. Both my father and sister began playing, then I started to teach my mother on Saturday mornings. I think part of the reason she joined in was that she was given so much laundry by the rest of us because of our almost daily sessions, that she might as well add some laundry to the pile and join the fun! The whole family would drive around Denmark to support me in various competitions. They were all there to cheer me on when I got to the finals of the national championships – and came second! Not winning was painful, but I kept reminding myself that at least I had made the finals.

I also played a lot of handball. It's a great team sport and led to a lot of social activities and opportunities to travel in and beyond Denmark. Lars also played and having his father, Jens, as our coach was an added benefit. Lars wrote very entertaining accounts of our exploits on these handball trips that we all read avidly, so I remember them in detail!

Family sporting activities were a regular fixture for us. Every Sunday, we would all get up early and go for a run in the woods together. After the run, we would go swimming in the local indoor pool and after that we would go home for a huge English breakfast with bacon and eggs. This was a great tradition, which meant a lot for us, and I often look back fondly on these Sunday mornings with my father full of energy and leading the way. Often on Saturdays, if there weren't any sports competitions scheduled, we would all go and play badminton. Those hours together, sharing an activity that we all enjoyed, seem today like the essence of our family life together.

I played some football, but without much success. I played basketball in high school and some tennis, and there was always a lot of running to get me in shape for badminton. In my early teens I was playing sports or training about 20 hours a week, a habit that has stood me in good stead. I feel I benefited from this training years later, especially during periods when I couldn't fit any regular exercise into my schedule because of travel and work commitments.

The social side of playing sports is a big part of my memories of our teenage years. There was a carefree, joyous atmosphere – we struggled with the usual teenage problems, but we were fortunate and very privileged in many ways. My life growing up was so much easier and more comfortable than it was for my father's upbringing, but I can honestly say we made the most of the opportunities we were presented with.

THE SOUTH
OF FRANCE

In August 1984, I set out on my next adventure and began studying at the local high school, Slagelse Gymnasium, where Jens, Lars' father, was the headmaster.

Once again, I had the sense of new worlds opening up to me. The academic level was higher, there was more room for debate and discussion, and more of my fellow students were genuinely committed to academic work. The teachers were enthusiastic and insightful, and often willing to enter into discussions that went above and beyond the curriculum. Obviously, I'm not equally interested in all subjects, but I genuinely love to learn, and if the environment is inspiring and friendly and the teacher is well-qualified and kind, I find that almost any topic can be of interest to me.

When I reread old letters from the time, it's clear that I was doing about four hours of homework every day, which might seem like a lot, but for me it was never a burden, always a pleasure. I was also quite comfortable with the higher level of study and raised my game accordingly. My favourite subjects were physics, history and philosophy – including classics, which was taught by Lars' father. He was a brilliant teacher, always a very clear and precise communicator, infectiously enthusiastic in presenting his subject. From an academic perspective, high school was the perfect challenge at exactly the right time for me.

My social life also developed at this time. I made friends easily, and I made use of the freedom my parents allowed me – I was able to go wherever I wanted, attend parties and socialize with young people of both sexes. As long as I continued to work hard at my studies and do my best at sports, they were happy that I was enjoying myself in the limited spare time I had. I was never especially conscious of the limits to my leisure time. I have always had the capacity (and the inclination) to work hard and play hard – something I would experience to the fullest when I later entered the world of investment banking! It makes for a very fast-paced life, but if you throw yourself wholeheartedly into everything, you get more out. At least, that's how it is for me.

My parents could see how involved I was in all kinds of different activities – academically, in sports and socially – but they never worried about it. They didn't try to rein me in or get me to focus on one or two areas, I think at least in part because they were happy with the academic results I was achieving. I was still always going for the highest grades in my class – which is almost like a sport in itself; it's more fun when you're winning! To the extent that they were ambitious for me, they were so in a quite unconventional way. Most parents who are eager for their children to succeed tend to insist on the child focusing on one or a few areas to be able to deliver better results. My parents recognized early on that I seemed to thrive as a person when I could commit myself to many different things at the same time, and they encouraged me – for which I am grateful to this day. They were a constant source of inspiration. Their influence on my choices and priorities in life shows itself far more in the values they helped instil in me rather than in any specific guidance on what I should do.

There were lots of parties at high school! Formal parties and informal parties; parties in sports clubs and in private homes – often when the parents were not around. Whenever we went on a sports trip, there would be spontaneous parties with other young teenagers of both sexes from other parts of the country. Some of my fondest memories from those years are of the trips I took with our handball club to Sweden. We would go to the city of Lund to participate in one of the biggest youth tournaments in Europe. We were very serious about the sport and would often do well in the competition, but we enjoyed the trips at least as much because of everything else that happened. I often think about the freedom we experienced during those trips and how much fun we had. The trips took place between Christmas and New Year's Day, and we would stay for five days and come home, completely exhausted, for more fun on the last evening of the year. While we were in Lund, all of our team, boys and girls, would sleep together in a gym hall, and although the adults who accompanied us tried (or pretended to try) to establish rules to keep boys and girls separated, once the lights were out, there were a lot of teenagers changing places and connecting with each other about things other than handball.

There were always lots of pranks, like stealing one another's pillows or sleeping bags or having candy fights. Whenever we weren't on a bus headed for the next match, we would improvise equally physically demanding games in the gym hall. When I think about the number of calories burned during a day like that, it's no wonder that I would eat three helpings of dinner, which I can't help but think back on fondly – while recognizing that today I probably wouldn't enjoy those dinners quite so much. We even found the time to visit the local discotheques, where we would try without much success to meet girls from the other participating countries.

Those trips were amazing experiences, full of fun for sure, but also opportunities to develop our social skills. I always felt that I thrived socially and was well-liked, although I would be at the receiving end of my fair share of the pranks and jokes. My interest in photography was a popular subject, especially after I had spent days bothering everybody with some very elaborate photoshoot arrangements, only to discover that I had forgotten to put film in the camera. I still have my first Canon A-1 camera from my teenage years which started this passion.

These were the days before texts, emails or social media, of course, and if we wanted to stay in touch with someone we met, we would write letters to each other. I like writing as an activity in itself, and I would find the time to write often quite elaborate letters when I met someone of interest. Often nothing would come of these new relationships and the paper trail they left, but sometimes it would lead to a deeper connection, which could last for years. I found myself growing up in many different ways, in a safe and trusting environment with friends and supportive adults. I think this has helped my ability to easily connect with and trust other people, something that is an important feature of my professional life.

At about this time, we began to consider ourselves more capable, as students, of organizing more than a party. First, we discovered alpine skiing. This was a time when high school students in Denmark first began to organize trips to the Alps for skiing – and partying – for themselves without any input from teachers or other adults. Things would often be a bit chaotic, but the trips were also very valuable lessons in how to navigate complicated situations, sometimes late at night, in a different language than your mother tongue and without any grownups around. More than anything we had fun, and the trips, which were also thoroughly and amusingly documented by Lars, really gave me an appetite for experiencing more of the world.

Between my second and third year of high school, in the summer of 1986, I decided to do something about my growing love for the French language by travelling to a language school in France.

The trip began with a flight to Paris, where I spent a couple of nights before going on by train to Cannes. We had three to four hours of language classes every day, and the rest of the time was spent shopping, playing tennis, which I had begun to enjoy, and windsurfing, a hobby that I had taken up only the year before at the Wimmer family summerhouse in Stillinge Strand, on the west coast of Zealand, not far from Slagelse. A group of us from the language school went on from Cannes to explore more of Provence, and then on to Monaco. I loved being part of a genuinely international crowd for the first time. The trip was such a great experience that it set a direction for my future plans. This was when I first set my sights on the idea of studying in the US. I reached out to some American connections in the fall of 1986, as I was beginning my last year of high school and started the process of applying to some US schools. The costs were significant, of course, and in the end, nothing came of it – until I rekindled that dream of studying in the US several years later, at a significantly higher academic level.

As I approached the end of my last year of high school, my mother's sister, Connie, offered me the chance to spend the summer in Thailand. She was an airline hostess for SAS, her husband was an airline captain, and they were to be stationed in Thailand over that summer.

I was more than happy to accept the invitation! It was an eye-opening experience. I was overwhelmed and touched by the hospitality and kindness of the locals, and I discovered that I was quite comfortable spending time with people whose ways of life and backgrounds were very different from my own. After many memorable experiences, I came home with an even deeper conviction that I wanted to travel extensively and experience life in different parts of the world. I also invested in my first Sony Video 8 camera to record my experiences, as I was beginning to pursue an interest in filmmaking!

I began to investigate other opportunities to see more of the world and came across an opportunity that was unusual, to say the least, but had all the elements I was looking for. In France, high school is a three-year education, just like in Denmark. It leads to a qualification called the *baccalauréat*, which is an internationally recognized and highly respected qualification, similar to a high school degree. I came up with the idea that I would go back to the South of France for a year before going on to university, study at a French school and take the *baccalauréat* examinations. I felt reasonably confident about my French after my three weeks of language study and my travels in France the previous summer. It seemed the ideal combination – and more than anything, it was an opportunity for me to continue life as a high school student before going on to university. It turned out, of course, that high school in France was quite different from high school in Denmark – but certainly no less amazing!

I was accepted into the Lycée Pierre et Marie Curie, a high school in Menton, a beautiful city in the southeast of France, on the Mediterranean coast on the border with Italy. My parents, generous as ever, were willing to pay for the trip, as they could see the new horizons it could open up and that it would be a great experience for me.

The trip was not altogether straightforward. I travelled with a friend and childhood neighbour, Lotte, who was bound for Toulon, by way of the night train to Paris and then the luxurious (and fast!) TGV – *Train á Grande Vitesse*. So far, so good. When I arrived in Menton, however, things went downhill. I couldn't find a place to stay, so I had to get a lift out of town with some locals to a small hotel with one remaining vacancy, high up in the surrounding mountains. The hotel unhelpfully chucked me out early the following morning, so I found myself up on a mountain with 80 kilos of luggage – including my encyclopaedia – and no place to go. I happened to find a discarded skateboard, so I heaved my heavy case onto the skateboard and dragged it slowly to the station to get a train back to Menton and continue my search for a hotel in town that had vacancies. I found a room, but at this point I was running low on cash, and I had no credit cards. Incredibly, I managed to persuade the hotel owner to allow me to check into this small hotel and even give me some much-needed cash to buy some food until more money could be wired from home. With close to zero French Francs in my pocket, I was additionally depressed to find that everybody in Menton seemed to be under the age of seven or over the age of 70, and there didn't seem to be anything to do by way of entertainment. I was missing my girlfriend, Henriette – by far my most serious relationship at the time – and as I sat around in the small hotel in Menton, bored, I missed her company even more.

One weekend some Danish friends and I went camping on what turned out to be an incredibly wet weekend. We endured a night in the tent as the rain found its way through the canvas of the tent and slowly soaked our sleeping bags. In the morning, we abandoned our camping adventure and crept, shivering, back to Menton, where the sun suddenly came out. I stretched out on a public bench on the main boulevard, lined with lemon trees, soaking up the warmth of the sun. I hadn't had much sleep the night before, and I soon dozed off. My friends decided I was too comfortable to be disturbed, and they headed back to the apartment. I was woken by a tap on the shoulder and looked up, groggily, to find two French gendarmes staring down at me. They got me to my feet and marched me off to the police station, where I was accused of being a homeless foreign vagrant. Once I had collected my wits enough to explain my situation, they were quite charming and assured me I was free to go.

But things got better soon enough. When the school opened, I managed to persuade the school to let me board on site, so in the early days I lived at the school during the week, surrounded by French-speaking students who very soon became friends. I was not particularly looking forward to sleeping in the dormitory with strict regulations – 'lights out' at 10.00pm, for example – but I found myself sharing with a French student, Michel Ghigo, whose parents lived in a village called Breil-sur-Roya in the mountains to the north-west of Menton, too far away for him to be able to commute on a daily basis. We became great friends. Michel used to call me *le grand danois* – the big Danish chap – which is a good joke, because *le Grand Danois* is the Great Dane dog, in French as in English. At weekends he would invite me back to stay at his parents' house in Breil. On my first visit, the family took me on a walking trip to show me the local area. It was an amazing experience. The countryside, in the foothills of the Alps, is amazingly beautiful. It's no wonder why the South of France has been a magnet for visitors for centuries and that I have kept returning to the South of France ever since. It was a huge privilege to have a very knowledgeable local guide in Michel's father, who spoke enthusiastically about everything we came across.

At one point he stopped in the middle of the road for no apparent reason. "I have to show you something," he said. We walked past a small, very picturesque waterfall and he opened an old, wooden gate and led me down a path. There, hidden from the road, was an ancient mill used to make olive oil, using the river to generate power to turn the great millstones. I was fascinated by the whole landscape and very thankful to Michel's family for taking the time to show me around.

The family house had a wine cellar, which we frequented several times over the weekend – not to drink the wine, but because the wine cellar was also where the table tennis was. A couple of other school friends, who lived close by, came over and we played several matches before the evening's entertainment at the local bingo night. If I remember correctly, we didn't win anything, but I can highly recommend playing bingo in a foreign language as a way to memorize all the numbers.

It was a great weekend, but the trip back to Menton on the bus ended up being very stressful. What I had failed to realize was that, to avoid the hairpin bends of the very mountainous road from Breil to Menton, the bus took a better road on a more direct route, which happened to run through Italy – the French-Italian border runs northeast from Menton toward Breil, and if you head south from Breil on the better road, you cross the border into Italy quite soon.

Because I had been unaware of this border crossing, I hadn't brought my passport. The customs officers certainly took their time talking to our driver as we were entering Italy, and they seemed rather keen on doing a thorough investigation, but in the end, they waved us through, to my great relief. We headed on south toward Ventimiglia on the Italian coast and then turned west toward Menton and France. Re-entering France, a well-nourished Italian customs officer barely managed to look up from his newspaper as he waved us through, and I swore to always bring my passport on future trips.

During my stay in Menton, I managed to significantly improve my skiing, thanks to the kind assistance of Michel and his family. Michel's father was an excellent instructor, and I was soon racing down the slopes, more than able to keep up with the locals and having a great time.

Michel and I got very tired of the regimented life in the school dormitory and managed to find an apartment in the Winter Palace in Menton, a glorious, huge, white-stuccoed Belle Époque hotel on a small hill with the mountains behind and beautiful landscaped gardens. Before World War I, it had been a favoured haunt of members of the Russian and European aristocracy, then it had become rundown and was later converted into apartments. The rent was affordable, and the apartment had wonderful views over the gardens with their tall palms, lemon and orange trees and the blue Mediterranean just beyond. I helped Michel with his English and German, and he helped me with my French – and also with history and philosophy, which I loved but found difficult studying in French. I have very fond memories of sitting in the gardens at the Winter Palace in the warm Mediterranean sunshine, far from home thinking about life and philosophy – ideally in French!

I did find the school to be far more formal than high school in Denmark, with a strict dress code and conventions around teacher/ student interactions that were very old-fashioned and strictly observed. But my command of the French language improved daily and, although I found it difficult at first to follow my fellow students' conversations with each other, this also threw me in at the deep end and was a valuable learning challenge. I had chosen one class, A1 – in human sciences – where by chance I was the only boy among 30 girls, which was not an entirely disastrous state of affairs and probably added to my enthusiasm for mastering the French language as quickly as possible!

I had been worried that things might be difficult for me socially as an outsider with some language difficulties, but the opposite turned out to be the case. My fellow students didn't know much about Denmark, and they were curious to learn more, and I soon made myself useful by doing some tutoring in English, which is like a second language for most Scandinavians. All in all, I was having a grand time as I asked my parents late in 1987 to find me some material on going to law school in Copenhagen at the end of my studies in France. I was constantly improving in all areas of my studies, and my hopes of graduating began to increase, even though the *baccalauréat* examinations are very stringent – between half and one third of students fail their exams every year.

My social life became easier and more varied once Michel and I had the apartment at the Winter Palace; we could party and hang out with friends whenever we wanted, especially in Nice at Marc Boussard's house. We could party with friends whenever we wanted and at weekends I was able to have friends over from Denmark to visit. We also often travelled to Nice to stay at a schoolfriend's house there.

It was lovely to go home that Christmas, but I honestly couldn't wait to get back to my life in Menton. I became even more settled there when I got a job teaching English at a local school. The story behind that was that during my English lessons at the French high school, I kept correcting my English teacher when her grammar or pronunciation were wrong. At high school in Denmark, such a critical, constructive and independent attitude was encouraged. Not in France! Quite the contrary: the teacher is the ultimate authority and source of wisdom. Simply put, students must take good notes, learn these by heart and repeat them during the exams. As a result, I got thrown out of English class and one day requested to see Mme La Cenceure, the headmistress of the school – who I was actually on good terms with. She proposed to take me out of English class and, instead, I could start teaching at a nearby French primary school. It was a great experience. I enjoyed the teaching itself, and the challenge of teaching a foreign language through another foreign language.

I had also met Carole, who became my girlfriend and a further inspiration to master the French language. We explored the area together and went on trips to neighbouring Italy.

Throughout that year, I had many amazing social experiences, partly because of my natural openness and ability to establish relations with the other students and their friends, but also because of their overwhelming kindness and hospitality. On one occasion, a group of us went to the carnival in Nice and then on to spend a few days in a country house high up in the mountains belonging to the family of a student called Christoph, whose family were friends of Michel's family. The Nice carnival is one the world's major carnival events, ranking alongside the carnival in Rio de Janeiro and Mardi Gras in New Orleans. It takes place in February, which tells you a lot about the climate of the South of France. Huge crowds turn out to watch the marching bands and groups of cheerleaders and dancers, people wearing huge masks and extravagant costumes, and elaborately decorated floats carrying giant models of animals or fairy tale characters or the famous politicians of the day. We watched the seemingly endless parade and danced and cheered and waved all evening.

The next morning, we travelled on to Christoph's family's house in the mountains. Christoph offered to take me horse riding. I readily accepted, always eager for a new adventure. At first, he rode on the horse, and I followed him on his moped – a kind of motorized bicycle. I'd never actually ridden a moped before and I never did find the clutch. It went along quite fast enough for me in what was presumably first gear, but the only way I could get it to stop was to switch off the engine. I wanted to get some photographs, and it was too much fuss stopping and starting the moped every time, so I managed to get some shots holding the camera in one hand and steering a bit erratically with the other.

Then Christoph suggested we should switch means of transport. I had very little previous horse-riding experience but figured it couldn't be that hard. It seemed I was right – at first. The horse set off at a walk and everything seemed fine. Then, as the horse's pace quickened slightly, I instinctively squeezed my legs a little tighter around the animal to help keep myself in the saddle. Mistake. As the horse broke into a trot, I squeezed tighter, and the trot soon enough turned into a gallop. The terrain was mountainous, and I tried every trick I could think of to get the horse to stop, while I began to panic. My last idea turned out not to be the best. We were galloping along a trail across the mountainside, and I decided to turn the horse off the trail and up the mountain to get it to slow down. The horse turned, all right – but it didn't slow down much, and the mountain was a lot steeper than I had thought. I ended up doing a nice backwards somersault and landed flat on my back on a patch of grass between a couple of nasty-looking rocks. I remember lying there for a while, enjoying my escape – though in a little pain – until my attention returned to the horse. I stood up and spotted the animal further up the mountainside. As I climbed toward it, very much out of breath, the horse moved further away. At this point, Christoph caught up with me, told me he had left the moped back on the trail and said he would fetch the horse and meet me further up the trail. As I rounded the next corner on the moped, we were happily reunited and made our way home, with Christoph on the horse and me on the moped, one more unforgettable experience the richer.

As the months passed and the studying intensified, I had my doubts about whether I would actually pass the exams because of the language problem. My teachers had been impressed by my commitment, which was encouraging, but I had to take some of the exams in Paris, which added to the stress. It was an extremely intense early summer. Work hard, play hard, which was to become quite a motto for me in the years to come.

When it was finally time to go home, my family came to visit and then we travelled back together, along with my friend Michel. It was a wrench to leave Menton; my year there had been an overwhelming, life-changing experience. It was very strange to find myself back home in Denmark. That July I received the wonderful news that I had passed my *baccalauréat*. I was saddened to learn that over half the class had not. I was proud of my achievement and, thinking myself very fortunate, I set out to enjoy the summer of 1988 in Denmark before a new chapter would begin.

COPENHAGEN, PARIS, LONDON AND BRUGES

I've always enjoyed the feeling of relaxing and kicking back when it's something you've really earned. When there's been a lot of pressure and high expectations both from yourself and from others to perform at a high level, whether in sport, study or professional life, and you succeed ... then you can really let go and enjoy yourself, knowing that now it's time to play just as hard as you have very recently worked.

I feel we managed to accomplish that, my friends and I, in the summer of 1988! Which meant that as September approached, I was really looking forward to beginning my studies. I had learned a bit about what I was capable of when I decided to really go for something, and I was excited to apply this to a new subject area, which I felt very enthusiastic about.

The University of Copenhagen is one of the oldest universities in Northern Europe. It was founded in 1479 by King Christian 1 and offered four faculties: theology, philosophy, medicine and law. The famous atomic physicist Niels Bohr studied there in the early 20th century before being awarded the Nobel Prize for his contributions to atomic and quantum theory. No wonder I felt slightly awed as I entered the sacred halls on 5 September 1988 to become a law student.

Though I was looking forward to studying law, I had a strong suspicion that I would never end up as a lawyer, let alone a professor of law in academia. One of my main reasons for choosing law was that it offered an invaluable background for a wide range of professional careers. I didn't yet have a clear vision of the direction my future would take, so it made sense to choose a subject that could lead to so many possible professional destinations.

I wasn't disappointed. The professors were insightful and enthusiastic, and the classes were excellent. There was a real effort to ensure that we could see how our studies related to real life and contemporary issues. This wasn't the case with absolutely every class, of course, but it dispelled any notion that the law was something remote from, or above, ordinary life. Studying law gives a useful methodology. You learn to appreciate both sides of the issue and understand how the arguments are constructed and where any weak spots lie. This discipline is very useful in negotiating business deals, and it's a skill I began learning all those years ago at the University of Copenhagen in the late 1980s and have been developing ever since.

I was surprised and a bit frustrated that many classes were compulsory up until the fourth year, and the potential for following one's own interests was restricted until then. I recognized the need to ensure that students were provided with a broad foundation of the subject, but I felt that by now each student could be expected to have quite clear ideas about where their specific interests lay. I, for one, certainly had well-defined ideas about what I found fascinating and what I did not.

It was a pleasure to become part of the social life at university, which quickly evolved into lots of parties, and I very much enjoyed Copenhagen, which was a lot shabbier in the 80s than it is today, but in a rather romantic and bohemian way. It remains one of the world's best cities for me. I lived in several small apartments and finally managed to find an apartment in Studiestræde, very close to the university in a particularly old and historic part of town.

We mostly had classes in the mornings and finished at noon, which meant that I had plenty of time to study. The lack of structure that went along with university life didn't suit all my fellow students. Some of them were not used to organizing their own time, got distracted by the amount of freedom we enjoyed and, as a result, took longer than intended to finish their studies. Luckily, the discipline I established early in my student life had stayed with me. I would attend classes in the morning and use my free time during the rest of the day to study and socialize. Plenty of socializing but also plenty of study!

I would often visit Slagelse on the weekends to spend time with friends from high school and visit my parents. There were always parties there, too, so I was constantly testing my ability to work hard on very little sleep. I had a fine opportunity to test this skill early in January 1989 as I celebrated New Year's Day in Menton for a couple of weeks, finally going straight from an epic party to catch the train to Copenhagen in order to deliver a big presentation in class later the same day. That summer, I went back to France again. I felt such a strong connection with the Menton crowd, and I missed them when I was in Copenhagen. I was lucky enough to have some friends from Copenhagen join us there during the summer. I guess being on the French Riviera with the sun and the beaches and having a personal guide to the local party scene was quite an appealing combination.

As I started my second year, I became a mentor for first-year students, which was a fun job, good for my résumé and also good for networking. I also worked for the Department of the Environment, which was somewhat dull but highly relevant to my studies and even gave me my own office for the first time in my life! When I finished my exams successfully in June 1990, I was keen to explore opportunities for studying in other countries. With that in mind, I visited Cambridge in England. It was an inspiring experience, and I resolved there and then to look for postgraduate education at one top university or another, though I was slowly beginning to realize that perhaps I wasn't quite Ivy-League material. Not yet.

For the summer, I worked as a legal secretary at a law firm in Paris. The hours were long and the work not especially interesting, but I loved being in Paris. I was able to continue to improve my business French and also acquire some of the specific vocabulary of French law. I returned to Copenhagen for my third and final year with a view to studying for a master's degree in law (LLM) in England the following year. The Danish education system allowed me to transfer my grades, and I continued to receive financial support from the state as I continued my higher education, something that was the envy of many other countries round the world.

I applied for places at Cambridge and Oxford but was not accepted and was delighted to be offered a place at Queen Mary College, part of the University of London and a member of the prestigious 'Russell Group' of universities and colleges to which Oxford and Cambridge Universities also belong. I was less disappointed than I would otherwise have been not to be accepted by Oxford or Cambridge if I hadn't already recognized that my résumé probably didn't stand out enough at this point in my life for acceptance by the very top-flight of the world's elite universities, but that there would be other opportunities to try again.

Before starting at the University of London, I spent three weeks at The Hague, home to the UN's International Court of Justice. Here I truly began to feel comfortable in academia – the hierarchies, the terminology and the social codes, which are all essential aspects of academic life – and how to navigate it successfully. I was also beginning to fully understand how much I thrived on being part of a genuinely international crowd. It really is a key thing for me. I feel most comfortable and relaxed in a very international setting, and it's a continuous source of inspiration to me when I am constantly meeting people with very different backgrounds from my own. After The Hague, there was a trip to the US East Coast with my French girlfriend at the time, Valerie. Having taken in New York, several East Coast universities, including Harvard, and some of the key 'sights,' such as Niagara Falls, I fell in love with this amazing part of the world and was determined to return to explore it more thoroughly.

Then London and Queen Mary College. Another great city. London suited me very well, though it was noticeably expensive, and financial concerns featured prominently in my letters to my family at the time! I did my usual share of hard partying and hard studying and finally passed my examinations, earning the right to call myself Master of Law.

It was in London that I first began to attract some media interest; something I was going to have to get used to. I gave an interview to a local newspaper about what it was like to have travelled so extensively at a young age and the benefits of studying abroad, not only academically but also having to negotiate new places, customs, languages and social skills. This was also a time of great spontaneous experiences. To name just one, I went on a wonderful trip to Gambia, of all places, simply because I saw by chance there were cheap flights available. With almost no preparation, I touched down in Banjul. Waiting for my luggage to appear on the carousel, I got chatting with a Gambian family. When they learned I had no accommodation arranged they invited me to stay with them, and I readily accepted. Their home turned out to be a shanty town house with a rusty tin roof, my bed turned out to be a straw mattress on the floor and there was an 'open air bathroom' – a bucket in the yard – but I wasn't complaining. I love adventure.

The following day, I set out to explore. I had a fancy to drive to Dakar, on the western coast of Gambia's northern neighbour, Senegal, but Avis refused to rent me a car. I decided to hire a taxi for the day. 'Hiring a taxi' makes the process sound a lot more formal than it actually was; my new family friends introduced me to someone who had a car and was happy to drive me around. I quickly discovered that the road to Dakar was littered with potholes the size and depth of a car tire and began to understand why Avis had been reluctant to rent me a car. After a six-hour drive with my new taxi-driving friend and several roadside puncture repairs, we ended up staying at the home of some of the driver's family, where we shared a massive bowl of rice with one fish on top. Because I was the evening's guest of honour, I was given the fish head, complete with eyes. I enjoyed the rice and toyed with the fish head while trying to find ways of ignoring the fish eyes.

The family had three daughters, and at the end of the meal the mother of the family told me that they would be happy for me to marry any of the three girls on one condition: that I would convert to Islam. I thanked her sincerely for the offer and told her that I would reflect on it and revert back as soon as I had the chance to give the offer my due consideration. I have still not reverted. The next day, I bought food for the family to say thank you for their kind hospitality and accommodation, which was very much appreciated.

I really enjoyed my unplanned and disorganized trip to Gambia – especially the sense of freedom and the feeling that the whole world was somehow *accessible*, if you simply took the chance and made the effort.

At the end of my year in London, I was keen to get home to Copenhagen. It was good to get comfortable again in familiar surroundings and reconnect with friends. But I still wanted more of the world, and I wasn't yet done with my studies. I began thinking about the College of Europe.

Founded in 1949 in Bruges in Belgium, it was the world's first institute of postgraduate studies in European affairs. It offered small classes, lots of time spent with professors who were all also leading consultants and advisors in the world of government and politics, and very high academic standards, all of which sounded great to me. I liked the idea of more individualized studies, and I knew that the college would definitely deliver on one of my key criteria: a genuinely international crowd!

First, I had to complete my thesis for the University of Copenhagen. It was nominally a master's thesis, but it was also a submission for a prize award for an original piece of research and was more like a mini-PhD. To make things even more challenging, I had only six months left of the allowed 12 months to complete the thesis, because of my studies in London. The theme was human rights in the EU. Fortunately, I had some grounding in the subject already, having photocopied half the library at the university and taken study trips to Strasbourg and Luxembourg. I rented an apartment in Havnegade in Copenhagen, which I shared with a French girl, and worked as intensively as I have ever done, despite distractions from drunken Swedes boarding the ferry at the portside below my window and a famous ballet dancer, Alexander Kølpin, doing his exercises in the apartment above! I emerged with a thesis that was deemed worthy of a silver medal by the University of Copenhagen. My family was very proud when the medal was presented to me by Her Majesty Queen Margrethe II.

I graduated from Copenhagen in 1994 with my second master's degree, and by then I had been accepted into the College of Europe, as I had hoped. This shift allowed me to change direction from the law to political science. I still loved the law, but I felt that political science would deliver a bigger picture.

Bruges is a beautiful, atmospheric city, with its medieval buildings and many canals – often called the Venice of the North. It is also quite small, which meant that my fellow students and I, who were from all over Europe, could socialize in an almost village environment. I felt that I belonged to a tribe of nomads who would descend somewhere to meet – as when we all attended our friend Allesandra's wedding in Rome – and then disperse to our respective corners of the globe before reconvening in some other destination at some future event, greeting each other warmly without considering how extreme our lives might seem at that time to people like my family and friends in Slagelse.

The way student life at the College of Europe is organized meant that you lived very closely with your fellow students, eating three meals a day together and studying in a very collaborative way. Many of us forged relationships there that lasted a lifetime. Some even got married. From the moment I left my room in the morning, I was surrounded by other students. At breakfast I would be greeted by the early risers, who had already done their 20 laps in the pool, and we would all interact very freely and informally with each other. After our studies, we basically partied a lot. We would go out to bars and clubs or visit each other's dorms for parties. Every Wednesday, my dorm, Gouden Haandstraat, which was the biggest and, in my opinion, also the best, would host the party. Like all the other dorms, we would share the cost of providing free beer and wine for all the guests, which of course significantly increased the quality of the atmosphere. On Fridays we would all meet at a bar modelled on ancient Greece called Palazzo, or the famous De Vuurmolen bar close to the central square of Bruges to the tunes of Dr Alban – "It's my life"; "Sing Hallelujah" – and 2 Unlimited with their inspirational lyrics, particularly relevant and meaningful to the title of this book and to me: "No Limit"! Saturdays were dedicated to theme parties such as pyjamas, Black/White or Latin.

The intensity of our social life, of course, meant that we got to know each other well very quickly. It also meant it felt a little like living inside a bubble, but it was a warm, comfortable and very friendly bubble. In a sense, we were being groomed for the senior positions in European institutions, which the majority of my fellow students would indeed occupy later in their lives. The service level was very high. Our rooms were cleaned every week, sheets were changed and new towels delivered. If you were in a hurry and had left your clothes scattered all over the floor, you could be sure that they would be tidied up and neatly folded when you came back. All our meals were prepared for us, and the food was of high quality, often even delicious, which was no small feat given the number of students.

The other students all had solid university backgrounds and spoke at least two languages fluently. I was surprised to discover how many of them had very international backgrounds and had lived in several different countries prior to arriving in Belgium. Many had only lived briefly in their home countries and had been raised in expat communities. There was a distinctly European feel, however, as the intake was done in quotas, favouring the bigger European countries. It was a perfect atmosphere for me, and the understanding I acquired of the finer nuances of cultural differences between countries was an extra benefit, something I would capitalize on later in my professional life when negotiating and closing international business deals. It was an intense experience, and European institutions are very fortunate to have a source of dedicated and skilled young people ready to become loyal civil servants in Brussels.

The students tended to develop a veneration for the institutions of Europe and the ideas on which they were founded, but to my mind, though I supported these ideas, the teaching in class lacked an element of critical thinking and debate about these ideas. I felt there was too much emphasis on the 'how' and not enough on the 'why' and a lack of openness of thinking that might challenge the whole concept of EU. I gave the farewell graduation speech on behalf of the students at the end of the course and shared some of these thoughts. The speech was very well received – though, in hindsight, I should perhaps have ended on a more positive note, because my stay in Bruges was a wonderful experience.

For me, my time in Bruges was significant in a number of ways. Not only did I tremendously enjoy the international student body and the teaching, but also the intimacy of living and studying together and the relative closeness to teachers and professors. I thrived there, and was very active academically, whether in the classroom, debating with my friends or simply studying alone in my small but very memorable Gouden Handsstraat room on the second floor – which later led to the publication of my first book, in French, about the future of European integration. During our 25 years reunion I visited my dorm again and was very sad to find that they had converted my room into a laundry room! I had hoped that other clever students would have been continuing great philosophical deliberations in that very room instead.

One of the highlights of my time there was meeting Bill Clinton in January 1994, when he was one year into his presidency of the United States. He spoke about the importance and potential of

COPENHAGEN, PARIS, LONDON AND BRUGES

future generations and their aspirations for positive change, so the 250 students at the college were the perfect audience, although what I remember most is not so much the speech itself but his charisma and charm and his ability to make each person in an audience feel special and to genuinely connect with everyone. Little did I know then that I would come very close to working in close proximity to President Clinton just a few short years later.

The experience of being a student in Bruges was so intense and rewarding that as I approached the completion of my third master's degree, I decided to stay in the EU-sphere and apply to become a *stagiaire* (intern) in Brussels. I managed to secure a position in the office of Henning Christophersen, who was vice president of the European Commission and highly respected, both for his understanding of economics and politics and for his skill in navigating the often-turbulent waters of Brussels. Once that was set up, I took a brief summer course with the United Nations in Geneva, where 10% of the 75 participants were graduates from the College of Europe – so I felt very much at home. The course was run like a mini-UN, and I truly enjoyed the experience of leading negotiations, working around the clock to reach a compromise acceptable for all parties. There had been a lot of partying in Bruges, but in Geneva we took it up a notch further, and once again I drew on my capacity to function on minimal sleep.

That summer, I travelled to Eastern Europe for the first time with Cathrine, who had been one of my teachers in Bruges and came to be my girlfriend. It was just a few years after the collapse of the Soviet Union, which had kickstarted a process of rapid transformation in this part of Europe. It was so close geographically but had for 50 years been a completely different world. It was an eye-opening experience to see, sadly, how far behind the rest of Europe Soviet-controlled Eastern Europe had fallen.

Working for Vice President Christophersen was as exciting and inspiring as I had hoped. I started in October 1994 and was involved in setting up aid programmes for Eastern Europe and the former Soviet Republics, a mission that was at the centre of European politics, trans-European networks and almost any other policy area – since when any financing was needed, the dossier had to pass through the cabinet of the Vice President responsible for the European budget.

We were able to access high-level meetings, including regular meetings of European finance and foreign ministers, and even participate in shaping the political future of the continent.

In January 1995, Christophersen was replaced by Ritt Bjerregaard in a very tumultuous process. Many members of the Commission were explicitly and vocally critical of Bjerregaard, as she had previously been less than enthusiastic about a lot of the work that was being done in Brussels. Where Christophersen was the well-respected, discreet senior diplomat at the top of the European Commission, Mrs Bjerregaard was a grassroots politician. The latter was never going to work well within the European Commission. For me and the other *stagiaires*, the switch also meant that for some, never explained reason, we were no longer allowed access to many of the high-level meetings, which had been one of the most stimulating and interesting aspects of the work. I began to think seriously about my next steps.

My long-held wish to study in the US and my visit to several of the key universities on the East Coast of the US had drawn me inescapably to one idea. I wanted to study at Harvard. I knew it was unrealistically ambitious – Harvard was probably the most respected and prestigious university in the world. There were also good reasons why applying to Harvard at this point in my life might not be a good idea. If I was accepted, I would be 29 years old by the time I graduated with my fourth master's degree. Even my father, who was in general very much in favour of higher education, felt that perhaps now was the time to start applying some of the skills I had acquired over the last decade instead of spending another two years studying. And a final reason why continuing my studies at Harvard might be a bad idea was the financial side of things. I figured that I needed more than £25,000 per year in college fees and living costs, which was a great deal of money at the time. Attending Harvard is a great deal more expensive now, of course.

Although Harvard was the dream, I knew I also needed to consider more realistic alternatives – both for studies at other universities than Harvard and for work opportunities. In spring 1995, I applied for Harvard and several other top East Coast universities armed with, I am proud to say, some excellent references from my teachers and professors at the College of Europe and from people I had worked with at the European Commission.

I also began a long dialogue with the European Environment Agency in Copenhagen, which seemed like a logical option, based on my experience. It would be nice to live closer to my family again and the salary was good, especially since I would have diplomatic status, which would very much influence the taxes I would have to pay.

I was also talking to Ford Europe in Brussels. They found my profile very interesting, especially because of my understanding of EU politics and my network of contacts in the European Commission. There would be a lot of travel between the European offices, and I would be working in an industry that my family was closely connected with. Ford even offered me my first company car!

All these options were appealing in their own way, but in my heart, there was no doubt about what I wanted most: Harvard.

While I was waiting for all of these alternative scenarios to turn into something tangible, I set to work writing a book based on my College of Europe thesis about the models and future of European integration for publication in Brussels. It was hard! The French language is tricky enough to speak, but to write about something as complicated as European political science and the European institutions in a language as complex and subtle as French was almost more than I could accomplish. I was doing this all by myself, as I had left the Commission and had no other affiliations at this point, and it was my first book, which is intimidating for anybody. I gave it everything I had, but it was one of the times where I felt I was pushing myself to my limits. My brain felt as if it might explode! The book did get published eventually with the title, *Vers une Europe à la carte après Maastricht?: Analyse des dérogations à l'acquis Communautaire.*

One day, as I sat in Bruges at my girlfriend Cathrine's place, buried in the complexities of the European human rights institutions and of the beautiful but sometimes infuriating French language, my mum called.

> *"Per, we have a letter for you here. It's from Harvard University.*
> *Can I open it?"*
> I jumped out of my chair and stopped breathing. An icy hand
> seemed to grip my insides.
> *"Of course. Thank you."*

I drew in a slow, shaky breath. I could hear the noise of the envelope being opened and the rustling of paper as my mother opened the letter.

"*Dear Mr Wimmer,*" she read. "*I am writing to …*"

My mum's English is not great; she stumbled and hesitated.

"*I am writing to … congratulate you on behalf of Harvard University …*"

"*Can you read that again?*"

"*I am writing to congratulate you on behalf of Harvard University for our acceptance of your application to enrol in our programme this year. We were very impressed by …*"

My mother stopped reading and her voice tailed off. I sank back onto my chair.

"*Per? Per? Are you still there?*"

"*I'm here.*"

"*Per, that's wonderful!*"

I found it hard to speak. This had been my goal for the last several years. I could feel an inner tension slowly beginning to unwind. I started to laugh.

"*Wow!*"

My mother sounded a little tearful.

"*That's wonderful, darling,*" she said in Danish. "*We're so proud of you.*"

We both began to giggle and talk at the same time. Dorte came on the phone and congratulated me, crying what were clearly tears of joy, and then Dad came to the phone, determined not to get emotional, and sounding very manly and matter of fact but obviously delighted.

I was going to Harvard. I couldn't believe it. This really was the dream come true. I had been offered a PhD at Georgetown in political science, which was extremely prestigious in itself, as the university is very well respected in the field (President Bill Clinton studied there) and as there were very few PhDs being offered I felt that if I went down the path of spending another five years in academia my fate would be settled, and I would end up as a college professor. I loved the academic world, but I felt certain that after an additional two years of intense studying at the best university in the world, and at the ripe age of 29, I would be ready to leave the ivory towers of academia for good.

HARVARD

The Cronkhite graduate student housing centre at Harvard is pretty much at the centre of the university. That is almost literally true, and it describes how I felt in September 1995, as I first entered what was to be my home for much of the next two years of my life. As soon as I heard the amazing news about my acceptance, I began searching for accommodation that would give me the best environment in which to pursue my studies. That is exactly what I found at the Cronkhite. The rooms were small but practical, which suited me fine, because they were only needed for studying and sleeping – in that order. There was a great cafeteria serving three meals a day with a wide variety of excellent food. It was great to know that I wouldn't have to worry about meals or doing the dishes, which is not my favourite thing in the world. The Cronkhite is very close to the famous Harvard Square, with its shops, theatres and restaurants, and to Harvard Yard, the historic centre of the campus. All the historic buildings where classes were held are a short stroll away, as is the Charles River, flowing through the city to Boston Harbour in the east. There were tennis courts nearby, and I started to play a game or two whenever I could with one of the very few other Danish students, though our free time was very limited. The old red brick buildings of the campus are stately and charming; the Cronkhite had a wonderful common room with a huge fireplace and is the home of 150 very smart young people. My fellow graduate students were a mixed crowd, very international. There were always interesting people to talk to. I felt right at home from the very first day.

I remembered how I had felt a little overawed seven years earlier when I began studying at the University of Copenhagen. Now I was a different person, more mature, with a broad academic background and some significant work experience ... but I think that everyone is slightly intimidated by Harvard at first. It is perhaps the most sought-after school in the academic world, with dauntingly high academic standards.

I was studying for a master's in public administration (MPA-2), a wonderful course that only admits 30–35 students each year. The great thing about the MPA-2 is that it effectively gives you carte blanche to study any course that Harvard has to offer. There are no mandatory courses. So although we were enrolled at the Harvard Kennedy School, we could take courses anywhere in the university. I could even choose to take classes at the famous Massachusetts' Institute of Technology (MIT) just down the road! There was a tremendous freedom to put together a highly bespoke package, and that's pretty much what I decided to do. I felt like a kid in a candy store.

During my time at the office of the vice president of the European Commission in Brussels, involved with the creation of the euro and the European Monetary Union, I had realized that I needed to learn a lot more about business and finance. I decided to devote roughly half of my studies to courses on international relations and US politics at the Harvard Kennedy School, which had been the original intended focus of my time at Harvard – but I seized the chance to spend the other 50% of my time on courses at Harvard Business School. I also threw in some courses in negotiation techniques, which were amazing and proved to be extremely valuable in my later career.

Harvard Kennedy School is on the north bank of the river, just down from the main campus. Harvard Business School is on the south bank, a short walk across the Anderson Memorial Bridge. As I walked from lecture to lecture and from one historic building to another, I felt a huge sense of privilege at being a student at this world-famous university where so many leading figures and world-class intellects had studied.

Because of the whole kid-in-the-candy-store scenario, I ended up signing on for three semesters-worth of course work with only two semesters to get through it: i.e., the first year. And studying at Harvard is different; a key feature is that the tasks students are given are impossible. There is so much course work that you can't get through all of it in time for your classes, so one of the most important things is to prioritize. You learn to familiarize yourself with an enormous amount of material very quickly, then figure out what is most important and focus your attention on that. It's a very useful skill once you've got the knack, and I have made use of it many times since those long and intense days of study on the East Coast of the US in the mid-1990s.

One thing I had to get used to was that you were called upon to answer in class regardless of whether you had something to offer or not (which was known as getting 'cold called'). You didn't get to put your hand up and volunteer something; you were put on the spot without warning. It was simply assumed that you came to class prepared. Harvard was also a far more individual academic experience than I had experienced before. In Bruges we had done everything together, and at Harvard that was a luxury you couldn't afford. There was so much work to get through that you had to do it alone. It sounds old school, and it is, but I have to admit it was extremely efficient. There is also a special way of reasoning at Harvard: a certain approach and a very sharp way of thinking. Interestingly, it is not dry and academic; in fact it's very dynamic – probably because so many of the professors and lecturers have active careers at very high levels within either business or politics. You get the feeling it's the real world addressing you, even while everything is done with extreme academic rigour. I felt more motivated than ever. When I had visited Harvard four years earlier as a tourist with Valerie, I had looked jealously around me, imagining what it would feel like to be a student there. Now I knew. It felt great! It felt like being at the top of the world.

In addition to all the new and exciting experiences I was going through at Harvard on a personal level, something else was happening at a more universal level: the arrival of the internet. The transformative technology was spreading like wildfire. I signed up for a course and spent as much time as possible in the computer room learning how to navigate the new digital world. Harvard felt like the perfect environment in which to experience this revolution. Many of the key technologies that drove the internet were being developed at MIT, a short walk away. I was surrounded by young, ambitious and technically savvy fellow students who were convinced the internet would change the world. It really did feel like the dawn of a new era.

At Harvard Business School, I had my first direct experience of the business world. Elite academia is highly competitive, probably more so than most people imagine, but Harvard Business School is at the extreme end of that continuum. People were desperate to attract attention and make a name for themselves, and the top performers were often not very well liked. They were so overeager, and their ambition was so naked, that it became socially embarrassing. I don't have a problem with this mentality on a personal level – there's nothing wrong with ambition – but I had always tried to achieve the highest possible academic grades while still involving myself socially and trying to be supportive and involved with my fellow students. I never felt that wanting to succeed means you have to be constantly scoring points off everyone else. I think this approach stood me in good stead in my later business career: everyone in business wants to win, but you also have to trust people and be comfortable doing business with them – and maybe even to like them a little bit.

Apart from being my first introduction to the world of naked ambition, the business school also gave me a high-level glimpse into the world of business that was becoming increasingly alluring. I remember my father taking evening classes to be better equipped for running the financial aspects of his business, and I also remember thinking at the time that I had no interest in that at all.

Now, I was not so sure. After being accepted at Harvard, I had begun the process of applying for all the endowments and grants I could think of that were available in Denmark. We were very fortunate to have a number of foundations and institutions that would consider such applications. I had previously done this successfully for my law studies in London, so I had some experience, and once again it turned out that my profile seemed relevant and qualified. In general, the people who decide who gets the funding are looking for Danes who are going places. Without bragging, I could honestly say at this point and based on my résumé, that I was going places. I got grants to cover my fees and provide me with a modest living allowance.

I was genuinely spending very little money at Harvard and had begun to invest some of my living allowance, thinking that I might as well see if I could improve my economic situation a little bit instead of just keeping the money in the bank. I invested entirely in US stocks, and of course the US stock market was doing extremely well in the 1990s. While I wasn't thinking seriously about a career in finance at this point, I liked what I was learning at the business school about the world of finance, and my first experience of 'playing the market' was going well – so much so that I was effectively able to finance my second year's studies from the profits of my investments.

One aspect of student life at Harvard had particularly surprised me: nobody partied! The Harvard version of a party was a polite cocktail reception, with people standing around sipping a glass of wine and having very intense, adult conversations. Nobody seemed to let their hair down and go out dancing till the early hours. I guess it makes sense when your studies take up 84 hours every week, but the disciplined attitude still came as a bit of a surprise. The annual balls were amazing events, with everyone dressed up to the nines, amazing entertainment and great food (and drinks), but even the balls were very quiet compared to what I had previously experienced in Bruges, Copenhagen, London or indeed Menton, back in the day. But the bright side, as I say, was that I really wasn't spending much money!

Studying at Harvard was extremely intense, but I felt that I learned something new every single day, which is how I liked it. Not one of my grades was below A-, and more than anything I genuinely felt that what I was doing every day was qualifying me for a professional life at the level I had my eyes set on. I successfully completed the three semesters worth of courses I had packed into my first two semesters and flew back to Copenhagen for what was intended as a brief interlude but ended up being nothing of the sort.

It was customary for business school students to find a relevant job for the summer to gain some professional experience. There was a global war for talent going on, and if you were studying at Harvard, you were a hot ticket. The recruiting process revolved around the Charles Hotel in Cambridge Massachussets and I would go there every other day to chat with the various companies that had set out their stalls and were looking for interesting new talent. I had several interesting options to choose from but the global consulting firm, McKinsey, seemed to appreciate my language skills and the breadth of my previous experience. McKinsey was happy with my wish to return to Denmark for the summer because they were just about to embark on a huge project for DR, the Danish equivalent of the BBC, helping them restructure the organization. The process would involve major cutbacks. It would be tough for DR but highly profitable for McKinsey, and young consultants (like me) would arrive at the national broadcaster's headquarters in Copenhagen in droves, brandishing their hot new Nokia phones, to trawl over the organization's operations.

My remuneration for my summer job with McKinsey was of a different order than anything I had experienced to date. I liked it. The work was interesting and educational and there were some pleasant 'perks.' We went to Rome for a conference, and I am honour-bound to say that we did a lot of hard work (we really did!), but the whole thing mainly felt like an intense and exciting vacation. I ended up with two American girls, and we went on to Venice together to keep the fun going – which we managed very successfully.

I became very involved with the DR project, and my new bosses at McKinsey seemed to appreciate that and recognize my commitment. They asked me to stay on to see the project through to the end. I was delighted to do so, not just because of the salary, but also because of the nature of the work and the magnitude of the project, which at the time was consuming around 25% of McKinsey's resources in Denmark. I felt that I was learning a lot, and it was nice to be out in the real world and enjoying Copenhagen whenever an opportunity presented itself.

I ended up staying until February 1997, which did not sit well with Harvard because I had missed the 1996 fall semester. I suggested that I could come back immediately and finish my courses by the summer, which was entirely feasible and no more of a workload than my first two, overloaded semesters at Harvard, but they refused. I had to wait until after the summer and come back for a second full year. While I was getting my head around this turn of events, McKinsey offered the DR team three weeks' paid vacation in Greece, as a reward for having worked so hard on the project. It seemed churlish to refuse. When that pleasant experience came to an end, I packed my bags and set off on a trip around the world, something I had been promising myself I would do since I was a young boy (a bucket list item!).

TO THE AMAZON

With my heart racing and a strong sense of the adrenaline coursing through my system, I was finally able to sit back on my flight from Copenhagen to New York and relax.

My departure had been a bit hectic; what a surprise! Before leaving Slagelse at 9.30 in the morning, I had to deal with some important last-minute emails, copy my latest updated travel plan and pay some urgent bills, but I made the train with a whole four minutes to spare. I was about to embark on the journey of a lifetime: a trip round the world.

At Copenhagen Central Station I had, probably ambitiously, scheduled two meetings for 11.00 and 12.00 and, naturally, the second meeting overran, so I missed the 12.30 bus to the airport. The next bus would leave at 12.45 and arrive at the airport at 13.05 and my flight was leaving at 13.30. The check-in desk for my flight was already closed when I arrived – but of course! I rushed to a Delta representative and was granted VIP access through security and given approval to check in at boarding. My luggage was loaded directly onto the plane at the gate. Everything done at full tilt with real American professionalism, and I was comfortably settled in my seat with a full 10 minutes to spare before take-off. Thank you, Delta!

So, this was to be my first lesson on my journey: I must learn to keep better track of time, allow more leeway for transport connections and anticipate the unexpected!

At JFK in New York I transferred to a flight to Boston and was lucky to be able to land there at all – Boston Logan Airport had been closed for a time after a huge snowfall. My first stop was a meeting with a Harvard friend, Anders Willhjelm, who was about to graduate and was facing an important career choice: whether to accept a role with McKinsey in London and South Africa, or another with a large chemical/health group in Brussels. Both had their own strong appeal. I was able to update him on the current situation at McKinsey; otherwise, I offered whatever advice I could. We had dinner at a wonderful seafood restaurant and talked until the late hours when I finally left for my hotel, exhausted after being awake for 24 hours because of the time difference. Over the next couple of days in Boston, I tidied up some personal financial arrangements and visited old friends and acquaintances at Harvard, then I caught a flight back to New York to connect with the flight to the first stop on my voyage: Rio de Janeiro in Brazil.

The first days in a new continent can be hard to describe. Everything is overwhelming and hurried and exciting. It is easy to form generalizations too quickly, but my first impression was simply of bright colours and beautiful people. I was staying at Ipanema – made famous by the 1960s *bossa nova* song, "The Girl from Ipanema" – and the girls were just as pretty as you might imagine. It was off-season and the weather was a little grey, but the upside was my hotel was relatively cheap, and I had the streets and cafés and the nearby Copacabana beach almost to myself. I strolled along the beautiful beach every evening, enjoying the gentle sea breeze.

I had arranged a trip up Sugarloaf Mountain, the dramatic peak on a small peninsula jutting out into Guanabara Bay and the Atlantic Ocean. I took a bus to the foot of the mountain, then two cable cars up the mountain. The view from the top is incredible. Blue waves break on the sandy beaches of Ipanema and Copacabana; across the bay to the east is another dramatic mountain, the 'Parrot's Beak'; boats sail in the beautiful sunlit bay between the two mountains.

From the top of the Sugarloaf, I also began to appreciate how immense Rio is – over nine million people at the time of my visit. I spent almost half a day at the top, then took an amazing helicopter ride down the mountain, floating round the 30 m statue of Christ the Redeemer on Corcovado Mountain to the west and sweeping on down to the city and the bay, snapping the most perfect photo opportunities imaginable. It was fantastic, wonderful.

Like any tourist destination, Rio had its downfalls. Everything seemed very expensive – even a ballpoint pen I needed to buy! The traffic is bad, and the buses are downright dangerous, driving at speed through densely populated areas – but they are cheap. Taxi fares are reasonable. Car hire is expensive. Motorbikes are so frequently stolen they cannot be insured. The language barrier was a challenge; Portuguese is quite difficult to the untrained ear. I got by with the little Spanish I knew, mixed in with some French and a lot of arm waving and gesticulating. I was conscious that my limited language skills were affecting my ability to get to grips with the local culture, and I resolved to improve during the trip.

On Wednesday morning, I picked up my friend Faith from Harvard, who had flown in from San Francisco. We had studied together in the US, and I was looking forward to having a travelling companion. The first day was spent catching up, walking around Copacabana and drinking Caipirinha – a refreshing Brazilian cocktail made with lime, sugar and rum. The next day, we made an eye-opening tour of the city's *favelas*, the huge slums that surround Rio. The thousands of ramshackle houses are built entirely without planning permission and crammed into every available space – even on top of other houses, when the owner of one building has sold the right for another house to be built on top of their home. None of these streets and houses appear on official city maps, even though they account for some 25% of Rio's inhabitants, and the government provides very little for them. On the other hand, the government doesn't interfere much with them either, and they don't pay any taxes. Most favela-dwellers also make illegal connections to the city's electricity grid and get their power for free. Life is hard, and the vast majority of people are dirt poor, but there is a great sense of solidarity and a real entrepreneurial spirit in this huge tax-free enclave. Perhaps surprisingly, the favelas are very safe places, because order is kept by the local drug gangs who don't want the city's police to have any reason to raid the area. If a tourist has a camera stolen, it is common for it to be quietly returned to its owner, the culprit having been summarily punished, perhaps with a gunshot through the hand. The city's police are corrupt and inefficient; the drug lords contribute handsomely to the wellbeing of the favelas in a way the government conspicuously does not. Many successful entrepreneurs from the favelas prefer to stay with their families in the slums rather than take their newfound wealth and move to the city centre.

The next morning, we were going hang gliding, which had been a dream of mine for many years. The previous evening, Faith and I had enjoyed dinner at a *Churrascaria* restaurant, with a seemingly endless stream of wonderful grilled meats carved at the table from huge skewers. It was wonderful, but it also cost a small fortune and the contrast with our recent experience of life in the favelas was embarrassing. We suffered first-world problems of stomachache and a bad conscience afterwards – but we couldn't quite bring ourselves to regret the wonderful meal.

Faith and I were picked up at the hotel and driven up to the top of one of the mountains that surround Rio. Before we had much chance to admire the stunning views, we were being given instructions for the flight. The take-off ramp looked challenging: some wooden boards jutting out from the cliff and then ... nothing. When the wind was finally good, we ran out onto the ramp and, before I knew it, I was hanging in the air in the tandem hang-glider alongside my instructor. I confess to some fluttery feelings in my stomach when we first launched ourselves off the mountain, but it quickly passed. Hanging up there in the triangular steel trapeze was just amazing. Absolutely amazing! It felt as if my weight had dissolved as we soared effortlessly up in the beautiful mountains and eventually spiralled slowly down to the beach for a soft landing. What an experience!

The next stop was a farm in Belo Horizonte, a regional capital in the mountains north of Rio, where Faith had acquaintances. With much effort, hassle and bureaucracy, we rented a beat-up old Ford Escort with no working radio and one non-functioning door. After a few early wrong turns and a stop to investigate some alarming noises from the engine, what was supposed to be a five-hour drive had already taken us seven hours and we were nowhere near our destination. The distances involved were immense. We phoned our hosts, Beto and Marzia, to let them know couldn't we get to them at a reasonable hour and were going to stay the night at the next village.

This turned out to be the pretty village of São João del Rei, an old gold-mining city from the colonial era with some wonderful buildings, including two Baroque churches, beautifully illuminated in the darkness. We stayed at an old hotel with beautiful wood panelling – but no hot water.

The hotel assured us that the drive to Belo Horizonte was only three hours, but we had learned to take these estimates with a pinch of salt. After six hours of driving and another wrong turn, we found the dirt road leading to the farm and our eyes lit up, relieved that we had reached our destination at last. How wrong we were! A half hour passed before we saw a sign confirming that we were indeed still headed to Beto and Marzia's Santa Maria farm. Our spirits rose again. We passed workers' cottages and stables, but there was still no sign of the main house.

We tried several other dirt roads that led nowhere, forcing us to turn back, and then decided to follow another road through the coffee fields because we could see a house in the distance, across the fields, and imagined it must be the farm. Mistake. We couldn't find a route through to the house, which we later discovered was not, in any case, Santa Maria, and then our dirt track simply came to an end. We tried to turn round but got stuck on some slippery grass with two trees in front of us and a steep slope behind us. The more we tried to get out, the deeper the tyres sunk into what was now clinging mud. At this point Faith failed to live up to her name and expressed some doubts about my driving and navigating skills and about the prospect of our finding a bed for the night.

But we persevered. Faith got behind the driving wheel, I used all my strength to lift the back end of the car out of the mud, and Faith stepped on the gas. Smoke came off the madly spinning tyres and, more alarmingly, out of the engine, but we suddenly broke free. I was covered with the mud that the tyres had very efficiently sprayed in my direction, but we were happy. Or at least happier than we had been a little earlier. We drove out of the coffee fields and stumbled completely by accident on the one dirt road that did indeed lead to the house, where our hosts sat and waited nervously to hear what had befallen us. We told the whole story over a glass of relaxing wine and, later, a lovely Brazilian dinner.

The next morning, Beto gave us a tour of the 300-acre plantation. It was great fun, and we learned everything I think we will ever need to know about coffee production in Brazil. Then Beto insisted on driving us to a little-known local beauty spot – an amazing waterfall on the São Francisco River, the longest river that runs entirely within Brazil's borders. The waterfall was an 80 km drive down yet another dirt road. Beto's Chevrolet pickup truck had no problem with the terrain, but it was a bumpy ride. At the falls, we swam in the freezing cold water (Faith tested the water and declined to join us) and had a wonderful al fresco lunch.

Sadly, we had to leave early that evening to start our 800 km drive back to Rio. We decided to take a small 150 km detour to the famous mining town of Ouro Preto for dinner. This may sound unwise, but the detour was worth it. In the charming UNESCO-protected village, each house seemed more beautiful than the last. We went to a local bar, where we fell into conversation with a local young couple in broken Spanish/Portuguese, and the evening sped by. At 1am we drove out of Ouro Preto with over 450 km of mountain roads ahead of us. The drive was long and gruelling, even with breaks, and we did not sleep at all that night. We got to Rio Airport at 10 in the morning, dropped off the car, got a fruit juice (still no real food since our lunch on the São Francisco River), and took the plane to Salvador de Bahia on the coast of northern Brazil, where we took the opportunity to rest up before catching a bus to Lençóis, 400 km into the interior. Lençóis is a kind of base camp for the Chapada Diamantina ('Diamond Plateau') National Park, a region full of high plains, deep canyons and dramatic waterfalls. The bus left at 10pm and arrived at 4am the next morning. We had booked a *pousada* – a kind of lodging or hostel. The door was unlocked; we let ourselves in and crashed, exhausted.

The first day was spent exploring the village, home to around 6,000 people. It was very impoverished. When we ordered a sandwich at a local café one evening, the owner had to go out to pick up some bread. Even the restaurants required diners to order their meals the day before. It was quite an awakening and reminded us to appreciate simple luxuries – like always being able to get a decent meal. The local diamond mines had recently closed, and now tourism was the only source of income. In the low season, when we were there, business was slow.

The next day began with a 14 km hike through rocks and boulders, making our way up a river to the Sossego Waterfall. The hike took all day, through stunning mountain scenery, but we were rewarded with an hour-long break at the waterfall, where we bathed, dried ourselves in the sun, ate lunch and rested our tired legs. As we marched back to Lençóis, a stunning sunset made a picture-perfect end to the day.

A few days later, my previously sunny outlook on Lençóis was being severely tested as Faith and I ventured out on what turned out to be a very demanding two-day hike. On the first day, we walked for about 10 km with a 10–15 kg pack carrying our sleeping bags, food and other gear; in the evening we cooked a primitive supper, then slept in our tents on the rocky ground. The next day, 8 km of pure mountain climbing, from rock to rock without any path. We abseiled 150 m down the middle of a giant waterfall in harnesses and helmets, which was great fun – but I inadvertently hit some kind of emergency brake on my equipment and spent several minutes stuck under a torrential 'waterfall shower' until a guide could abseil down to set me free. I was soaked through, though still in good spirits; my mistake, after all! Then we climbed the cliffs again and followed the river back to our camp. It was about eight in the evening, and we had started out at eight that morning. We were exhausted, suffering from sunburn and mosquito bites, and ready to crawl back into our sleeping bags. Alas, this trip was only a one-night excursion because some group members needed to work the next day. We put our packs back on to travel the 10 km back. My feet hurt, my legs ached horribly and the weight on my shoulders seemed heavier and heavier; I was carrying Faith's pack as well as my own because her knee was causing her real problems. We made it back to our hotel – and Faith enticed me out to eat. I can't believe I let her persuade me, especially since the restaurant food in Lençóis was not wonderful, to say the least, but we were both ravenously hungry, and we hobbled off together into town and wolfed down our meal.

The next day, I was still in recovery: my feet screamed in pain with every step I took. We joined another short walk with some other guests at the hotel, but after feeling the sun on my already burned legs, the mosquitos beginning to bite and (the final straw) grabbing an extremely prickly cactus to prevent myself from falling after a stumble, I decided to turn back. Faith did not object. We found a bar by the river, ordered some sodas and enjoyed the view from the shade of the terrace. Enough was enough!

The next few days were spent licking our wounds on the island of Morro de São Paolo. We seemed to be almost the only tourists on the island and got good discounts and service as a result. We spent our time walking, swimming, snorkelling and eating, which was absolutely fine by us. On the Thursday morning we took a ferry to Valença on the mainland, then a two-hour bus journey to the north back toward Salvador de Bahia, where we had left some luggage, then a ferry trip across the Bay of All Saints to Salvador itself, and finally a half-hour taxi journey to our hotel. After a trip to the post office and the currency exchange, followed by a taxi to the airport, we arrived just in time for our one-hour flight to Recife, where we took a final taxi to the colonial city of Olinda.

Olinda was once the capital of the Portuguese region, or 'Captaincy,' of Pernambuco, and got rich from sugar cane and cheap slave labour. We were staying in another pousada; this time an old, colonial-style building converted into a hotel with a charming patio and, best of all, really hot water! It may sound simple, but the two things I had tired of most on this journey so far were the cold or at best lukewarm showers and the mosquitos; I was thrilled to get a few days' break from both. After a day of strolling around the town, we rented a car and spent Saturday at the market in Caruaru, followed by the coral beaches at Porto Galinhas. We had originally planned to spend only a few hours at the market, but it took us a long time to find our way there. The market was worth the journey, but the sun was setting as we set off for Porto de Galinhas. The name translates as 'the port of chickens.' The harbour had long been used as a port for ships bringing slaves from Africa to work on the sugar plantations, and the trade in slaves continued even after the official abolition of slavery. To cover this up, the human cargo on board the slave ships were logged as 'chickens.' Today, it is a well-developed holiday destination with all the usual tourist attractions: expensive restaurants, beach buggies, jet skiing. I do love jet skis, which to me are like a cross between cross-country skiing and riding a motorcycle on water. Later, we went snorkelling on the wonderful coral reefs. I felt nervous at first swimming in maybe half a metre above the coral, where the risk of being stung by sea urchins or getting scratched by the coral is much higher, but Faith was an experienced diver and an excellent instructor. By the end of the day, I felt confident diving in both shallow and deeper waters – several metres down. The corals are beautiful in themselves, and they teem with brightly coloured fish and other marine life.

We spent a day in Porto de Galinhas before heading back to Olinda and parting ways. Faith was heading back to the United States; the next stop for me was Manaus and the Amazon.

The flight to Manaus took nearly eight hours and involved many stops and changes of plane. At the airport in Manaus, I was immediately hijacked by tour operators selling jungle tours. I navigated my way through the crowd, politely declining their offers, and moved on to tackle my more immediate problem: cash. I had brought very little cash with me and quickly found that drawing cash on my cards was not straightforward. Visa was not accepted; the bank that would usually give cash on Mastercard had gone bankrupt – and in those days, the Brazilian economy worked largely on a cash basis. I could stay in a hotel in Manaus and pay for everything by card, but that wasn't why I had come to Brazil. My last resort was American Express, which had an office in the city. After just one phone call, I was given $1,000 in travellers' cheques. I made sure to upgrade to gold membership before leaving. Great service! My dad was never a great believer in credit cards – especially not in having several different credit cards – but on a trip like this, it was very handy to have a selection.

With my funds sorted, I bought some recommended items: an antidote for snake bites and scorpion stings (alarming); mosquito repellent (essential); and some toothpaste (civilizing). I would come to wish that I had also bought some toilet paper, for reasons you will shortly understand.

Leaving my luggage at the hotel, I took a taxi to the riverfront, intending to catch the ferry to Tefé, 600 km up the Solimões River to the west. At Manaus, the Solimões and the Rio Negro meet to form the Amazon – though most people outside Brazil call the Solimões 'the Amazon' also. All of the Solimões region lies within the state of Amazonas and consists entirely of tropical rainforest.

The guidebook said that the ferry left at 6pm and, for once, I was ahead of schedule. I arrived at the jetty at 5.10pm feeling relaxed and in control – only to be told the boat had left at 5.00pm. I had seen enough of Manaus by that time – it's quite industrial, despite some beautiful colonial-style buildings – and I wanted to experience the real Amazon. I gazed forlornly up the river, but the ferry was already out of sight. A local boatman offered a solution. He had one of those long, narrow, wooden boats you've probably seen pictures of, with a powerful outboard motor and a long propeller shaft sticking into the water. They're light and not very stable but pretty fast at full throttle. The boatman offered to catch up with the ferry. We haggled over the price; he was very sharp, and I was very desperate. We settled on USD$40 – a lot of money on my student budget, but I was thrilled to have the chance to catch the ferry.

I handed my backpack to the boatman, stepped gingerly into the boat and sat down as soon as I could. And then we were off! We raced up the river at high speed. It was fantastic! When we caught up with the ferry, it was much bigger than I had expected; three decks high. The boatman pulled up alongside as it chugged on up the river. I put on my backpack, steadied myself, and reached for a kind of ladder that ran up the side of the boat. The precise moment when I had to leave the small boat for the larger one was interesting; I could very easily have ended up in the river, but I made it. I clung to the ladder as I turned to wave my thanks to the boatman. He waved back, turned the nose of his boat into the downstream current, peeled away from the ferry and headed back for Manaus.

The first deck of the ferry was reserved for animals; mainly goats and javelinas – a kind of pig. They didn't pay much attention to the crazy gringo climbing up the side of the ferry. At the next deck, a kind of 'economy class,' there was a lot more interest from the assembled passengers as they watched 'Indiana Jones' continue his climb up the side of the ferry. I reached the top deck and swung over the rail; I hope with some panache. Among the other 'upper class' passengers were 12 stunningly beautiful Brazilian models on their way to a photoshoot. You couldn't make it up: Indiana Jones was transformed into James Bond! "I was just passing, and I thought I should drop by. The name's Wimmer; Per Wimmer ..."

The girls all gathered round to hear the story of this crazy guy who had sailed up the Amazon in a speedboat to catch up with the ferry. That evening, we had a great party. The next day the girls all disembarked and we said goodbye, while I carried on upriver to Tefé, a two day journey in all. Funnily enough, the ferry didn't have any system for charging passengers who joined the trip by speedboat, so I was never charged for the ferry, which made my $40 speedboat trip much more of a bargain – though, obviously, I also did not have a cabin reserved, and spent a cold night sleeping as best I could on a hard bench with my backpack for a pillow.

When I arrived in Tefé, I asked how I could visit the rainforest and meet the indigenous people, and the locals told me that I needed to meet Joaquim, who lived five streets down to the left past the house with the blue door, etc., etc. I found what looked like the house they had described, knocked on the door and was greeted by a charming but clearly blind Indian man: Joaquim. He invited me in and told me that he had family in the jungle and could take me upriver to stay with them. I politely pointed out that he seemed to be blind and asked how he could act as my guide, but he assured me that all would be well. We negotiated a price, I handed over the money with some trepidation, and Joaquim invited me to stay at his house before we set off the next day. He was the sweetest, nicest guy – but the way he lived made me revise my ideas on comfort and hygiene. I slept in a hammock in the 'living room,' which consisted of a space with a hammock strung between two walls and two plastic chairs. That was it. We ate fish and cornmeal for supper, accompanied by a kind of sweet wine that didn't encourage me to ask for seconds. The toilet was a bucket. The shower was filthy and had only cold water. But Joaquim's house did have electricity and a stove; his family's 'house' in the jungle would have neither of those luxuries.

The next day we found a boatman and headed upriver. After some time, Joaquim told the boatman to turn off into a smaller tributary of the main river; then we took another turn up a creek, then another ... I was already completely lost. I don't know if Joaquim had some residual sight – he really did seem to be completely blind – but he seemed able to 'sense' where we were and which turns on the river we should take. He led us without any problem to his family's house – a wooden building raised up many metres on stilts to cope with flooding and keep the inhabitants out of the way of wild animals.

The family welcomed me warmly: a mother and father and five children. I later learned that it was not uncommon for families to have as many as 10 or 12 children. On arrival, Joaquim and I took a 'bath' – that is to say, a quick dip in the muddy river. It soon became obvious that personal hygiene in the jungle was pretty rudimentary.

For dinner we had fish, meat and rice that we had brought with us, sitting on the wooden floor of the primitive house up above the forest floor and eating straight out of the pots the food had been cooked in. We talked about Denmark, which they were curious about, but chiefly about their main topic of interest and expertise: the flora and fauna of the rainforest. Joaquim was clearly an expert in the healing properties of plants – a real 'medicine man.' It was a fascinating glimpse into the priorities of these people's lives and their 'knowledge base' – very different from my own. The adults talked and the children listened politely without saying anything. By 9.00pm, it was time for bed. I slept, like everyone, in a hammock, enveloped in the essential mosquito net. All around me I could hear frogs, grasshoppers and birds; the constant noise was surprisingly soothing.

I had already discovered that the only toilet was a now-familiar bucket. The next morning, I also discovered the lack of toilet paper. Joaquim suggested I find a convenient spot in the rainforest, as everyone else did, and make do with leaves. I was not keen. I resolved not to 'go' for the duration of my stay. I wasn't eating much anyway; breakfast consisted of bread and rock-hard corn cakes. There were ants everywhere – in the food, on the wooden floor; everywhere. Toothbrushing was done with bottled water on the veranda of the house; the only other water available came from the river.

We went fishing for piranha in a small wooden boat. I got quite good at it during the four days I was with the family. You put a tiny piece of bait on a hook on the end of a piece of string and put it in the water; there's your high-tech fishing rod. If you don't get a bite, you try somewhere else on the river, and if you catch one piranha you will almost certainly catch several, because they live in big shoals. They have very sharp, powerful teeth and if they do bite you, they draw blood. The stories about shoals of piranha stripping anything that falls into the water to the bones within seconds are not true, but people have been killed by piranha on occasions if they were drunk or incapacitated in some way, and many people who inadvertently end up in the water near a shoal of piranha get very nasty bites. On this fishing excursion, we caught three. It rained – but of course; this was the rainforest – and we took shelter under some plastic sheeting, dozing off and on in our little boat as the rain poured down. The rain wasn't like any other kind of rain I had experienced; it was as if the air had turned into water. Lunch was two oranges, some salted fish and cornmeal.

The vegetation in the jungle is astonishing; you can almost see it grow as you watch. Trees seemed to pile up almost on top of each other, as if they were in a race to get to the sky – which, of course, they were. Between the taller trees, smaller palm-like trees, shrubs and vines fill every available inch of space and grow down into the water. Birds are everywhere. We saw toucans, with their huge colourful bills; delicate hummingbirds that hovered in the air; large parrots – blue, yellow and red – and many other bird species I didn't recognize. There were astonishingly beautiful butterflies. We heard crocodiles grunting and bellowing at each other, though I never spotted one; in the water, they are almost invisible.

That evening, the father, Alberto, came back from a day's hunting and proudly showed us his prize: a large, otter-like creature that he had killed with his spear. Alberto's wife prepared the fish and meat by the riverbank and then cooked it over an open fire. Piranha taste good – especially when you have caught them yourself; a bit like eel but less oily, though there are many annoying bones. The meat from Alberto's kill was tough and chewy and had a strong fishy taste; I wasn't enamoured. We ate our meal with rice and cornmeal, as usual. To drink we had the juice of some cocoa-like fruit.

The family was almost completely self-sufficient. I soon discovered the unimportance of money to them; it would allow them to buy some manufactured items from local traders, but it wasn't essential. They had no bills to pay; they also had no deadlines to meet and little to worry about. The family had some small clearings in the vicinity, a short boat ride way from the house, where they grew corn; the jungle provided everything else they needed. I can think of multimillionaires who are not as happy and contented as these people and who would do well by spending some time there.

My back – and my backside – were getting sore from sitting on wooden floors and in the wooden boat. I longed to sink into a deep upholstered armchair and to sleep in a bed between sheets. The mosquitos were a constant nuisance; I spent all day in jeans, socks and a long-sleeved sweater, despite the heat and humidity, trying to avoid their bites, but they managed to find their way through to the skin of my ankles, wrists and neck. They also seemed to be able to bite right through my clothes. They are bigger than the mosquitos back home; everything in the Amazon is bigger!

We had arrived on the Friday and were due to leave on Tuesday. By the Monday, my clothes were smelling pretty ripe. And on Monday, despite my light diet and my resolve not to have to 'go' in the jungle, nature prevailed and I went – in the soggy jungle undergrowth with some leaves to serve as toilet paper. I won't dwell on the experience, but it was not pleasant.

I was also beginning to get bored. There is literally nothing to do in the jungle. The children were curious to see me writing in my diaries in the evening; none of them could read or write. When it was time to leave, I was happy to have shared the family's simple life and experienced life in the jungle, but I was ready to go. As we sailed back down the river to Tefé, I felt dirty, unshaven and sweaty. I was tired of ants in hard bread and mosquitos down my neck – but it had been an amazing experience.

Back in Tefé, I found a decent-looking restaurant and treated myself to a huge meal. I finished it off with the largest sundae on the menu in an ice cream parlour across the road. And I slept in a nice bed in my hotel with hot and cold running water ... and toilets.

ON THE INCA TRAIL

After my experience of life in the Amazonian rainforest, I flew from Tefé back to Manaus in one of the 15-seater 'jungle planes' and then on to Brasilia, the country's capital. Brasilia is a huge, modernist city, built from scratch in less than four years, starting in 1956, and financed by billions in debt from the World Bank and other international institutions. It's an architect's paradise, with dramatic, futuristic public buildings, skyscrapers and bridges, and a huge artificial lake, but it is a little soulless, laid out in a strict grid format with no street names. Although this makes it easy to navigate, I missed the charm and history of street names and real neighbourhoods. But the hosts at my lodgings took me to an enjoyable Brazilian guitar concert followed by a lively party with a group of young, likeable locals, where I chatted, joked, danced and drank well into the night.

The next day I was off to São Paulo, 1,000 km to the south, near the coast. Despite being dead tired when I arrived, I could not say no to the invitation of my wonderful new hostess and ended up in town. The disco bar we went to was nothing special, but nearly all the *Pãolistas*, as the locals are called, were like international models: tall, chic, good looking, well educated. I was too tired to do more than chat to everyone over a few beers, and then I was happy to head home for bed.

I woke up the next morning feeling as sick as a dog. Soon I was violently ill; food poisoning, most likely. I couldn't keep anything down.

The doctor prescribed no food for two days and a regime of water, sugar-salt solution, pills and acid drops every four hours (horrible!). I was due to leave after four days and spent nearly all the time lying horizontal, taking my acid drops and sugar-salt solution and getting steadily thinner. All I saw of the city was the disco bar, some traffic jams and the airport. However, I did get a sense of its size – one of the largest cities in the world by population – and of the huge gulf between rich and poor.

My next stop was Foz do Iguaçu and the famous Iguaçu Falls on the border between Brazil and Argentina. By the time I arrived, I was feeling significantly better. The worst of my stomach problems seemed to be over. Now my body just needed to readjust to eating solid food again!

I was staying at a lodging owned by a friendly and entertaining lady called Laura. She came highly recommended in my guidebook, and rightly so! She was immensely helpful and made everyone staying with her feel right at home. I met a Danish couple who were travelling roughly the same route as me but in the opposite direction. It was a great opportunity to exchange advice and ideas over a restaurant dinner in excellent company. I was also able to help another boarder, Christina, with advice about London, where she was due to start university in September.

I spent the whole of Thursday and Friday at Iguaçu Falls. I have seen both Niagara Falls in the US/Canada and Victoria Falls in Zimbabwe/Zambia, and the Iguaçu Falls are more beautiful and impressive, with 275 falls spread over 3 km, the largest waterfall in the world.

You get the best view of the falls on the Brazilian side, but there are not many activities on offer. I paid for a helicopter ride over the falls and walked along the canyon and up through the falls to the forest above. It was indescribably beautiful. Over on the Argentinian side, there were more activities available. I bought a one-day combo ticket. I sailed in a rubber inflatable at the top of the falls right up to the edge of the waterfalls and down at the base almost underneath the torrential falls. I drove in a Jeep along a trail through the forest before racing down the Iguaçu River in the back of a tiny dingy powered by two V6 engines. That was the most fun, almost like jet skiing in a larger format. I could have spent more than the two days at the falls;

they were astonishing. At the end of my visit, I sat quietly in a small, deserted café and drank a couple of Fantas while I enjoyed the view of the confluence of the Iguaçu and Paraná rivers, which forms the borders of Brazil, Argentina and Paraguay.

On Saturday I was up early to see one of the world's largest and most expensive dams, the Itaipu Dam on the Paraná River between Brazil and Paraguay. It is huge – 8 km in length and taller than a high-rise building – and cost an astonishing $20 billion to build. They say the concrete used to construct the dam would have been enough to build a two-lane highway from Moscow to Lisbon! It generates 12 million kilowatts, enough to supply the whole of Paraguay's consumption and one third of Brazil's, but at a devastating cost to the natural environment: a waterfall higher than the Iguaçu Falls was sacrificed to construct the dam.

My next stop was Buenos Aires, the capital of Argentina. The city was perhaps the greatest discovery of the whole expedition. I arrived on Saturday with no preconceptions, but soon discovered how lovely and exciting this city is. It reminded me more of Europe than any other South American city I had visited. Almost half of the inhabitants were of Italian or Spanish descent and European influences can be seen everywhere. The city has many Parisian-style buildings designed by French architects around the turn of the century, including the beautiful opera house, Teatro Colón.

The people are friendly, and things work in a relatively orderly way – as opposed to Brazil, where things seem to work despite everything seeming to be in a state of permanent chaos. The locals are beautiful, charming and stylish. The inhabitants of Buenos Aires are known as *porteños*, or 'people of the port' and *porteños* cuisine is based heavily on beef, because of the country's wonderful beef cattle; the restaurants are famous for their mouth-watering giant steaks. Incidentally, my guidebook described the *porteños* as "Italians who speak Spanish, wish they were English and behave like Frenchmen," which is amusing but also quite accurate. Most of the population are of Italian descent, but everyone speaks Spanish; they value everything from The Old World, including old furniture and 'English' sports such as polo, rugby, golf, etc.; their school system is built on the English boarding school model – but the inhabitants are just as preoccupied with fashion, food and culture as the French. After 11 days in Buenos Aires, the city has been promoted to the prestigious league of cities in which I would like to spend more than a short vacation.

On Wednesday morning, I flew to Rio Gallegos on the far south-eastern coast of Argentina in a province of Patagonia, just north of Tierra del Fuego, the southernmost tip of the Americas. Unfortunately, I had needed to make a change to my original reservation with Aerolíneas Argentinas, and in the process had unknowingly been switched to an economy class airline, Austral, that Aerolíneas works with, and my direct flight of two-and-a-half hours turned into a seven-hour journey with several plane changes, lousy food and cramped seats. When I finally stepped out of the plane into the cold air of Rio Gallegos, I was starving, and my entire body was tired.

Rio Gallegos is not a particularly interesting place, and I was eager to make the most of my time. I was keen to see the famous Perito Moreno glacier and was soon headed there on a small bus with 12 others – one of my few officially organized trips! On the two-hour drive to the glacier, we saw eagles, falcons and condors – the world's heaviest birds, with the second largest wingspan (3.2 m) after the albatros. When we reached the glacier, I spent the rest of the day transfixed. The huge body of ice was beautifully coloured by minerals in the water, giving it a wonderful turquoise hue. The glacier is fed by an ice field in the Andes and flows down into Lake Argentino, cutting the lake in two like a huge dam, with the water level on one side building up by as much as 30 m above the level on the far side of the glacier, where water flows out to the Atlantic Ocean through the Santa Cruz River. At intervals of between one and 10 years, the glacier ruptures dramatically, and water pours out with huge force into the lower side of the lake.

My next excursion was to the city of Ushuaia, in Tierra del Fuego, near the southernmost tip of South America. The town is sometimes called "the End of the World." I flew in an old Norwegian Fokker plane that was so small I couldn't sit fully upright, and so noisy that my ears were still ringing for some time after we landed. The landing itself – at the southernmost international airport in the world – was a bit hair-raising: the landing strip is right next to the ocean and is notorious for its strong crosswinds and tailwinds.

Ushuaia is stunningly beautiful. The huge snow-capped Martial Mountains dwarf the city. The light is unlike anywhere else I have seen; the sky is a unique blue-grey colour. Just south of the city is the Beagle Channel, the strait of water that separates Ushuaia from the desolate islands that make up the rest of the tip of continent. There are many small rocky islands in the channel. The whole scene is incredibly beautiful.

I stayed in a modest $11 hotel with a $1,000 view of the bay and met a couple of Danish backpackers and a few Australians who had travelled from Sydney. I spent Friday walking around the main street visiting the (few) local sights. My original hope had been to visit the South Pole, but there were no regular flights at this time of year. I decided that this was as far south as I would venture and that I would head back north to the next stop on my itinerary, Puerto Natales in southern Chile, nearly 800 km to the north, at the edge of the Torres del Paine National Park. The Australians strongly recommended the three-day cargo ferry journey north from Puerto Natales to another Pacific port, Puerto Montt, a famous jumping-off point for Chile's 'Lake District.' It was likely to be a demanding, stressful and nerve-wracking journey in a part of the world where transport links are not entirely reliable, to put it mildly, but I decided to try. The famous glacier in Torres del Paine National Park was the same glacier I had seen flowing into Lake Argentino on the Argentine side. I decided to give the National Park a miss and experience the wonderful cargo ferry trip to Puerto Montt and the Lake District instead. Here's the story:

I had already planned to visit Puerto Montt and had booked a plane ticket there from Punta Arenas, just across the Strait of Magellan from Tierra del Fuego – but that would mean missing out on the wonderful ferry journey that my Australian friends were so insistent I should experience. Maybe I could get a refund on my plane ticket. I decided to go for it. The decision was made on Saturday morning. The next ferry to leave Puerto Natales was due to leave on Sunday at 6am, but a call to the ferry company revealed that all passengers needed to be onboard by 9pm on Saturday evening – later that very same day. That was very tight! The best options seemed to be a direct flight, if there was one, from Ushuaia to Puerto Natales or, failing that, a flight to Punta Arenas and then a bus north to Puerto Natales. But I found there were no flights between the Argentinian city of Ushuaia and the Chilean cities of Punta Arenas or Puerto Natales – or indeed to any destination in Chile – because of a dispute between the Argentine and Chilean airlines.

It was 11am by now, and it seemed I was stuck in Ushuaia. I went to the travel agent, who went into creative overdrive. I could fly back to the Argentinian city of Rio Gallegos, arriving at 1.50pm, but there was no bus from Rio Gallegos to Puerto Natales on Saturday. However, there was a bus leaving 10 minutes after the plane landed that would take me to the town of Rio Turbin, on the border of Chile, arriving at 7.30pm. I could then catch another local bus at 8.00pm, which would arrive at Puerto Natales a half hour later, just before the ticket office for the 9.00pm ferry would close. It was going to be tense – but this was supposed to be an adventure, after all!

As we flew into Rio Gallagos, we learned that the runway was shrouded in fog, and we were unable to land. We circled and waited. The time passed 2.00pm: I had missed my bus. Catastrophe! Eventually we were able to land. I ran to the bus stand. The bus company had decided to wait, knowing the plane had been delayed. Joy! I boarded the bus. The journey took over five hours, with three stops. The landscape seemed beautiful at first, then became monotonous. I had eaten nothing since breakfast that morning – a bowl of cornflakes and some malaria tablets. I was ravenous. I managed to get some coffee and dry bread at one of the stops. I arrived at Rio Turbin and caught the 8.00pm bus with seconds to spare. The last supposedly short leg of the journey was especially nerve-wracking. The bus was completely full and there were two border posts to pass, where everyone had to disembark to have their passports examined. Mine, with its many different stamps, seemed especially interesting to the border controllers, who also debated among themselves as to whether I needed a visa to enter Chile. They eventually gave me permission to get back on the bus and continue my journey, but by then I was 45 minutes late. I would miss the ferry. Disaster!

As the bus left, I listened idly and despondently to the other passengers chatting. I realized that they were talking about changing their watches: Argentina had a one-hour time difference with Chile

– I had 'gained' an extra hour! Euphoria! I got to the ticket office with once more only seconds to spare and finally boarded the ferry with some other backpackers, including some English girls, an American guy and a couple from Hong Kong.

I don't know why my Australian friends in Ushuaia had been so keen for me to take the wonderful cargo ferry trip; it was awful! The food was dreadful. Our first breakfast – when I was starving hungry – was a cup of cold instant coffee and some lukewarm toast with rubbery cheese. At lunch my new friends and I tried but failed, despite our hunger, to eat a hamburger-like object served with rice and cabbage. We ate the rice and cabbage, but the hamburger was literally inedible. Dinner was an improvement: one sausage each with some watery instant mashed potatoes.

Puerto Natales is sheltered from the open ocean by many islands, inlets and fjords, but soon our ferry reached the open Pacific and started to head north. The swell was significant: big, Pacific Ocean waves. A particularly miserable cheese lasagne saw the light of day again. I was OK lying down but standing up for any reason at all brought on waves of nausea. I was losing a huge amount of weight on this trip – especially after the São Paulo disaster – and I started to wish we were ashore. The biggest plus was the company: me, the English girls and the American teacher formed a great bond as we endured our ferry ordeal together and, when we finally arrived at Puerto Montt, we all got breakfast together (bacon and eggs – that's more like it!) before renting a car and driving down to Chiloé Island in the Lake District. We spent a few days driving around the island's bumpy gravel roads past the many lakes, admiring the colourful fishing boats and beautiful wooden churches. We stayed in small inns with good food but literally freezing cold bedrooms and saw the astonishingly beautiful, snow-capped – and active – Osorno Volcano on the shores of Lake Llanquihue. Unfortunately, our road trip also involved a small collision with another vehicle (thankfully, no one was injured) but the negotiations involved, combined with the long drive back, meant that I missed my flight to Santiago, where I was supposed to be skiing at the highest-altitude ski resort in the world. However, I managed to get to Santiago the following day and had a wonderful time with my Danish friend, Bab, who lives in the city and had offered to put me up at his apartment. Bab went to school with my sister, Dorte, and became a friend of all the family. He had moved to Santiago. When I knew I was going to be travelling there, I got in touch, and he immediately invited me to stay. We had a great few days eating, drinking and partying in the local bars. We joined up with another Dane, Martin, and fell in with three lovely Chilean girls at a local live music bar, where we danced until the early hours. The next day we all got together again at Bab's place to watch Chile play Ecuador at football while Bab cooked steaks and the girls made salads. Exquisite. Then it was back to the airport and off to Easter Island to continue my travels – and the whole gang came to the airport to see me off.

Easter Island, or *Rapa Nui*, lies more than 2,000 miles to the west of Chile. It is the easternmost island in Polynesia, the region of the central and southern Pacific Ocean containing over 1,000 islands, from New Zealand in the southwest to Hawaii in the north and Rapa Nui to the east. Although tourism is gradually increasing, it remains largely unspoiled. The residents of Rapa Nui speak a beautiful Polynesian dialect (as well as Spanish, English and French) and have a profound respect for their heritage, and especially for the magnificent stone sculptures known as *mo'ai* for which the island is best known.

I found some lodgings, where I met a crazy Chilean, and we headed out for a night on the town. The main town in Rapa Nui is Hanga Roa, which has one main street. There was only one bar open with no more than eight people drinking there that Sunday evening. We had a few drinks and then the beer ran out. We decided to head back for an early night. The following day we rented an old Jeep and spent our time exploring the island.

We visited Rano Raraku – a volcanic crater filled with solidified volcanic ash or 'tuff' from which the mo'ai were carved. At the base of the slopes are sculptures in various stages of completion, apparently abandoned by their creators – though some exceptionally huge statues may never have been intended to be transported and erected elsewhere on the island and were always meant to be stay put, part of their native rock. After hundreds of years, they seem just part of the landscape now. It was fascinating to see the various stages of production. At the foot of the 'factory', 15 beautiful mo'ai, restored in the 1990s, stand facing inland, guarding the island just as the originals, all toppled in the 18th and 19th centuries, stood for centuries around the island's perimeter after their construction in what we would call the late Middle Ages and early Renaissance period in Europe.

We stopped at a local market and were invited to dinner by a local family. The crazy Chilean and I had arranged to meet some local park rangers, who covered their 'beat' on horseback. I was keen to hear more about the island from these local experts, but my new Chilean friend hijacked the entire conversation. He talked quickly and constantly in a mixture of Spanish and schoolboy English, could not sit still and waved his arms around violently in his urgent need to communicate the thousands of ideas he was having every minute. He had already driven a jeep into a rock (luckily, I wasn't with him) and fallen off his motorcycle three times. But he was very entertaining. We ended the day at a part of paradise called Anakena beach, where we swam in crystal-clear water surrounded by white sand, palm trees and several mo'ai, restored to their standing positions.

That evening we went for dinner with our new local friends – our hostess Rachel, the uncle and aunt she lived with, a friend of hers and a few other tourists – which was delightful. We were served excellent local fish specialities, drank wine, listened to music, sang and danced. Rachel and I got on especially well – she spoke excellent French.

The following days were spent mostly in the company of Rachel and her lovely family, who invited me to spend the rest of my stay with them. Rachel drove a huge Honda motorcycle, and we drove all over the island together with me on the back. That evening we all gathered in a restaurant to say goodbye to someone who was leaving for Tahiti, and the evening developed into a party as we danced and drank until the early hours – and then went to a local disco and danced until closing time. The next day, complete with a literal and financial hangover from our excesses the day before, I set out with Rachel's uncle (a tourist guide) to go horse riding – a fantastic experience, if a little challenging. We rode through lava rocks and grassy hills, admiring the sea, cliffs and volcanoes. We stopped on the way back to see some cave paintings that are inaccessible by road – a huge benefit of travelling by horse. I came home exhilarated but exhausted with sore thigh muscles and a backside covered with bruises and a few lesions. Every time I sat down, it felt as if I was sitting on an open wound. I only had energy for dinner and a few drinks before packing my bag and heading to bed, but it had been a truly wonderful day.

On the following day, I flew back to Santiago. Bab collected me from the airport, and that evening we had a wonderful dinner at his apartment with four other Danes. The next day, Bab and I headed to the airport for our flight to La Paz, 2,400 km to the north in Bolivia. La Paz is just south of Lake Titicaca, on the edge of the Andean Plateau. The flight was incredibly turbulent, and Bab wasn't able to keep his airline lunch down. I managed, but only just. At La Paz, we checked into a cheap hotel; the toilet didn't work, there were no towels and no water came out of the shower, but otherwise it was excellent. We tried to explore the city, but the air was incredibly thin. La Paz is 3,640 m above sea level, the highest capital city in the world, and we were constantly pausing for gasps of air, but we had a delicious dinner and there was a free concert of Bolivian folk music in the town square. I woke up in the night feeling breathless – a strange and unsettling feeling. I also had a bad headache from the lack of oxygen; the headache was still there the next morning. We visited a market, complete with local women wearing their famous bowler hats. Then we rented a taxi and were driven the hour's journey to the world's highest ski resort at Chacaltaya: 5,500 m above sea level. The taxi ride up small, narrow and dangerous roads was scary, with our wheels often inches from a terrifying drop, but the views were incredible, with huge snow-capped mountains.

At the ski station, we rented equipment and took the ancient rope tow lift. Nothing could match the view that greeted us. We were the only skiers on the one slope the resort has to offer. Conditions were not ideal: there was too much ice and the trail itself was only 300 m long. The thin air continued to challenge us; after a few runs, we were exhausted. But we were satisfied. We had skied at the world's highest ski resort; what an experience! The Chacaltaya ski resort closed in 2009 when the glacier on which it stood finally melted completely. I'm glad we had the opportunity to experience it while it was there.

After another freezing cold night at our hotel, which gave me a cold and a sore throat to go with my constant headache, we took the beautifully scenic bus journey through the Andes from La Paz to Copacabana on Lake Titicaca. We had lunch in Copacabana, and then drove on to Puno, further up the western edge of the lake, in Peru. The next day we sailed on the lake, with its clear, blue water, and sunbathed and relaxed on the top deck of the boat. We visited two floating islands, created by nature and improved by the locals, using reeds. In fact, they use reeds to make everything – houses, clothing, shoes, souvenirs and even boats.

We sailed back across the lake in a wonderful sunset and had pizza and sangria for supper with a group of Brazilian girls and a few Australians we had met on the boat. The hotel in Puno seemed even colder than the one in La Paz. My cold, sore throat and headache all got worse.

The next day we were up early taking a cold shower (not by choice!) before catching the 7.30 train to Cuzco in southern Peru, which was once the capital of the Inca Empire. We were at the station on time, but the train was apparently being repaired. When we finally set off, it took all day to travel the 650 km northwest through the Andes to Cuzco, but the views of Lake Titicaca and the snow-covered mountains made it all worthwhile. We played cards and drank beer with the Brazilian girls, who were making the same rail journey. We arrived at 9.30pm and booked an 'Inca Trail' trek for the very next morning before heading into town, where we ran into the girls again and went for a quick beer, which turned into many beers. We got back to the hotel at 2am, with only three hours of sleep before the trek began.

The Inca Trail was 50 km long. It seemed easy going at first. The mountains, the cacti and the river formed a breathtakingly beautiful backdrop, and we stopped for lunch along the way in an old Incan village. As the day went on the route became increasingly tough, as we started to climb into the mountains. We pitched camp for the night, and Bab and I shared a small tent with a Frenchman. Harking back to my trip up the Amazon, I had already been reintroduced to the questionable joys of going to the toilet *al fresco*. I woke feeling frozen and miserable. I was wearing five layers of clothes, including an Icelandic sweater and a quilted jacket, but was still as cold as I could ever remember feeling. The rest of the day was one of the most physically demanding days of my entire life. Even Bab, who is as strong as an ox and has been in the military, agreed.

We started at an altitude of 2,000 m and gradually climbed up to 4,050 m on steep and treacherous paths, carrying 25 kg packs. I had become a little acclimatized to the altitude since La Paz – but a hike with a full pack at that altitude was very hard. It became a great ordeal, bordering on the unbearable. I could barely walk 10 ft without taking a five-minute break. I felt I was on the verge of collapse, which was a bad feeling, since the nearest hospital was a day's walk away. Bab could see I was in a bad state, and even offered to carry my pack, but I was determined to push on and conquer my burned-out leg muscles, sore shoulders and collapsing lungs. One of the worst moments came when we reached what I thought was the top of the mountain pass we had been climbing toward – only to find there was another 200 m climb ahead. I staggered up to the top at the rate of about two steps every 10 seconds. At the saddle point, I took in the unbelievably beautiful view of the surrounding valleys and snowy mountains. I was completely burned out: blisters on my feet, dry lips, a constant cough and sore throat. But we had made it!

We slept as best we could. The third day started at 6.30am with a cup of water, chocolate and some bread, and I lifted the backpack again onto my tired shoulders as we trudged toward the second pass of the trip. The first hour was hard and steep and, to make matters worse, I had run out of water. I had no iodine tablets and so no way to purify meltwater or snow water; two other Danes in our group did fall ill, perhaps because of drinking iodine-purified water – the iodine isn't 100% effective. My throat was like sandpaper, and my thoughts became more and more fixated on how many litres of Fanta I would drink at the end of the trek that evening.

At lunch we had soup and coca tea, which helped our hydration. Coca tea contains very small amounts of the alkaloids that make cocaine; it's a mild stimulant but it also makes you feel less thirsty, which was very welcome. There was also pasta on offer, but I couldn't eat; I was thirsty, not hungry. Bab and I grabbed some sleep during the lunch break.

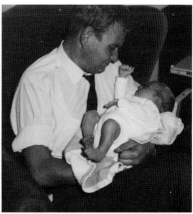

As a baby with mum, Lis, and dad, Leif, at home at Slotsalléen 11, Slagelse.

Getting a taste for speed in my first go-kart (with teddy).

At kindergarten loading sand *(bottom left)* and looking serious *(bottom right)*.

This page
Top: My rain gauge in my grandparents' garden. When granddad asked how much it had rained, I would pour the rainwater onto the grass and point to the puddle for the answer.

Second row: Posing for the press with the SBI-sponsored junior football team (second from left back row).

At Legoland with Dorte in 1979.

My maternal grandfather, Thorkild, working on the farm in Stillinge.

My maternal grandmother, Else, watering flowers in the garden.

Off to school Class 2, 1976.

1981
Glædelig
jul
Godt
nytår.

Opposite page
(Top to bottom left to right)
13th birthday with Dorte.

The school handball team in 1980.

With Dorte and pet budgerigar, Christmas 1981.

My room in Slotsalléen.

More handball – getting taller!

Graduating from Slagelse Gymnasium in 1987.

This page
Top right: Mum with her sisters.

Third row right: With my best friend and flatmate Michel Ghigo
while studying at the Lycée in Menton, France.

Third row left: In Menton, France, for French high school in 1987-88.

Bottom: The Winter Palace, Menton, my home at high school.

This page
(Opposite and above)
Top: With my cousins at the Christmas family get together.

Top right: Mum at home at Slotsalleen 11, Slagelse.

Second row: With mum and dad and Dorte.

Third row left: '*Mor Mads*' ('mother Mads') and Preben Madsen at Stenstuegade 6, Slagelse.

My maternal grandmother, Else Larsen.

Opposite page
(*Left to right from top*)
With grandma and grandad Larsen.

My grandparents' farm at Hvidstensgaarden.

My grandparents at their farm with me and mum's sister Connie.

My parents moving into Stenstuegade 6, Slagelse (c. 1992) and renovating.

Family Christmas.

Grandma Kristine.

Dad with his mother, Kristine Nielsen.

University of Copenhagen, Law Faculty, Denmark.

Opposite page
(Left to right from top)
The family on a Nile cruise in Egypt (with Dorte's boyfriend Jesper). March 1990.

Middle left. Tennis with dad in Egypt. March 1990.

Middle right. Setting off for London to study for my first Masters of Law. Aug 1991.

Mum and dad in London and on the beach at home in winter.

This page
Studying in in London for the LL.M. (1991-92)

This page
In 1992, I drove 15,000km across southern Africa from Johannesburg to Cape Town, Port Elizabeth and Durban, on through Namibia and Zambia and the Victoria Falls, then back to Johannesburg via Zimbabwe.

Top two rows: Visiting local tribes in Namibia.

Third row: Having run out of petrol in Namibia at 3.00 in the morning we hitched a lift to the nearest petrol station to find... NO PETROL.

Bottom: Getting stuck at the South African-Namibian border and having to stay with drunken soldiers in their tent overnight.

Opposite page
A trip to Gambia during the Autumn break from my law studies in London, 1991.

Middle row: Repairing punctures on the road to Dakar, Senegal; dining with my Gambian hosts.

Bottom row: The 'open air bathroom' of my Gambian hosts; back in my student room in London.

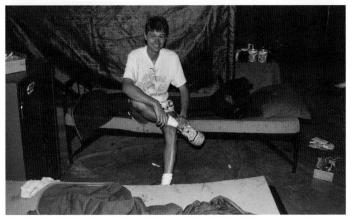

This page
At the College of Europe, Bruges, 1993-94.

Second row right: My student dorm at Gouden Handstraat, Bruges, College of Europe, 1994.

Third row: Scandinavian Viking party at the College of Europe, Spring 1994.

Opposite page
Top left: Taking part in an international law competition in my final Master's year at the University of Copenhagen, Spring 1993.

Top right: Presenting at the Adventurers' Club, Copenhagen.

Second row: Awarded the Academic Silver Medal by Queen Margarethe II for legal 'mini-PhD' on EU human rights, University of Copenhagen, 1995.

Third row right: writing my paper on EU human rights, Copenhagen, 1993.

Bottom left: Studying at the College of Europe, Bruges, 1993-94.

Bottom right: The Pee Wee (Per Wimmer) Club at the beach, College of Europe, Bruges, Belgium 1994

Top: Working for the Cabinet of the Vice President of the European Commission, Brussels 1994-1995.

Middle left: Internship at the United Nations, Geneva, summer 1994.

Bottom left: Starting at the European Commission, September 1994.

Bottom right: Official visit to Austria with the European Commission, Spring 1995.

Opposite page
With friends at the College of Europe, Bruges.

Bottom left: Graduation speech, College of Europe, June 1994.

Third row right: Moving from Belgium back to Denmark before heading for Harvard, summer 1995.

Bottom right: In my student dorm on Gouden Handstraat, Bruges.

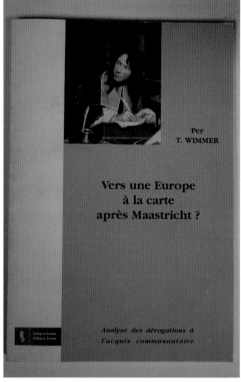

Top left: At the Cabinet of the Vice President of the European Commission, Brussels, Autumn 1994.

Top right: Christmas party at the home of Henning Christophersen.

Second row: With incoming Danish Commissioner Ritt Bjerregaard and outgoing Vice President Henning Christophersen, European Commission, Brussels, 1995.

Bottom left: Model UN competition, Luxembourg, while studying at College of Europe, Bruges, 1994.

Bottom right: My first book in French about the future of European integration (July 1995).

Per
T. WIMMER

**Vers une Europe
à la carte
après Maastricht ?**

*Analyse des dérogations à
l'acquis communautaire*

The view, as ever, was astonishing: green valleys and mountain peaks dotted with Inca ruins, a brilliant blue sky as the background to everything. We had been promised an easier day's hiking, and some of it was indeed downhill – but going downhill was also strenuous and just uses a different set of muscles. The whole trek was significantly harder than we had expected. When we got to the camp, I bought and drank five Fantas, one after the other. We ate dinner indoors – for the first time on the trek – and the evening turned into a lively celebration, with each participant obliged to sing their national anthem. I was, of course, not the only Dane in the group, and we got very enthusiastic. In fact, we were so loud that we were eventually asked to turn it down by another group at the camp!

Despite our exhaustion, Bab, the Frenchman and I started out the next day before dawn with battery torches to walk the last portion of the Inca Trail to the world-famous Machu Picchu ruins, arriving at sunrise. We stumbled many times in the dark, but after one and a half hours of walking, we got there. I had taken a bottle of champagne in my pack, and we toasted the first rays of the sun as they suddenly lit up the astonishing ruins, the tips of the sublime green-clad peaks and the ancient terraces, while the valleys still lay in darkness below … that bottle of champagne had come very close to being left on a mountainside several times during the trek, but that meant nothing now. Now, we would celebrate.

We took a bus down from Machu Picchu and stopped off at the Aguas Calientes hot springs to bathe. It felt so good! We hadn't showered in six days. We ordered a couple of beers and some freshly squeezed juice cocktails and stayed in the water until we almost dissolved.

The next stage of the journey was by rail. We arrived at what seemed to be a large goat market but turned out to be the Aguas Calientes train station. Everyone milled around, walking across the tracks and buying things from various stalls. When the train arrived, it was already full, and now around 200 more people had to be squeezed inside – often literally; people even climbed onto the roof and clung on there. Bab and I were forced to stand on the step board, backpacks and all, and hang on. The first one and a half hours went well. We were in good spirits and glad that we were not in the stuffy, cramped carriages. The train wound through the valley, and we soon found ourselves sharing our precarious space with several locals. Then came sunset, and the temperature dropped sharply. We were freezing, but still laughing. We were hugely impressed by the ticket inspector, who checked the tickets of everyone crammed into the carriages and hanging out of the windows – and then climbed onto the roof, crawled along, checking everyone's ticket sthere also. Those of us on the step boards escaped his attentions – but were checked the moment we were able to get into a carriage, after about two and a half hours. We stood for most of the rest of the five-hour journey, until we finally got to sit on a sack of potatoes and onions, squeezed alongside the locals. When we arrived in Cuzco, we went straight to bed and slept like lambs.

The next few days were spent first in Lima, the capital of Peru. I quickly got tired of the traffic, noise and pollution, although I enjoyed the Gold Museum, with its collection of Incan gold sceptres, gold-woven rugs and antique weapons. The next day was spent in Quito in Ecuador, a city filled with charming colonial buildings from the Spanish era, pretty churches and monasteries. It is a beautiful place to walk around, though clearly very poor and undeveloped. It was a good opportunity to unwind and destress before what I hoped would be one of the highlights of my trip: the Galápagos Islands.

My first day on the islands began with a walk around the east coast of San Cristóbal, where we saw the island's famous blue-footed booby birds, with their astonishing bright blue feet. Like the rest of the wildlife on the island, they are uniquely tame. You can get so close to them with your camera that you could almost ask them to pose! Next up was a snorkelling expedition. We saw hundreds of brightly coloured fish, while pointer sharks and hammerhead sharks circled beneath us in among the many scuba divers. We were assured that these were not a danger to humans, and the divers seemed unperturbed. We swam among the sea lions, who were very tame and playful, spinning effortlessly around us and often swimming toward us at great speed before turning away at the last moment, as if that was a great joke – which, of course, it was!

The next day was just as exciting: another snorkelling trip where I swam in a shoal of perhaps 200 blue angelfish with bright yellow tails and alongside sea turtles moving slowly and gracefully through the water. We also saw penguins and pelicans.

The following day was to be my first scuba dive. I was given a brief set of instructions on the boat before plunging into the crystal-clear ocean, where manta rays were circling. A whole new world opened up. How beautiful it was to be there, and how incredible to swim under water like a fish. Over the next few days, you could hardly keep me out of the water. I saw more corals, turtles, starfish and squid and spent my time between dives enjoying the local discos and the wonderful food. My trip to the Galápagos was so fantastic that I ended up extending my trip by an entire day.

After leaving the Galápagos, I stopped off briefly in Quito, before moving on to Bogota, Colombia. Bogota is located on a high plateau and is the third-highest capital city in South America, after Quito and La Paz. It is also one of the world's largest cities with around 7–8 million inhabitants when I visited. I was struck by the heavy traffic, but I was impressed by the charming old town, with its brightly coloured houses, charming balconies and small cafés. I visited Simón Bolívar's presidential home and learned about the country's road to independence from Spain in the early 19th century. State power is weak and largely corrupt. Guerrilla groups control parts of the country, functioning as both police and tax authorities. Drug cartels are extremely powerful, and the drugs trade fuels much of the Columbian economy.

I had been lucky to avoid any experience of corruption in Colombia, but I was about to experience this for the first time in Venezuela, when I arrived in Caracas. After arriving at my hotel, I went to a local café before deciding to stroll alone down the street in a nice, touristy neighbourhood when I was stopped by some distinctly unfriendly police officers. They ordered me to empty my pockets and began searching me, looking ostensibly for drugs. When they found nothing, they asked me to accompany them to a nearby hotel with an intimidating iron lattice door, which was locked behind us. I found the situation unnerving, to put it mildly, especially since the police were all armed and wore bulletproof vests. I could see that cooperation would be my best strategy.

Inside the hotel, I was told to remove all my clothes. I even had to take off my underwear and turn my socks inside out. I felt incredibly uncomfortable and vulnerable. When they found no trace of drugs, they asked for my passport. I avoid carrying important documents on my person where possible for safety reasons, and this gave them the excuse they had been looking for to issue a 'fine.'

I decided to apply some of the bargaining principles I had learned at Harvard, focusing on what our tutors used to call "expressed and underlying interests." I let them speak first, listened to what they said and then made my counterarguments. I began to sense that one of the two senior officers was either beginning to understand my argument or was getting tired of listening to me. I focused my attention on him until he finally let me go. I think they must have decided I was potentially more trouble than I was worth. I subsequently found out that these sorts of incidents are not unusual. I found it very disturbing to find that law enforcement there could not be trusted. Nevertheless, the rest of my time in Caracas was extremely pleasant: I met an interesting girl named Sara, and we spent time together exploring the Museum of Modern Art, a Picasso exhibition and the various cafés, bars and restaurants. Caracas has an efficient, French-style metro, good roads and many pedestrian streets and nice squares. There was a relaxed atmosphere in most places and the town was easy and pleasant to navigate.

Caracas was the final stop on my tour of South America. My journey continued with a 24-hour stop in Mexico City, before I flew on to Los Angeles the next day. Faith met me at the airport, having flown down from San Francisco. She had arranged everything, including a fantastic hotel in Santa Monica and car rental. We went shopping on Rodeo Drive and, unfortunately, I stumbled upon a super cool black suit with a crisp white shirt that I couldn't resist. It was so nice that I was even willing to carry it with me for the rest of the trip. All of Sunday was spent at Disneyland, just outside Anaheim. On Monday, we relaxed on the famous Venice Beach. It was here, however, that a large portion of our luggage, including my brand-new supercool black suit and white shirt, was stolen from the trunk of the car. We tried not to dwell on this and spent the rest of the time chatting and catching up on each other's experiences over the past few weeks.

The final, big stop on my trip was Fiji, where I had the chance to develop my diving skills. On the first two days, I experienced the three absolute best dives I have ever done. My favourite was on the famous Great White Wall. We descended 10 m before gliding through a 4-metre tunnel, then swam down even further to 30 m; usually the current is very strong at the White Wall, and it's rare to be able to descend so far. Then we basically stood still in the water and let the current sweep us across the face of the wall. To begin with, we saw corals of all colours and then suddenly the entire wall was filled with white corals in every possible shape, as far as the eye could see. These amazing corals are naturally white and have no connection to the 'bleaching' of coral reefs that is becoming an increasingly common problem as a result of rising ocean temperatures. We swam up through another tunnel – it was a wonderful feeling to fly up, feeling weightless. The next day we went to see the so-called cabbage head coral – a huge coral about 20 m in diameter. The third dive was very special and took place at an incredible dive site called Jerry's Jelly. The famous diving pioneer Jacques Cousteau used to dive there, and his son built a resort nearby. On my final dives in Teveuni, I saw the deadly poisonous lionfish and huge tuna, over 2 m long.

At my next stop, on the Kadavu Group archipelago, I took my diving certificate. The diving here was just as good as in Teveuni, with countless coral cliffs. I stayed in a wicker hut with only a kerosene lamp for light in the evenings – a little spooky when the wind was howling and the waves were crashing on the beaches; we experienced some storm-strength winds during my stay. Then to Suva, Fiji's largest city, and to Beqa Lagoon for two more days of diving. Finally, to Sydney for a few days' sightseeing, then to Copenhagen via Bangkok and Vietnam.

By the end, I was looking forward to getting back home. I was tired of airplane food, restaurant food and fast food and yearned for some plain and simple home cooking. More than that, I longed to see my family and friends. I couldn't wait to fill them in on all the details on my adventures and to hear how they had been since I left. After five months, I had visited around 20 different countries and even more cities, travelling by plane, train, car, horse, helicopter, bus, boat and on foot, for a total of around 60,000 km.

I was poorer financially but richer in many other ways: I had learned about other people's cultures, gained deeper insight into their values and questioned some of my own. I had seen many man-made and natural wonders and stored up a wealth of experiences I would be able to look back on at any time with pleasure. I had more clarity on what I wanted from my final year at Harvard and was keen to begin my professional career – though still undecided as to whether that career should follow the diplomatic route or a business path. I also felt the journey had matured me and – surprisingly – had to some extent made me more disciplined. Tight time frames had instilled some additional self-discipline, and potential dangers had helped develop my common sense and practical skills and brought home to me that I alone was responsible for the consequences of the choices I make and had to think carefully before making those choices. I was also very grateful for the help, backing and support of my family, without which the journey would not have been possible. I was aware of being privileged.

Looking back, there was almost nothing I would have changed about the trip – besides not leaving my backpack in the unlocked trunk of a car in Los Angeles!

GOLDMAN SACHS

I went back to Harvard in September 1997, full of energy from my trip round the world. My second year at the university was to be a very different experience. I only had one semester's work to do in twice the amount of time, so the pace of my studies was far less hectic, and I had time to take on some extracurricular activities for the first time. I started taking piano lessons. I set up the Scandinavian Society at Harvard to create a hub for the many Scandinavians studying at the university and to offer other students a greater understanding of Scandinavian culture through films, meetings, discussions and the like. Plus, of course, the all-important Scandinavian beer-tasting evening. I became involved in some charity work through the business school, where we had an outreach project providing landscaping and gardening to nursing homes and other institutions. Philanthropic work has been an important thing for me, ever since I was young. I've always been inspired by my mother, who was always involved in helping the local community in some way through various organizations.

As winter turned to spring, however, one question came to dominate my thoughts. What should the next chapter of my life be? Which direction should I take?

Spring at Harvard is hunting season for some of the most prestigious companies in the world, who come to the university hoping to attract bright new talent. They would set up their booths and hand out glossy brochures setting out the exciting possibilities of a career with them; senior members of staff would give talks about their organization; in the evenings they would host cocktail parties and senior staff and recruitment consultants would mingle with students, hoping to spot the most interesting talent and entice them to consider a career with them. I went to the career fair of spring 1998. I read the brochures, I watched the presentations, and I drank the cocktails – obviously – and I mingled with the senior executives and the recruitment consultants.

For business school graduates, one of the most important and appealing employers was the world-famous investment bank, Goldman Sachs. The other favoured banks were companies like Merrill and Morgan Stanley. In the world of management consultancy – another favourite destination for HBS graduates – firms like BCG, McKinsey and Bain were preeminent. But if investment banking was your thing, few opportunities in those days were as exciting or prestigious as a role at Goldman Sachs. The Goldman Sachs boys were a kind of elite, and a job at the bank could set you on the path to a glittering career. I met the Goldman Sachs team at the fair and, amazingly, I met and chatted with Abby Cohen, who was then the bank's chief investment strategist and something of a national figure as one of the country's leading financial analysts. The fact that Abby Cohen would make herself available to attend the fair says a lot about how seriously top employers take the recruitment drive at Harvard. She and I seemed to hit it off, and the Goldman Sachs team made it clear that they were interested in talking further. At that time, as I was saying earlier, the internet revolution was well underway. In fact, the dot.com bubble was starting to inflate, but nobody – literally nobody – saw that coming. Everyone thought (quite rightly) that the internet was going to change the world and that we could be part of that epoch-making moment.

My time at the Harvard Business School had opened my eyes to the potential of the financial sector – I found it fascinating and exciting – and Wall Street was booming. There were also rumours that Goldman Sachs were considering 'going public' in the near future; turning the organization from a partnership into a publicly traded company listed on the stock market. The main beneficiaries would be the partners – the effective 'owners' of the company – but less senior members could also hope to be given shares and share options.

Even the possibility of a role at Goldman Sachs seemed like something I would be foolish not to go for.

But there was another, intriguing opportunity. Another prestigious organization was present at the career fair, looking for talent ... the White House. President Bill Clinton was in his second term of office and the Clinton Administration was looking for bright young things from Harvard who were interested in working as interns for the Clinton Administration. They expressed interest and invited me for an interview.

An intern's pay is not very exciting – but many fabled careers have been launched by a few formative years spent working as an intern in the White House. My early studies and my work with the European Commission – and my current studies for a master's in public administration at Harvard – had all stemmed from a genuine fascination with the law and government and affairs of the state. I went for an interview ... and then five more interviews, one at the White House itself. It was exciting and flattering – surprising, since I was a foreigner, not a US national.

But in the meantime, the Goldman Sachs recruiting process was gathering steam. I had an interview in Boston. Then they flew me to London for two more rounds of interviews. They gave me first-class tickets for the flight and booked me into the famous Savoy Hotel on The Strand in London's central Covent Garden area for my stay. It was all very glamorous and high-powered. It was impossible not to feel exhilarated, but also anxious – it was like being given a glimpse of a wonderful possible future while knowing all the while that the next interview might be the one where you finally said the wrong thing or failed to 'bond' with someone very senior. Then there were several rounds of interviews in New York, including interviews with Bob Steel (Robert K. Steel) who was cohead of the Equities Division at the time. Bob went on to be on the board of Barclays PLC and to be president and CEO of the financial service company Wachovia, which he led into a merger with Wells Fargo. Bob is a wonderful person; we had a fabulous time.

Goldman Sachs take their corporate culture very seriously, which is why they devote so much time to the recruitment process. They believe in teamwork and a collaborative approach that will best serve the long-term interests of the firm, and they look for people with well-rounded characters – not the kind of brash, arrogant, ruthless character that is the (not entirely false) caricature of a Wall Street banker. From memory, I went through 38 different interviews. I met nearly every senior executive at the bank, except for the CEO, Jon Corzine. I once estimated that the process of vetting me must have cost Goldman Sachs around $1 million in expenses and executive time. The final rounds of interviews with Bob and the senior team in New York were clearly successful; I was offered a role as one of that year's new associates. I was being given the chance to become part of the Goldman Sachs family. But now there was a choice to be made – because I had also been offered a job at the Clinton White House.

I genuinely agonized about that choice. Both roles were wonderful, potentially life-changing opportunities. Before my time at Harvard, I believe that my instinctive choice would have been for the White House. It opened up the possibility of future roles close to the heart of government, something that I had always imagined was my dream career. But Harvard had introduced me to the world of finance. I was excited by it, I understood it, and I thought I would be good at it. I had attended lectures given by people who were both thought leaders in their field and active senior professionals in leading financial organizations. I had rubbed shoulders with the people who made the decisions and closed the deals that were reshaping the world of modern business. I was smitten. With great regret, I thanked the White House team effusively for their offer but said that I had decided to seek my fortune elsewhere.

I was to learn later that one of my Harvard classmates had accepted one of the White House intern roles. Her name was Monica Lewinsky. After President Clinton was impeached as a result of his romantic involvement with Ms Lewinsky, some of my colleagues speculated that, had I joined the White House along with Monica, she and I might have dated, and President Clinton could have been spared a great deal of trouble. Then again, President Clinton would have been pretty serious competition, even if Monica had shown any remote interest in dating her Danish ex-classmate and new fellow intern.

The world will never know how that particular alternative universe might have played out. I accepted the role at Goldman Sachs.

———

In my very early days at Goldman Sachs, I was given an apartment in Battery Park, organized and paid for by Goldman Sachs, on the southern tip of Manhattan Island. There was a wonderful view over New York Harbour, and it was a 10-minute walk through the park to the company's HQ at 1, New York Plaza, in the heart of Manhattan's financial district. The physical Wall Street was a few blocks walk away. The metaphorical Wall Street – the entirety of the United States' financial markets – was all around me. I felt as if I was living and working at the centre of the financial universe.

The next three months would be a crash course in investment banking the Goldman Sachs way. There was a strong focus on business culture and ethics; Goldman Sachs has always prided itself on its level of client service; on a constant striving for excellence; on business integrity; and on teamwork. It was drummed into us that mistakes could be forgiven, because everyone makes mistakes from time to time, but any behaviour that damaged Goldman Sachs' reputation was unforgiveable. We were given presentations by senior figures; famous former partners came to tell us their personal stories and talk about the company's history and culture. We were taught about all of the company's global activities, to give us the bigger picture. Even if you would be working exclusively with US equities, you also learned about the Japanese derivatives market. It was a wonderful introduction to the world of global finance.

Life outside the intensive induction course was pretty heady, I have to say. I was single. I was making more money than I had ever thought possible. Goldman Sachs paid for our apartments, our food, our entertainment. I had tons of cash coming in every month and no living expenses. I don't smoke and I don't do drugs but, as you might imagine, we were partying like there was no tomorrow every single day. In those days, especially, working at Goldman Sachs was an entry ticket to the most glamorous nightclubs in town. You would just mention the magic words to the doorman and get shown to the best tables, because they knew that Goldman Sachs' staff would expect nothing less and would be happy to pay for it. We were all young men and women, nearly all of us single, earning extremely good money and with none of the boring distractions of normal life. We had, as you might imagine, a great deal of fun. And then we worked till we should have dropped – but we never dropped. In those days, I could get by on three hours of sleep and still be in the office at 6.15 the next morning, bright eyed and bushy tailed and ready to take on the world. It was super intense and hugely exciting.

In November 1998, I relocated to London to work in European equities. Goldman Sachs put me up in a penthouse flat next to the Dorchester Hotel on London's famous Park Lane, the western boundary of the city's prestigious Mayfair district. I think there were five or six bedrooms. I shared the apartment with one of my colleagues, but we could just about manage. We had marble and gold in the bathrooms and a balcony overlooking Hyde Park. The rent for the apartment was around £10,000 per month. I dread to think what it would cost today, but that was still serious money in those days. The time did come, of course, when we had to find – and, sadly, pay for – our own accommodation, but those early days were happy times.

The equities market was also experiencing happy times. Back in 1994, a company called Netscape had launched a web browser that would dominate the market for a time. Only 16 months after the company had been formed, it launched on the stock market with an extremely successful IPO. Shares were originally planned to be offered at $14; a last-minute decision saw this raised to $28; on the first day of trading, shares reached $75, before closing the day at $58.25.

Netscape had yet to make a profit, though its earnings were picking up. In 'the old days' (the days before the internet revolution), it was virtually unheard of for a company that was not making a profit to be able to launch on the stock market at all. The key indicator of whether a company's stock represented good value or not had always been the 'price to earnings ratio' – the price of an individual share, which would dictate the company's total value depending on how many shares had been issued, relative to its 'earnings' (profits). But Netscape didn't have any 'earnings.' The old way of assessing whether a company's stock was good value or not had gone out of the window. Netscape, it was argued, was the future. The old 'bricks-and-mortar' economy was obsolete – the successful companies of the future would do business via the internet, and it would be a mistake to value them by the old measures. All that mattered was the *potential* these new early movers had to grab a share of what would become a whole new economy.

It's worth remembering that there was a great deal of truth in this – the internet changed the world in many ways, and it absolutely did change the way that people acquired information and goods and services. The companies that got it right in the early days – Amazon springs to mind – now rank among the world's most valuable companies. The problem was, back in 1998, nobody knew which new internet company might go on to become a world leader in its field, and which companies were more likely to crash and burn. What people were very focused on was that new internet businesses like Netscape were making investors who bought shares in those businesses very rich indeed. A successful IPO could see share prices double overnight – as Netscape's had. Doubling your money overnight was a very appealing concept. New ways of assessing the new companies' worth were devised, such as judging the potential future success of a new internet company by the number of 'clicks' they were attracting: the number of times consumers would visit the pages of their websites via a click on their computer's mouse.

But the reality was that nobody had any sure-fire way of telling which of the new internet companies were going to succeed and which would not. It became generally accepted that any 'dot.com' venture that could dominate a particular market sector was here to stay and would eventually reap the rewards. More importantly, its share value could only ever increase.

For quite some time, as with any bubble on the market, this became a self-fulfilling prophecy.

I remember those days on the London desk very well. I was working in the Scandinavian market, placing shares with major Scandi institutions. We were selling what we called 'paper' (i.e. shares) all day long. It was paper in 'blahblah.com' and 'nothing.com' and 'godknowswhat.com.' Whatever people used to do in the old world of business was going online: home deliveries; fashion; pet food; sports equipment; car hire; travel; financial information ... and they all had a business plan; our only problem was that all of the companies launching into these areas were very young, by definition. They had no track record of being able to attract enough customers – nor, significantly, of being able to run a successful business even if they got the customers. So there was no real way of telling if the business plan had any chance of turning into reality or if it was just fantasy; making up numbers about customers and clicks and revenues and (maybe even) profits.

But it didn't matter! Anybody who said these companies were not going to succeed was just an out-of-touch hack who didn't understand the new online world. And these were not billion-dollar deals. Compared to many old-fashioned industries, internet companies were not that capital hungry. A typical share offering might raise £100 million or so, which was the kind of deal we would expect to wrap up before lunch. And everybody wanted in on those deals, so the relatively low amount of capital required meant that supply was limited – and demand was high. I talked just now about doubling your money overnight, but increasingly new share offerings were trading up three, four, five and even seven times in the aftermarket. It was as if you couldn't lose, and you were guaranteed to win big. I remember we were just selling those deals all day long. There was not enough capacity. On some deals, I would call up sophisticated institutional investors on a Friday afternoon when the book was closing that same day and say, "I'm so sorry, I'm a bit late and I haven't had time to get around to you. I do apologize. We're handling the IPO for nonsensenonsense.com and the book is already 30 times oversubscribed, but do you want to be part of it?" And they would ask, "What is it? What does nonsensenonsense.com do?" And I would say, "It's something to do with nonsense, and it's going to be great. They probably won't make money until year eight or something, but the shares will trade really well." And my clients would say, "All right, put me in for 20 million euros." I'm being flippant ... but not entirely so; there were times when it was literally just like that. And I was telling the truth; shares in nonsensenonsense.com would definitely soar in value once they got onto the market and everyone would be happy.

There were some other aspects to the 'self-fulfilling prophecy' of the dot.com bubble at its height. Because nearly every dot.com share offering was hugely oversubscribed, we would do our best to allocate a decent number of shares to our most important clients, but it was common for major clients to want, say, €50 million worth of shares and for us to be able to allocate only €30 million. It was possible to persuade clients to buy a lower amount of stock in the IPO than they would ideally want, on the promise that they would buy more stock once the shares had gone public and begun to increase in price. So an investor might buy three million shares in an IPO at €10 per share, having promised to buy an additional two million shares once they were trading on the market at a higher price – say €15. This additional locked-in demand would quickly push share prices higher still.

At a more basic level, the excess of demand for shares over supply generated its own momentum. We would, for obvious reasons, advise our clients to ask for more stock than they actually wanted, because we would only be able to allocate a proportion of their original request. This created a false impression of the level of demand for any new share issue, pushing the initial price higher. We were also able to use the fact that the share price of any dot.com IPO would increase in the aftermarket to help us get IPO business from new clients. We could entice the owners of new dot.com enterprises to place their IPO with us by offering an option on stock with another new company on our books – stock that would 'inevitably' increase in value, making our potential new clients an additional killing.

I liked the competition, and my portfolio of Scandinavian clients was happy with my services. I thrived in this atmosphere. My career was going well, and I was soon made executive director with a sizeable team under me. I was on course to be made partner within a reasonable number of years. Becoming a full partner at Goldman Sachs was a big deal. As I was now responsible for the success of the people on my team and not simply for myself, I cut back a little on the social activities. I thought it was best to get a bit more sleep and let the younger team members do more of the partying. Also, the nature of my social life was shifting a bit, as I was developing a personal network of interesting, successful people. There were more private occasions and less clubbing. My personal relations with the top tier of Scandinavian business were growing stronger; relations that are professionally very valuable to me even today.

I was also put in charge of recruitment on the East Coast of the US, including, of course, the recruitment of Harvard graduates, which was great fun. When I was interviewing students, I could vividly picture myself sitting on the other side of the table, and I was able to conduct interviews with a great deal of empathy and an understanding of the candidates' hopes and aspirations – and whether they were likely to be a good fit with the Goldman Sachs' culture.

THE BUBBLE
BURSTS

This was also the time when Goldman Sachs would finally decide to go public; the last major investment bank to do so. The debate had raged internally for three decades. It was a major decision, with strong opinions on both sides of the argument.

One of the key features of Goldman Sachs up until this point had been its willingness to make investments that might be unattractive in the short term, because they were convinced of the benefits in the long term. The bank simply didn't have to care what its numbers might look like in any particular quarter. For publicly traded companies, of course, the latter was just about the only item on the agenda. A public company's market valuation lives and dies on the strength or otherwise of its next quarterly figures. On the upside, being a publicly traded company would give Goldman Sachs access to more capital and allow it to use its own shares to help finance strategic acquisitions. As the market became increasingly global, 'the right size' for an international investment bank kept growing and going public would give Goldman Sachs more clout.

The current partners would, of course, become extremely rich as a result of taking the company public, and it was argued that this would be unfair to the previous generations of partners who had built the company and helped bring it to its current preeminent position. Then again, those previous generations of partners were not the ones calling the shots right now.

In the spring of 1999, Goldman Sachs put 69 million shares on the market – 15% of its equity – raising $3.66 billion. Shares opened at $53 and closed at over $70, valuing the company at around $33 billion.

That day fundamentally changed my personal financial situation. Though the partners at the company were the biggest share owners, I had been given shares and share options as part of my remuneration package. When Goldman Sachs went public, I went from being very well paid to being essentially economically independent. It was a significant shift on a personal level. I felt, almost physically, how my priorities and thinking about the future had begun to change.

This was also the time when the opportunity for space travel presented itself – something that had never previously been an option for any private individual. With my passion for adventure, this was the ultimate goal: a truly 'out of this world' adventure. I started to fly out to Russia on the weekends to do my space-training flights in MiG-25 jet fighters, as I described at the beginning of the book, but this wasn't something I made very public at work. It was amusing to turn up at work and ask colleagues about their weekend and be told about the great party I had missed or whatever – but when asked in return what I had been up to, I would say something like, "Oh, nothing much; very quiet really," when in fact I had been flying at Mach 3 at the edge of space!

After Goldman Sachs went public, the bank had new strategic opportunities, but the pressure to deliver also immediately went up. Short-term results were now essential, which didn't fit easily with the bank's established culture. The partners had stock options, which meant that they were strongly incentivized to deliver exceptional results in the next couple of years. Nevertheless, a significant number of partners simply cashed in their shares and left after their shares lock-up period had expired. There comes a point when one has so much money that the opportunity to earn even more money is not necessarily an incentive.

From my professional point of view, things couldn't have been much better. As I entered what would turn out to be my final year with Goldman Sachs, our researchers worldwide elected me as the bank's best salesperson of European stocks. I was particularly successful within the Technology, Media, Telco (TMT) sector, of which the dot.com sector was a part of. We were all intrinsically bullish about the potential of TMT. We were young, we had only ever known a bull market and we were a part of the internet generation. We saw ourselves as part of the revolution; a mindset that doesn't always lead to the most clearheaded analysis. I and all my colleagues were also investing our own money in internet companies; it would have seemed crazy not to get our own share of the action as well as our professional rewards. On an intellectual and emotional level, we genuinely believed in the world-shattering potential of what we were selling – certainly in 1999, when the market reached what would be its peak. In late 1999, when I had been in charge of the distribution for the listing of Danish IT company, *Damgaard Data*, for example, it was oversubscribed by 16 times. When the market began to falter in early 2000 and share prices started falling, we saw this as a buying opportunity. The US Federal Reserve had raised interest rates to hold back rising inflation, making money more expensive; Japan had entered a recession and a worldwide sell-off of shares had disproportionately affected technology stocks; a planned merger between Yahoo! and eBay came to nothing. In April, NASDAQ, the key market for technology stocks, lost over 25% of its value in one week. We still saw this as an overreaction to unrelated pieces of financial news, not as proof that tech stocks were fundamentally overvalued and that a crash was around the corner.

Then, of course, on September 11, 2001, American Airlines Flights 11 and 175 crashed into the North and South Towers of the World Trade Centre in Lower Manhattan in a terrorist attack masterminded by the Islamic extremist terror organization al-Qaeda, and the world became a darker and scarier place. All US stock markets closed until September 17. When they reopened, the Dow Jones Industrial Average index fell by 7.1%. By the end of the week, it had fallen by 14.3% – the largest ever weekly fall of the index until that time.

It was as if the shock of that awful day had opened everyone's eyes. In November, the pet supplies venture, pets.com, went into liquidation only nine months after its February IPO. The company had spent a fortune on advertising and achieved excellent brand recognition, but it was selling goods to consumers at less than the price it had to pay for them. It was becoming clear that having a well-known URL, good web traffic and lots of lovely 'clicks' was not, after all, a substitute for a sound business plan, and that the huge amounts of money that had been spent on advertising to make pets.com a household name had been wasted. Maybe getting dominance of any business sector online was not guaranteed to turn into profitability.

It was as if we had been collectively partying so hard that it had taken us almost a year to realize that the music had stopped playing and everyone else had gone home. The champagne had gone flat, and the hangovers were beginning to kick in. The mood became low very quickly.

———————

One great upside of that difficult time following the burst of the dot. com bubble was the birth of the idea that would become Wimmer Space – an entrepreneurial organization devoted to my flight into space and my other planned adventures but, more importantly, to using these as a way of inspiring children around the world to live out their dreams, whatever they may be, and to stimulate their interest in space and science generally. Further, Wimmer Space became the test bed and the source of inspiration for my becoming a true entrepreneur, which eventually materialized when I set up my first company, Wimmer Financial, on 4 October 2007.

Even though very few of my colleagues knew at first about my having bought a ticket to space, I was getting an increasing number of phone calls from the press saying, "We hear you're involved with a private space venture. Is that true?" and I would say, "Yes I am, but not many people at Goldman Sachs know about it," and in general I played it down.

But one day, somehow, the fact that I was going into space made it onto the Reuters newsfeed and one of our Belgian traders picked it up and posted it to Goldman Sachs worldwide: "Per Wimmer from Goldman Sachs is going into space!" Boom! There it was. At that point, I had to make a decision. Was I going to shut down the media completely, or was I going to use the press coverage and make something out of it? Could I use people's interest in my trip to space to create something of value?

I decided to go for it. I would be happy talking about space all day long to anyone who would listen: why not?! And maybe people would find it interesting and inspiring – especially young people – and I could even use the media interest to promote certain charities and charitable efforts. But it was quite difficult doing that while still working at Goldman Sachs, because they liked to control the media narrative, and they were wary of anyone getting too much individual attention in ways that might not fit exactly with the corporate brand.

I left Goldman Sachs in 2002. Not because of their reluctance to let me make too much about my trip to space, though it was exciting to be able to throw myself into that once I was outside Goldman Sachs. It was simply that my work there was not fun any more. I had gone from the most exuberant of markets, when institutional investors were queuing up to get a slice of the exciting new ventures, to a market that was quite literally depressed – in both senses of the word. Nothing was happening. The culture shift at Goldman Sachs after the IPO was not helping, either. There were a lot of internal politics, a lot of pressure to do deals that would deliver short-term results and a new penny-pinching atmosphere where every expense was scrutinized; a very different experience from the days when any amount of money spent in the course of doing business was simply dwarfed by the amount of money we were making.

I decided to take some time off. I felt tired for, I think, the first time in my entire life. You feel tired after a hard game of badminton – but you also feel invigorated. I felt tired when I finally completed my book in French on the European Union after a very intensive spell of work – but after a good night's sleep, I was raring to go again. This was different. I needed some new challenges and new perspectives.

I had some decent money in the bank, and I went home for a spell. It was great being back home, but not everything was perfect there. My father had sold his car dealership to a 'trusted' colleague and should have been looking forward to his retirement, but he discovered that bad things had been going on behind the scenes at the company and that his 'trusted' colleague – who had bought the company at a very advantageous price – was maybe not so trustworthy after all. It affected him badly. He was smoking too much, for one thing. It upset and annoyed me to see what should have been the triumphant end of a great career spoiled by unpleasantness. The family rallied round. We did our best to remind Dad that he had nothing to reproach himself for, but you could sense that it was nagging at him. Still, I had a wonderful time with the family, and I caught up with old friends in Copenhagen and elsewhere. Then I went back to London and did some serious partying. It was a great time. I felt free and unfettered. I felt that I had made the right decision and earned the right to enjoy myself for a time. I began to feel refreshed and ready for a new challenge.

In early 2003, I went back into the world of finance with a UK company called Collins Stewart (now called Canaccord Genuity), where the culture was very entrepreneurial. Collins Stewart were one of the biggest issuers of shares on London's Alternative Investment Market, part of the London Stock Exchange that specializes in small- and medium-size growth companies – a very exciting market. The company was best known for their unique cash-flow model, which argued that a company's annual 'earnings' could paint a slightly rosy picture of the financial reality. A company might, for example, have done $50 million worth of business in a particular financial period – but when were they actually going to collect the money? The model suggested that cash flow – money in the bank at any point in time – was a far better indicator of a company's true financial health. Collins Stewart built a clever computer-based cash-flow model called 'Quest' that could analyse companies' performance from a cash-flow perspective and highlight the companies whose stock represented exceptionally good value on that basis.

At Collins Stewart, I was working as an investment advisor for my Scandinavian client base, and I was given far more freedom and responsibility than at Goldman Sachs, which I found liberating. I also enjoyed the more transparent commission system. At Goldman Sachs, a relatively complex system rewarded individuals not only on their own performance but also partly on the performance of the wider team and the company as a whole (with a good measure of discretionary 'political' input). This meant that an individual might deliver exceptional individual results and not see any exceptional benefit. It was also true that Goldman Sachs felt, with justification, that the Goldman Sachs name was largely responsible for opening doors to new clients and guaranteeing the level of service and results that a new client could confidently expect, and that, as a result, any individual working at the company should not be rewarded too lavishly for bringing in new business. Collins Stewart was far smaller and less renowned than Goldman Sachs, and they believed wholeheartedly in rewarding individual contributions to growth. There was a company saying: "You eat what you kill" – meaning that if your hunting was successful, you got your fair share of the subsequent feast.

The markets had recovered remarkably quickly after the bursting of the dot.com. The US Federal Reserve ('The Fed') had reduced interest rates to 1% – the lowest since 1958. Money was cheap and, as The Fed had intended, the appetite for risk returned.

The more entrepreneurial approach I learned at Collins Stewart certainly fed into my thinking about how I could develop my trip to space and my thirst for adventure into something extra. Something that could generate money and make a contribution to society in some way. Collins Stewart was not only far more flexible than Goldman Sachs about my involvement in the private space industry, they also thought it was very cool! This allowed me to get more creative. I started doing small presentations at schools, and some motivational talks for businesses. I would show some very amateurish videos I had shot of my training in Russia. They were unedited and shaky, and the sound quality was terrible – but people loved them! I began to get more requests from schools, but also from business connections, saying, "We'd really love you to come and speak to some of our colleagues or our clients about this because we think they would find it very inspirational. And we'll pay you for it." And I said, "OK, sure; why not? How much would you want to pay?" And then I thought, well, if people are paying me for this, I'd better get it right. I mean, I can't keep showing up with this raw video; it's embarrassing! I hired a professional video company and we produced some professional-quality videos and hooked up with a number of speaker agencies, and what was now established as Wimmer Space developed into a small motivational speaking business. Interestingly, I noticed that work tended to follow the economic cycle. When times were good, businesses wanted to hear about 'the sky is no limit' and think bold and adventurous thoughts. And when business was not so good, they tended toward looking inwards and finding themselves and doing yoga. I was clearly more of a 'bull market' flavour!

In these bullish periods, I would do a lot of presentations and meet a lot of very interesting people – often pioneers in their field, which is why they were interested in bold ventures such as the private exploration of space. And over time I began to add other ideas and activities to the Wimmer Space vehicle, including my books and projects related to my other adventure activities, such as films, DVDs and TV documentaries.

The most exciting aspect of Wimmer Space is still my work with young people and the charitable initiatives. Back then, together with *Jyllands-Posten*, the Danish broadsheet newspaper, and a Danish space education organization, we put together a roadshow that travelled across Denmark visiting schools. At the time I was the only Danish astronaut, and the kids would get very excited to see me in my spacesuit and space helmet, with the Danish flag on the shoulder of my space suit. We invited classes to create their own designs for a future moon base and submit them to a panel of judges; the winning team of children would win a trip to London.

In London itself, Wimmer Space was involved with the Ideas Foundation Creative Space programme, which worked with schoolchildren from the inner-city London Borough of Tower Hamlets on another competition designed to generate interest in science and technology and encourage creativity in science. In that case, the winning teenagers got to travel to the Houston and Kennedy Space Centres in the US to meet with leading people at NASA. It was genuinely inspiring to see these young kids from a traditionally deprived area get excited about space travel and science and technology in general, potentially opening up whole new futures for them and providing them with new hope, goals and aspirations. For me, the sky is no limit and I have always followed my dreams. Sharing that passion and philosophy with these young people, hoping they would take them on board and expand their current horizons would be a rewarding outcome for both me and them.

After a couple of exciting years at Collin Stewart I moved to the MAN Group, one of the biggest hedge funds in the world with assets under management north of US$60 billion. Their AHL Quant fund was one of the pioneers in computer-driven Quant investing. The company was founded in the 18th century to trade in sugar after the founder, James Man, won the contract to supply the British Navy with rum for the entire fleet's daily 'rum-tot.' The company still has a commodity trading division, but the hedge fund was the most significant division. Today, Man Group is the largest publicly traded hedge fund in the world, with over $100 billion funds under its management.

I joined the company in 2005 as a senior European equities advisor in their Man Securities division, working with large institutional investors. Nostalgically, given the company's history, my office was at Sugar Quay on the River Thames, right next to the Tower of London. I had a wonderful view of Tower Bridge from my office window. My salary was pretty amazing, and I could earn an additional six to seven times my basic salary in a good year. Man Securities was another highly entrepreneurial company. There was as much international travel as ever, especially to Scandinavia but also all over the world to meet personally with the key executives of companies with opportunities that might be attractive investments for my clients.

I helped to build up a substantial equities business, which was something new for the MAN Group. I had the freedom to spend any money I felt necessary to grow the business – and MAN would talk very much in those terms: "It's your business; do whatever you think is necessary." I was also pretty much free to spend my time however I wanted, provided I delivered the results, and I was able to pursue my interests in Wimmer Space as much as I chose to. But Wimmer Space was starting to get bigger. There was more and more activity, and it was starting to cause a little bit of friction at the edges. Even though I was as free as I possibly could be in any employment I can think of, I was still boxed in, to some extent. I still couldn't go someplace on Thursday afternoon because there was something happening at Man Securities, so it would have to be Friday. Small, unimportant things really – but they reminded me that working in even the freest, most entrepreneurial setting was not the same as running my own shop. I was still not entirely my own boss. I was beginning to think that it was time to branch out on my own. It was a scary thought, but also an exhilarating one.

Toward the end of my time at Man Securities, the group floated what was to become MF Global on the New York Stock Exchange. It was the second IPO I had been part of, and I did well out of it, but I had to leave all my vesting shares and options behind, since I was ready to set up my own firm.

THE FIRST PRIVATE SPACECRAFT

We arrived at Mojave Air and Space Port in California before dawn after a 90-minute drive from my Los Angeles hotel. The date was 4 October 2004. I was still employed by Collins Stewart, but I was not in California on company business: I had come to witness space history in the making.

As the road climbed into the southern foothills of the Sierra Nevada, the night sky grew darker as we left the lights of Los Angeles behind. As we approached Mojave, the billions of stars that make up the Milky Way were shining brightly in a velvet night sky. I was tired but exhilarated. We were about to witness an important step in the history of man's journey toward those stars.

Mojave is a small town in the southwestern region of the Mojave Desert, America's driest desert. The town started life in the 19th century as a construction camp for the Southern Pacific Railroad; later it was used as the headquarters for the construction of the Los Angeles Aqueduct. During the Great Depression, a small airport with two dirt runways was built there to service the gold and silver mines that had first been dug in California's Gold Rush. During World War II, the airport was taken over by the US Marine Corps and developed and expanded. Many of the Corps' WWII fliers received their gunnery training there.

This little town on the edge of a desert has played its part in the development of America's railroads, its infrastructure and its air force.

Mojave Air and Space Port was the first facility to be licensed by the Federal Aviation Authority for the launch of reusable spacecraft.

As you drive into the airport today, a sign over the roadway proudly proclaims that it is "The Home of SpaceShipOne." That sign was not there when we drove into the airport in the early hours to witness a historic launch of that very spacecraft: SpaceShipOne – the world's first private spacecraft.

SpaceShipOne had already made two flights into space from Mojave. In June 2004, the craft had flown to a height of 100 km above the Earth, crossing the 'Kármán line' that is the accepted boundary between the Earth's atmosphere and space. It had flown again on 29 September, only five days earlier. A successful flight today would allow the team behind the spaceship to claim the Ansari X Prize for developing the first commercial manned spacecraft to enter space twice within a period of two weeks.

Because of my commitment to commercial space travel, I was desperate for the flight to be a success and anxious at the possibility of failure or – far worse – disaster. I was providing live commentary of the event for BBC television, who were increasingly turning to me to provide comment and background on matters concerning the private space industry. I was proud to be a witness to the historic endeavour.

Dawn began to break, and the stars began to fade as the sky lightened from deep black through shades of blue and turquoise. As the sun's first rays fell on the Tehachapi Mountains to the west of the space port, I joined the crowd of assembled journalists and camera crews to offer my own commentary for the launch.

After a long wait, WhiteKnightOne, the mothership that carries SpaceShipOne to the edge of the Earth's atmosphere, began to taxi down the runway.

WhiteKnightOne looks ungainly on the ground with Space-ShipOne slung beneath it. It is only when it is in flight that the mothership's true elegance is revealed, with its twin tail planes and huge 82 ft (25 m) wingspan in a distinctive 'flattened W' shape. The sharp-nosed central cockpit is raised above the twin tail planes by the upward slope of the inner section of the W-shaped wings, and SpaceShipOne is carried directly beneath this raised cockpit.

SpaceShipOne itself is like a schoolboy's drawing of a rocket ship: cigar-shaped, with a more sharply pointed nose than its mothership and two stubby wings that extend into twin tail planes. The tail plane portion of the wings can be tilted upward to increase drag as the spaceship re-enters the Earth's atmosphere and then lowered again to allow the craft to glide to a landing.

WhiteKnightOne's twin turbojets powered the craft down the runway as it quickly picked up speed. As the mothership took off, all sense of ungainliness vanished as its giant wings gently lifted its heavy burden into the blue desert sky, with the sun burning brightly now on the horizon, turning the eastern skies pink and orange. The crowd of onlookers clapped and cheered, and I struggled to contain my emotions enough to be able to deliver a relatively coherent commentary as the BBC cameras filmed the ascent.

We all had a chance to catch our breath as WhiteKnightOne made its 60-minute ascent, climbing to around 14 km (around 46,000 ft). If the mission has to be aborted, the mothership is capable of landing with SpaceShipOne still attached. The pilots' voices were being livestreamed to us, and we cheered again when we heard that Space-ShipOne had been successfully released from the mothership. The spaceship glides for a few seconds; if its rocket fails to ignite, it can glide safely all the way back to Earth. But the rocket ignited flawlessly, blasting into life and powering the spaceship up into space with an acceleration of around 1.7 G, reaching a velocity of over three times the speed of sound (Mach 3). After the burn, the rocket continues to climb like a bullet, reaching the apogee of its climb at over 100 km – the all-important Kármán line and the border of space.

We cheered again as we heard pilot Brian Binnie calmly announce that the spaceship had passed the line.

At this point in the flight, future passengers in the spaceship will experience 10–20 minutes of weightlessness. I have experienced this myself as part of my astronaut training, along with high G-force experiences in centrifuges. I tried to imagine what Brian Binnie was experiencing and wished I was his passenger today.

As SpaceShipOne begins its descent, it reconfigures its wings into 'high drag' mode to slow its speed, just like a badminton shuttle-cock. As it hurtles into the Earth's upper atmosphere, it experiences extreme deceleration: over 5 G; far more than the G forces experienced on the ascent into space.

About 20 minutes later, we all got our first glimpse of a small white dot in the sky: the spaceship gliding back toward the airstrip, its wings now down in 'lower drag' mode. It touched down smoothly, nose up, followed a little later by WhiteKnightOne, which takes longer to make the descent.

I watched and continued my commentary as three pivotal figures in the programme drove out in the back of a pickup truck to greet the returning spacecraft: Burt Rutan, the brilliant aerospace designer and engineer behind the development of SpaceShipOne; his company's backer, Paul Allen, cofounder of Microsoft; and Richard Branson, whose Virgin Galactic enterprise would be the company's first customer – and who would shortly give me the opportunity to become their 'founding astronaut' with a ticket to fly into space on the commercial spacecraft, SpaceShipTwo.

I had noticed Burt Rutan, the Dr Einstein of spaceship building, weeping quiet tears of joy earlier as SpaceShipOne made its historic ascent, marking the winning of the Ansari X Prize and the accomplishment of his dreams. It had been an emotional and amazing day for me also, in my own small way: another milestone cleared on the path to my first flight in space. Fantastic!

————————

Let me take you back in time a little while, to the birth of commercial air travel.

In the early years of powered flight, the only real customers for aircraft were the military and the US Post Office, which had seen the potential for an airmail service that could deliver mail faster and cheaper than the railroads – and who were supported in this idea by the military, who saw that regular airmail flights could increase the supply of trained and experienced pilots.

In 1925, the US Congress passed "An Act to encourage commercial aviation and to authorize the Postmaster General to contract for Air Mail Service" – and commercial Contract Air Mail was born. The first two routes were awarded to the Ford Motor Company, flying a fleet of six Ford-built Stout 2-AT aircraft. A later contract, to carry mail from St Louis, Missouri, to Chicago, was awarded to the Robertson Aircraft Company, who employed a young flight instructor called Charles Lindbergh to lay out and subsequently fly the route between the two cities.

Now, let's go back a little further in time, to 1919, when a French-born New York hotelier called Raymond Orteig is listening to a speech by World War 1 American fighter ace, Eddie Rickenbacker, given to the Aero Club of America. Rickenbacker looked forward to a day when America and France might be linked by air travel. Orteig was inspired by the idea. He offered a $25,000 prize to anyone who made a nonstop flight from New York City to Paris (or in the other direction) in the next five years.

Charles Lindbergh, our young airmail pilot, became determined to win the prize. He managed to persuade two St Louis businessmen to raise a bank loan of $15,000, committed $2,000 saved from his salary and also persuaded his company, Robertson Aircraft, to back the venture. The small and money-strapped team commissioned a custom-built aircraft, *The Spirit of St Louis* – and the rest is history.

On 20 May 1927, Lindbergh took off from Roosevelt Field, Long Island, and completed the 33-hour flight to Le Bourget Aerodrome near Paris. He was dragged from his cockpit and carried head-high for over half an hour by a huge crowd gathered to witness his historic arrival.

Lindbergh's flight captured the public imagination and had a dramatic, worldwide impact. People everywhere were caught up in the excitement of a vision of a world in which men and women could fly across oceans and between continents. As Lindbergh said, "I was astonished at the effect my successful landing in France had on the nations of the world. To me, it was like a match lighting a bonfire." Bankers began to see the potential returns from new aircraft technologies and the development of commercial air travel; money began to flow into the aviation industry.

In 1927, the year of Lindbergh's epic flight, pioneering aircraft manufacturer William Boeing won the bid to carry airmail from Chicago to San Francisco. By the end of the 1920s, he was carrying one quarter of all US Airmail and an increasing number of passengers. In 1929, he launched a 12-passenger biplane, the world's first passenger aircraft. In 1933, the company launched its Model 247, the world's first modern passenger aircraft.

The entrepreneurial spirit of commerce was beginning to drive innovation and turn into reality the dream of air travel that had so inspired the world after Lindbergh's epoch-defining flight. These early days of commercial flight were the province of the rich and famous. Beautiful people sipped cocktails in the hotel-like lounges of Pan American Airways and other operators, en route to impossibly glamorous destinations: the Caribbean, Honolulu, Manila, the Far East!

And then, very quickly, air travel became available to all. Businessmen and women could meet their colleagues and trading partners in far-flung corners of the Earth at the cost of a few days out of their busy schedules. Ordinary working families began to travel to exotic destinations (especially exotic and *sunny* destinations for people in the northern hemisphere) as a matter of routine.

The commercialization of air travel had transformed the aviation industry from an intriguing new innovation of great symbolic significance, with perhaps some minor role to play in the armed forces and for delivering mail and other interesting developments, into something that would transform the world economy and become a part of everyday life for millions of people.

I believe that commercial space travel is at *exactly* the same inflection point. We are currently at the beginning of a new dawn: a revolution in private space travel.

In the late 1990s, Greek American engineer and entrepreneur Peter Diamandis conceived a prize that would mirror the Orteig prize that galvanized Charles Lindbergh's transatlantic attempt: the X Prize for the first nongovernmental team to develop a reusable spaceship. He believed – quite rightly, as events are beginning to prove – that such a prize would drive innovation in space travel and unleash its commercial potential in exactly the same way the Orteig prize had stimulated the growth of the aircraft industry earlier in the century. Seed money was raised, and the venture was called "The New Spirit of St Louis Organization." Later, two Iranian American entrepreneurs and space fans from the Ansari family put up $10 million in prize money for the winning team, and the prize became known as the Ansari X Prize. (On 18 September 2006, my friend Anousheh Ansari went up to the International Space Station as the first Iranian-born astronaut and the fourth private space traveller on a Soyuz rocket.)

Over 20 teams competed to win the prize: some of them real 'garage' operations; some of them well-funded and sophisticated. That, to me, is the joy of commercial, entrepreneurial endeavours. Lindbergh won the Orteig prize on a shoestring budget, beating projects with far higher funding. With innovation and invention, money helps, but it doesn't guarantee success. You never know when some crazy people with a good idea and lots of determination might sneak in and win the prize!

As it was, on that day in October 2004, SpaceShipOne and the Scaled Composites team – a bunch of people with some crazy ideas *and* some serious backing from Paul Allen ($25 million) – won the prize and opened up a thrilling new future for space travel.

Seen in the light of history, private aviation really took off when private enterprise got involved: it drove up the number of flights, passengers and miles flown. Levels of customer service went up and costs and prices came down, as they do in the early days of any successful new industry. Precisely the same thing will happen in the emerging commercial space industry. Few people today realize how revolutionary this is, but a growing number of us feel the excitement and see the potential. In fact, we are probably underestimating what is really to come. For me, this has all the excitement of the early days of aviation and the ground-breaking efforts (and eccentricities!) of visionaries like Howard Hughes, and the starlit glamour of the early days of air travel, with celebrities and excitement and adventure.

But, just as air travel moved on from those heady, glamorous days and soon got down to the serious business of changing and improving the lives of huge numbers of people, I am convinced that commercial space travel will also change the world, in ways we cannot yet imagine. Making a trip into space will be affordable for more and more people, like a trip on a cruise ship or a luxury holiday to exotic destinations: things that were once the preserve of the wealthy but are now enjoyed by many of us.

It is my personal belief that when increasing numbers of people leave the Earth's atmosphere and see our beautiful, fragile planet from space, they will come back to Earth with a different perspective ('The Overview Effect'). And I am absolutely certain that younger generations will be fascinated and inspired by the increasing familiarity of space travel. I believe that this will be the catalyst that creates new levels of interest in science, engineering and technology in today's schoolchildren and students. And once they see that space travel is something they can aspire to and hope for in their own lives, who knows what new ideas and initiatives may spring from their fertile young minds?

I see and feel this when I make motivational speeches at schools and universities, talking about my involvement with the private space programme. If just half of us future astronauts do our bit in bringing the excitement and potential of commercial space travel to young audiences, I truly believe we could make a big contribution to the next generation.

I am certainly committed to doing my bit to pass on the torch to the young would-be astronauts of the future.

CAPE CANAVERAL

It is July 2005, and I am closing the front door of my home in London to set off on a momentous trip. First, I am travelling to Miami and on to Cape Canaveral to witness the historic launch of the Space Shuttle *Discovery* – the first 'Return to Flight' mission for the Space Shuttle since the *Columbia* disaster in 2003, when that Space Shuttle disintegrated on re-entry into the Earth's atmosphere, killing all seven crew members. The *Discovery* was also the Return to Flight craft chosen after the Space Shuttle *Challenger* broke up 73 seconds into its flight in January 1986, again killing all seven crew members. After that appalling disaster, *Discovery's* Return to Flight had happened in 1988. I had feared, with many others, that the 2003 *Columbia* disaster would be the end of the Space Shuttle programme and, with my commitment to the idea of travelling into space becoming a part of our 'normal' lives, I was hugely excited to see the Space Shuttle, the world's first reusable spacecraft, travelling back to space.

After my trip to Cape Canaveral, I was setting off on a wonderful – though far more mundane – adventure of my own: another voyage of discovery, travelling from Miami to the United Arab Emirates, Vietnam and China. I was looking forward to it. I had also made the decision to move from Collins Stewart to Man Securities. The trip would be the perfect break between employments; a chance to unwind and refocus.

Standing on the doorstep of my apartment in Islington, London, I did the usual mental check. Wallet. Keys. Phone. Essential business papers. Reading material for the flight. Tickets. Itinerary. Passport.

Passport.

Passport!

Where the **** was my passport?!

I had flown into London Heathrow only a couple of days before. I had come safely through passport control. Must have put the passport back in my jacket pocket. Somewhere else? No, jacket pocket. Then what? Taxi into London. Had I taken my jacket off? Yes; hot day. Maybe it had fallen out in the taxi? I started to run through my options – and then I felt like bursting into tears. I had been so looking forward to witnessing the launch of *Discovery*.

There was the slimmest chance that I could retrieve the passport from the Transport for London Lost Property Office, if I had indeed lost my passport in the taxi. But I remembered from somewhere that lost passports are sent first to the police, and then forwarded to the Lost Property Office, which takes a week or so. The other alternative was to apply for a new passport. Getting a new passport from the Danish embassy normally takes five to six weeks and the *Discovery* launch was in a few days' time.

It was hopeless. Or, as we say in Danish, *håbløst*. Or, again, as we say in English, it seemed I was stuffed. Snookered. Done for. Buggered.

I forced myself to focus on the available options and got to work. I rang the Lost Property office and the Danish embassy. The embassy people were very helpful and promised to get right onto it. The Lost Property Office was polite, but all they could tell me was to try again in a week's time.

As it happens, I was saved by a piece of 'unluck.' I can't call it 'good luck,' because it was bad luck for NASA: *Discovery* had a problem with its fuel sensors, which NASA were racing to fix. This piece of unluck had the potential to repair my first piece of unluck in losing my passport. But it would be a close-run thing.

I filled out my new passport application on July 11. By July 14, the passport production company in Denmark had received all relevant material and had started the physical production. Everyone was really pulling out all the stops for me. I was so grateful. In the end,

I went to the embassy on Friday, 22 July 2005, only 11 days later, having been told the passport had arrived – in about a third of the time one would normally expect to have to wait. I thanked the embassy staff warmly and went straight to the travel agent to confirm my flights for the following Monday morning, 25 July 2005.

Everything just fell into place in the last hours of that Friday afternoon. Sometimes, I believe I must have been born under a lucky star ... which is also why I must try to fly a little closer to it, to be able to say thank you!

I now had a weekend to pack and get ready for my trip. A hang-gliding trip planned for the Saturday was cancelled because of bad weather, which gave me some useful time to get ready. But on Sunday I had been invited to attend one of the key events in the British summer calendar: the Cartier Queen's Cup Final of the Guards Polo Club, which takes place on the Chukkas Lawn in Windsor Great Park, the ancient hunting grounds beside Windsor Palace, one of the royal residences. Her Majesty Queen Elizabeth II would be attending, as would her younger grandson, Prince Harry. As social occasions go, it doesn't get much swankier. And now, after the latest piece of unluck, I would be able to attend!

The polo was excellent, I'm sure, but I have to confess that most of the focus was on the VIP China White area, which was packed with celebrities, actors and actresses and a fair number of people from the world of finance, like myself. I knew a lot of people there and had a good catch up with a number of them. With Prince Harry partying rather quietly at the bar, we partied slightly harder until late into the night. The next day, Monday 25 July, a little jaded but very excited, I was in the air on my way to Miami to witness the launch of *Discovery* the following day.

I have watched various Space Shuttle launches a hundred times on various TV programmes, but I have never seen one 'live' at Cape Canaveral. I guess part of the reason is that trainee private astronauts like me do most of our space training in Russia so, rather bizarrely, I have more connection with the Russian space programme than I do with NASA and Cape Canaveral. As a result, I am looking forward to tomorrow's launch like a small boy looks forward to Christmas the night before. Which is making up for my almost tearful disappointment when I realized I had lost my passport nearly two weeks earlier and that Christmas had apparently been cancelled!

What I *had* missed, unfortunately, was a dinner scheduled around the original launch date celebrating the 30-year anniversary of the Russian-US cosmonauts'/astronauts' rendezvous in orbit and the shaking of hands in space for the first time. That was a shame. I would have loved to have heard some of the stories from that time.

As I thought about the next day's launch and about *Discovery's* 'Return to Flight' after the two previous deadly Space Shuttle disasters, I remembered a quote from the early Project Gemini and Apollo astronaut, Gus Grissom, about the risks and costs of space travel. "The conquest of space is worth the risk of life," wrote Gus. Gus himself died, along with two fellow astronauts, when a fire broke out in the capsule of Apollo 1 on the launchpad during a prelaunch test in 1967. But Gus was right: continuing the quest for space and continuing to push the space frontier ever further justifies and honours the earlier sacrifices of the space pioneers. This, after all, is what they strove for. This is what some of them died for.

If my own flight to space turns out to be a disaster and a mortal failure, I would fervently hope that lessons would be learned and that other space enthusiasts would add to the impetus to continue the private exploration of space and to reach further than ever before. Like any pioneering activity, the exploration of space is dangerous and carries risks. We have to face those risks, accept disasters when they occur – as they inevitably will – and soldier on.

---

26 July 2005.
5.15am. Wake-up call!
Why do these historic space events always have to take place in the middle of the night?!

One good reason is that the weather conditions are more conducive, before the day gets too misty and clouded. However, this time, a further reason was hitting the right orbit. *Discovery's* scheduled launch time of 10.39am had a window of only 10 minutes to hit the right orbit in order to dock with the International Space Station.

Not much room for error.

At Cape Canaveral today, I was to be the guest of Space Adventures. Their executives, Tim Franta and Chuck Sammons, were driving me via a scenic back route through the Cape Canaveral peninsula to the Cape Canaveral Air Force Station to avoid the inevitable traffic. On the original launch date, 13 July, it was estimated that about a quarter of a million people had shown up – sadly in vain! Similar numbers were expected for today's launch. Fortunately, Tim is incredibly well-connected within NASA (and elsewhere for that matter; he calls former governor Jeb Bush at home) so we were given the full VIP treatment: VIP car parking in spaces allocated for NASA staff; a VIP breakfast; VIP transfer to absolutely the best and closest launch viewing site – the Saturn V hangar, about 6 km from the launch site itself. That may sound a long way away but, believe me, you wouldn't want to be any closer! Our VIP status got its final confirmation when Laura Bush arrived with an escort of police and secret service to join our party at the hangar.

I had to smile to myself as I watched the previous First Lady of the United States of America take her seat quite close to us. I had been partying with Prince Harry at Windsor on Sunday. Today I was a VIP guest of NASA with Laura Bush to watch the launch of *Discovery*. What would the rest of the week hold, I wondered?!

We waited eagerly for the launch. Heavy photographing began in front of launchpad 39B and in front of the famous countdown clock, which was showing nine minutes to launch. An Air Force band struck up America's national anthem, and the mood became more intense. The solemnity of the occasion hit us all: a daring return to space after the tragic ending of Space Shuttle *Columbia's* last flight; a celebration of the dedication and ingenuity of the NASA team and of mankind's indomitable will to persevere in our exploration of space, regardless of risks and setbacks.

Then came the passing of the five-minute mark! This was the point of no return. Now the launch must proceed. I went live on TV, providing voice commentary for the Danish TV station DR-1.

We all fell silent as the calm voice of the NASA Vehicle Manager was broadcast to us all for the final countdown. "Ten, nine, eight, seven, six, five, four, three, two, one ... lift-off. We have lift-off."

What a truly historic moment and a huge relief for everyone at NASA, and for the world. We were back in space! And out came the biggest water clouds on both sides of the shuttle that one can imagine. About 300,000 gallons of water sprayed in huge volumes close to the rocket engines as they ignited to counter the worst of the potentially damaging soundwaves. Slowly, yet elegantly, this huge colossus of steel carefully ascended into the sky – smooth and easy and bang on time: 10.39.

And then an incredible wall of sound hit us, despite the damping effect of the clouds of water spray. I had never experienced anything like it. The noise itself was unimaginably loud – but it was more than a noise; it was like an assault. My clothes actually moved and shook. The air in my lungs seemed to vibrate and it felt hard to breathe.

Discovery was rapidly disappearing into the sky on a column of smoke.

A new chapter in space history could now begin. Regular visits to the International Space Station could be resumed.

For me personally, this seemed like another milestone paving the way to my own flight into space in a few years' time. I could not wait to go.

I arrived in Abu Dhabi, capital of the United Arab Emirates, on 6 August. The timing wasn't great. It is very hot in the Arabian Peninsula in August. Who knew? Obviously, I did know in theory, but I was still taken aback. The temperature was 49°C and the humidity was very high. I had never experienced anything like it. Even getting from one's comfortable beach chair into the beautiful clear waters of the Arabian Gulf a few metres away can be a challenge – the baking hot sand literally burns your feet. You sweat all the time because of the humidity; I gave up trying to keep fresh with an endless stream of showers because it is a battle one is bound to lose. Most of the locals, who are more sensible than us beach-mad Europeans, rarely leave an air-conditioned environment in the summer months – they go straight from their air-conditioned apartments into their air-conditioned cars, and on to an air-conditioned office or mall or restaurant.

I hired a 4WD Toyota and did some sightseeing: oases filled with palm trees, historic forts, goat markets and the like. I discovered that patience is a necessary virtue. Everyone seems very happy and good-humoured and are very helpful, but nothing happens very quickly. Perhaps it's the heat. There was a very real sense of how recently the country has become wealthy and modernized. The region used to depend mainly on pearl-fishing for its income; the industry only finally died out after the end of World War II. Then in the 1950s came oil exploration. In 1958 a floating oil rig was towed from Hamburg in Germany and positioned over the ancient pearl bed ... and struck oil. Oil and money began to flow, fast and furious, utterly transforming the economy.

I drove 500 km east to Muscat, on the Gulf of Oman. Muscat is huge and sprawling and a bit like Los Angeles but without the downtown skyscrapers. I checked into a downtown hotel and went for a quick beer at the hotel. The many male immigrant workers were having a big Thursday night out (Thursday in Oman is like Friday in the West). About 100 men were quietly having a drink while watching four women dancing an Arabic dance. From time to time, one of the men would buy a silver-coloured necklace for one of the dancers as a sign of appreciation. Very few of the men seemed to talk to each other as they sat quietly, watching the dancers and sipping their drinks. It wasn't the wildest night on the town. The Copacabana Club at the beautiful Hyatt Hotel did seem to offer something close to a nightclub, with Western music, a dance floor with an enthusiastic DJ playing hits from the 1970s and 1980s. Men and women were strictly separated. The women danced together, and the men stood at the edge of the dance floor watching the women dance with a rather forlorn look. There were also quite a few older men dressed in traditional Arab clothing: a quite surreal scene. A bouncer walked constantly up and down the edge of the dance floor to make sure the men stayed well clear of the dancing women.

The next day, I took an early morning drive along the coast of Muscat. There were beautiful fishing villages surrounded by mountains and, not surprisingly, the Sultan's residence situated in an especially prime location! I travelled on to Abu Dhabi to attend the wedding of some Sudanese friends, then transferred to Dubai to stay at the famous Burj Al Arab hotel with its famous 'sail-like' architecture – the world's only self-proclaimed seven-star hotel. The level of service was genuinely impressive and included the attentions of a personal butler.

The 'rooms' were more like apartments, and there was a great deal of gold everywhere – real 24-carat gold. The spa on the 18th floor had spectacular views over Dubai, the beach and the ocean.

My next stop was Phnom Penh in Cambodia and then on to Siam Reap in the north of the country. My dear friend from the Lycée in Menton, Michel Ghigo, had settled in Cambodia and done an amazing job of building up a Cambodian version of 'Yellow Pages' – the business telephone directory that was so successful in the days before the internet when we needed a way to look up the phone number of businesses that could supply the goods and services we needed. Michel had sold his stake in the company he had built up and seemed contentedly settled in Cambodia with his wife and three children. The country's recovery from the dark days of the communist Khmer Rouge regime was remarkable, with an economy driven mainly by small enterprise and a tireless workforce eager to make a better life for themselves. Although there had been a gap of many years, Michel and I fell immediately back into our old friendly ways. I was touched that he still called me *min bror* – Danish for 'my brother' – a habit he had got into back in Menton.

The Cambodians still suffer horribly from the landmines planted by both sides during three decades of conflict: there were many people who had lost legs to be seen begging on the streets of Siam Reap; the country has one of the highest casualty rates from landmines in the world. It was impressive how the Cambodian people, who had suffered so much, were so welcoming and seemingly happy. Tourism was beginning to have a significant impact, but corruption remained a problem; every single public official seemed to have their hands 'in the till' in one way or another and the higher the position, the bigger the scale of the corruption. This was a particular problem in the legal system, obviously, because it meant that the richer party in any dispute would always come out on top. At a lower level, it looked as though ordinary people had very little protection from the authorities: I saw one lady carrying a basket of fish, presumably heading for the market, when she was stopped by the police. I don't know what the supposed problem was, but I noticed it was quickly solved when she handed over two of her fish. I also learned from the many 'unofficial' guides to the various tourist sites – many of them students trying to earn a bit of extra cash – that they had to make payments to the local police to be allowed to continue to offer their services. Nevertheless, my general impression of Cambodia was very positive. China's influence was strong and likely to grow – there were direct flights to Beijing from Siam Reap seven days a week – but the historic involvement of France and the US in Cambodia had left a noticeable legacy, international aid was clearly having an impact, and I felt the country's future looked bright.

I had a wonderful time catching up with Michel and his family in Siam Reap, and the rest of the time I spent on the tourist trail – mainly visiting the country's many amazing Buddhist temples. The famous Angkor Wat temple, built in the 12th century, is the centre of a complex of over 80 temples, large and small, scattered over a large area, much of it now forest or agricultural land. The *Lonely Planet* guidebook – my bible for the trip – had created a new phrase to describe the experiences of the dedicated temple visitor: the possibility of being 'templed out.' The largest temples can easily take three hours to explore properly and most feature very steep flights of stairs: they are built as symbolic representations of the sacred five-peaked Mount Meru, the centre of the physical and spiritual universes, and it is necessary to suffer and struggle to reach the peak, where Śakra, the ruler of heaven, presides. At the end of several days, with sore feet and tired legs, I did feel I was close to being 'templed out,' but it was worth it.

The easiest way to travel was either by the ubiquitous tuk tuks – three-wheeled motorized rickshaws that get you around very cheaply and efficiently – or, for longer trips, on the back of a motorcycle taxi. I travelled by motorbike to the beautiful Kbal Spean creek and waterfall 60–70 km outside Siem Reap. The drive was considerably longer than I had imagined, and the dirt roads and potholes didn't make matters any easier, but travelling by motorbike gets you close to the local environment and gives you a real feel for a place that you miss from the cocooned comfort of a car.

From Siem Reap, I flew to Beijing. The welcome in China was in marked contrast to the happy smiles of Cambodia. Many Chinese seem to try to rip you off whenever they get an opportunity and are frequently rude or, at best, impolite. When I arrived at Beijing Airport, a taxi driver grabbed the luggage from my trolley without asking and set off toward his vehicle, He suggested a fare that was four times the correct amount and lied outright about the cost of the shuttle bus, telling me that it cost Y80, when the actual fare was Y16.

There are rogue taxi drivers in every country, but my general impression of the Chinese didn't improve greatly. They are, in general, extremely loud and seem to shout without reason or any consideration of the people around them. They are aggressive – but not threatening – and extremely selfish and inconsiderate. They will jump any queue if they can get away with it (to the great annoyance of any British!) and will walk straight in front of the camera if you are trying to take a photograph without batting an eyelid. In shops and markets, very few prices are displayed, so everything has to be negotiated, which becomes very tiring – especially since the negotiating style, again, is unpleasant and aggressive and, of course, the opening offer for any tourist is unreasonably high.

Beijing is also physically demanding because of the large distances between the main tourist sites (Tiananmen Square, the Forbidden City, the Great Hall, etc.). One can easily end up walking miles and finish the day exhausted. I was also suffering from persistent diarrhoea, which didn't help. The Chinese really do seem to eat everything – scorpions, intestines, silkworms (fried), duck brains – and although I balked at trying some of the more exotic offerings, I did try to be a bit adventurous. My stomach was clearly not grateful for my bravery. To top everything off, on my visit to the Forbidden City, it poured with rain the whole time, ruining the visit.

Still, my mood was hugely improved when, by a truly extraordinary coincidence, I bumped into Elena, a fellow College of Europe student from my class in Bruges 10 years previously. She was travelling with a group of other tourists but had got separated from them – easily done, because of the huge crowds of visitors – and she suddenly spotted me at the exact moment I spotted her. We couldn't believe our eyes. We hugged and talked incoherently over each other for a while: "What on Earth …?" "Where did you …?" "I can't believe …!" "What are you …?" And then we calmed down and briefly told our stories.

We spent some time pushing our way through the crowd, looking for Elena's group to reassure them that she was safe and well, but it was hopeless. She decided that she would put in a call when she got back to the hotel to tell them she was OK, and we headed off to get some lunch at a local restaurant. Over a rather indifferent lunch (perhaps we ordered too conservatively and should have gone for the pigs' intestines with scorpion) we talked nonstop, filling each other in on the details of our lives for the past decade. Then we decided to visit the Lama Temple, which was 'only' about 5 km away from the Forbidden City. The correct name of the temple is the Yonghe Temple – the Palace of Peace and Harmony. It has particular significance to Tibetan Buddhists, as it became the national centre of Lama administration (a Lama was originally the head of a Buddhist monastery). When the latest incarnation of the Dalai Lama is identified, this must be confirmed at the temple. It houses an astonishing 18-metre-high statue of Buddha carved from a single white sandalwood tree, a gift from the seventh Dalai Lama. We toured the great halls and then said our goodbyes, promised to stay in touch with each and other headed back to our hotels, the rain still bucketing down on us.

I must confess that I was delighted to have found a Starbucks café in a shopping plaza near my hotel. The 'culturally interesting' Chinese breakfast served at the hotel was a bit too interesting for my suffering digestive system and I was glad to at least be able to start my day with some familiar and comforting foods. A lot of other Westerners seemed to have had the same idea.

I did some more sightseeing, including a second visit to the Forbidden City on a day when it was not actually raining, and I was able to properly appreciate the astonishing palace complex and its beautiful gardens and parks. Then on 18 August 2005, my 37th birthday, I decided I would celebrate with a visit to the Great Wall of China.

Mao Zedong, the founder of the People's Republic of China and chairman of the Chinese Communist Party wrote a poem containing a line that translates to something like, "Until you reach the Great Wall, you are not a proper person." This has come to be used as a saying meaning that to be an admirable or a great person, one must overcome difficulties. Partly as a result, huge numbers of Chinese people visit the Great Wall, which meant standing in a truly huge queue with a lot of pushing and queue-jumping and a constant battle to avoid having one's eye put out by the sun umbrellas of fellow queuers.

I met up with a German and a Turk, and we managed to break away from the group we were with to walk along the wall at our own pace and without our guide's not-very-interesting commentary. The wall, built over many centuries as a defence against marauding nomads from the Eurasian Steppe, runs along the peaks of the mountains that mark the edge of the Mongolian Steppe. It is an awe-inspiring sight and truly one of the architectural wonders of the world. It is also very tough walking, with steep climbs and descents. We walked a loop of a few kilometres. Our legs ached but the experience was unforgettable.

Unfortunately, the fact that we split from our group meant that we had to take a taxi to get to the place where we were all to have lunch. This led to a negotiation with the most aggressive, unpleasant, opportunistic taxi driver I have ever come across. We haggled the price down from Y300 to Y100, which was a reasonable fare, but the taxi driver was so upset and vengeful that he refused to turn on the car air conditioning during our drive. After lunch, there was a forced stop on our return to Beijing at the Chinese Herbal & Acupuncture Medicine Research Institute, where the main 'research' going on seemed to be into how to take a maximum amount of money from the captive tourists who had been marched into their establishment. We all returned exhausted, and most of us slept on the bus on the way back to Beijing. That evening I sought refuge with some fresh fruit at Starbucks. Some revitalizing was in order and my stomach couldn't handle any more interesting culinary experiences.

I went to bed well exhausted after a week of 'hard work' as a tourist in China, but it had been a fascinating experience and an exciting way to celebrate my 37th birthday. I looked back on my life to date with satisfaction, on the whole. I had achieved more than I would have thought possible when I was a young student trying to figure out which course my life should take and there had been, literally, never a dull moment. Now I was looking forward to my return to Europe and my new job with Man Securities.

There was a final small annoyance before leaving China: my wake-up call was 30 minutes early at a time when I was keen on getting all the sleep I could, and there was no food available on my nine-hour flight back to London! The bright spot was that the taxi taking me to the airport actually charged the correct amount: Y90.

WIMMERSVEJ

In March 2006, I found myself in four countries in just one day.

I woke up in London at 4.30am and headed to the airport to catch a flight to Gothenburg, Sweden. I went straight from the airport to a meeting with AP2, one of Sweden's national pension funds, to discuss global oil and energy markets. Then I was straight back to the airport and onto a flight to Denmark for a meeting with the investment arm of Norde Bank. Finally, a flight from Copenhagen to the Norwegian capital, Oslo, took me to my last destination of the day, where I had dinner at the Hotel Continental. I had had enough of airports for one day!

The next morning, I had a client meeting scheduled in central Oslo. The office was nearby, so I decided to walk. The morning frost was biting; it felt like Siberia. The client was Norway's largest hedge fund, specialists in global oil and energy. It was a great meeting: the atmosphere was friendly and the level of detail we talked about was stimulating; fertile ground for new ideas. I left feeling energized.

The last meeting of the day was with KLP, the asset management company of the Norwegian municipalities. I gave a presentation about the global uranium market, which was a neglected area at the time, but it was a fascinating and compelling topic in investment terms and my presentation on global supply and demand over the next 10–15 years was met with great interest.

My break from airports didn't last long. That afternoon I was on another flight, heading back to Copenhagen for another full day of meetings with institutional investors. None of the investors were based in Copenhagen and in the evening they were keen to visit a Spanish-inspired restaurant they had read good reports about. They were not disappointed; after an excellent dinner, we went back to the Hotel D'Angleterre – my usual base when I am in Copenhagen – for drinks. They noticed a list of famous guests who had stayed at the hotel. The list included kings and queens; presidents; famous actors and film stars ... and Per Wimmer! They were so excited they took out their phones and started taking pictures and selfies.

If they like that, I thought, I have another surprise in store: the bar at the D'Angleterre stocks a special range of 'Per Wimmer' Cuban cigars labelled with my name. I am not a smoker personally, but I find these little touches go down very well with clients.

After another full day of finance meetings the following day, I 'changed uniform' so to speak, trading my tailored suit for a space-suit: I had a meeting with the CEO of a Danish fashion retailer to discuss the design of a new spacesuit and possible joint ventures, distribution and merchandising agreements and marketing.

Later that evening, I took a client and a colleague on a tour of the current spots of Copenhagen nightlife, including Zeze, Grillbaren and Club 8. The evening didn't finish until 6am the following morning.

I snatched a few hours' sleep before brunch later that morning at a cosy Østerbro café with my Wimmer Space team. We were discussing a space presentation I would be delivering at a high-end VIP conference in May with some very important exhibitors including Ferrari, Bentley, Omega, Louis Vuitton and other luxury brands. It was a very enjoyable and inspiring session with my colleagues, with a lot of good idea generation about potential synergies. Finally, by taxi I went to my sister's house to borrow her car for a journey I had to make the following day. While I was there, I joined in some fun 'cooking' with my niece Filippa, who was then three years old. Filippa always loved to pretend to cook when she was little. These days she is a very real and very good cook indeed!

That evening, I joined my cousin and another friend at the Danish Music Awards in the KB Hallen arena. One of my old favourite

Danish groups was the toast of the evening: TV-2, one of Denmark's most successful bands. They were having a comeback with a new album reprising their original 80s New Wave style. Their latest single was called "*De Første Kærester På Månen*" ("The First Sweethearts on the Moon"). Perfect! Their awards were well-deserved and, sitting in the audience, I vividly remembered TV-2 playing a gig at my old high school, Slagelse Gymnasium, in the mid-80s. I was always a big fan of their lyrics, which had a very cynical take on the conformity and consumerism of the Danish middle class. I still love TV-2's music, even now I am a fully signed-up member of the middle class and no longer a rebellious teenager!

The next morning, I was off again, this time driving up to Risskov near Aarhus in Jutland. The musical theme to my weekend was to continue: I was meeting the late Flemming 'Bamse' Jørgensen, of the band Bamses Venner, to record a song especially for my trip to space. Bamses Venner were a hugely successful Danish band that performed together for nearly 40 years, starting back in the 70s. They represented Denmark in the 1980 Eurovision Song Contest.

One of their biggest hits was a cover of "The Lion Sleeps Tonight" in 1975, translated into Danish and titled "*Vimmersvej*." For what happens next to make any sense to you, I'm going to have to delve into a bit of pop history.

Back in the 1930s in South Africa, a man called Solomon Linda recorded a song in the Zulu language called "*Mbube*" ("Lion"). The song featured voices only, without musical instruments – what we call *a capella* (church-style) in Europe. Linda's work gave rise to the style of African popular music popularized by bands like Ladysmith Black Mambazo.

Throughout the song *Mbube*, there is a kind of background chant: *uyimbube, uyimbube, uyimbube, uyimbube* ... which means "you are a lion" in Zulu. Over this chant there is a powerful lead vocal, which you may have heard in the English-language version: "*In the jungle, the mighty jungle, the lion sleeps tonight...*"

In the 1940s, a musical director working for Decca records brought the song to the attention of folk-music star Pete Seeger and his band, The Weavers. They recorded an instrumental version with the background chorus or chant, and they called it "Wimoweh," which was how they misheard the Zulu chant of *uyimbube*. The English lyrics *"The lion sleeps tonight"* weren't written until the 1960s, when a doo-wop band called The Tokens had a massive hit with the song.

If I tell you that the chant *wimoweh, uh-wimmoweh, uh-wim-moweh, uh-wimmoweh* sounds exactly like *Wimmer way, uh-Wimmer way, uh-Wimmer way, uh-Wimmer way* – I think you'll begin to see where we were coming from with this! It works perfectly in Danish also: *Wimmervej* still sounds just like 'Wimmer's Way.' We decided to record a special version of the Bamses Venner version of the song to celebrate my trip into space. Bamse was going to write a new version of the lyrics and record it with me later in the year.

Bamse, his wife Kate and the rest of the family welcomed me with wonderful hospitality. I ended up spending pretty much all day at the Bamses and was given a tour of their music studios. Bamse is a man of action who doesn't waste time: just my type of person. Lots of suggestions that came to light in our brainstorming session were put straight in the calendar. Recording studio prices and availability were checked; some other 'follow-up' ideas were delegated. We settled on a recording date in August. It was a pleasure to work with someone with whom I had such good chemistry, where good ideas were executed without delay. Before I left, Kate prepared a superb, home-cooked Danish dinner, which for a Dane living abroad is a special treat. I didn't get back to Copenhagen until 1.30am and was up again at 6.30 for a presentation I was due to give at a conference called 'Innovation Forum.'

And so it was that I returned to Aarhus in August with my space-suit and my musical talent in tow (the latter didn't take up much room.) I drove from Copenhagen across the island of Fyn and onto the Jutland peninsula and north to Aarhus – Denmark's second-largest city. I stayed at the Hotel Royal in the heart of Aarhus, just a few steps away from the famous cathedral and the city's beautiful Venice-like canals. A big plus of my space project had been discovering wonderful parts of my home country that I never would have visited otherwise. Just a few miles south of Aarhus are the Marselisborg Forests, 1,400 acres of beautiful woodlands next to the Bay of Aarhus. I spent the afternoon on a beach at the edge of the forest – the Danish summer at its best.

The next morning, I drove back to the forest and the beach for an early morning jog before picking up my documentary crew, which would be filming the recording session and driving to Risskov to meet Bamse. We exchanged excited hellos, put his guitar in the boot and drove north to the famous PUK Studios, named after its founder, John 'Puk' Quist. The studio is very remote. You can only reach it by car, down country roads and through tiny villages I had never heard of. A final turn onto a dirt road, past an isolated farmstead. Finally, you have reached your destination. It was worth the journey. A long list of musicians has made it this far to record in PUK Studios, including Elton John, George Michael, Wet Wet Wet, Depeche Mode and Judas Priest. Not to mention a who's who of Danish pop: Bamses Venner, Shu-bi-dua, Kim Larsen, Carpark North.

When I got inside the studios, I understood why. The two main recording studios, a mastering room, one smaller studio and numerous recording rooms were furnished with all the equipment a musician could wish for. Outside there was a beautiful garden overlooking apparently endless cornfields. The housing accommodation was all kitted out with top-end Bang & Olufsen hi-fi. An idyllic retreat deep in the country and a musician's dream! PUK was run by producer Peter Iversen, a kind of walking encyclopaedia of music history. He seemed to know an astonishing amount about anything related to music-making, from the chemical composition of a cassette tape to the economics of the music value chain. Bamse gave us a quick guided tour of the studios as, one by one, his fellow musicians from Bamses Venner arrived. To my surprise, when we got chatting about the project, I was met with a flow of interesting questions about my space project, particularly from the drummer, Frank Thøgersen. Everyone settled into the studio and started warming up. Then Bamse kicked off proceedings quite spontaneously. The recording was underway. Listening to my music heroes, Bamses Venner, playing a song about me was surreal; this was a long way from anything I had previously been involved in.

It turns out that making a song is like making a layer cake. I had always thought, naively, that to record a song, a band would play it together over and over again until everything was near faultless. That couldn't be further from the truth. In fact – as you probably know

– each musician records their part alone: the drums, the guitars, the special effects, etc., etc. Even the shouts of 'hep hep' (including my own enthusiastic contribution!) were recorded separately. It was a great insight into the creative process of making music, a world away from the busy trading floor that provided my usual background music.

We had a lot of fun together. Without Peter's mixing expertise, we couldn't have made it. Just before we were meant to take a break for dinner, we were all focused on finding the exact rocket noise for the intro. Everyone was so absorbed that no one wanted to break off! It was a real privilege to share such creative enthusiasm and drive. Bamse kept coming up with great ideas, down to the ad libs at the end of the song: "Per Wimmer calling Horsens" (Horsens is a town on the east coast of Jutland) was the new "Houston, we have a problem." We even added a 'knock-knock' on the rocket using a stainless-steel coffee can from the kitchen. Very high-tech sound effects!

We finished the day at around 10.30pm in a great mood. By 4.30pm the next day, having watched Peter and Bamse complete the mastering of the recording at the studio's high-tech 'desk' – another fascinating aspect of the creative process – I had the final product in my hands.

In 2020, PUK Studios were burned down in a fire. I was truly fortunate to have visited and recorded somewhere with such a unique place in Danish cultural history before it was too late. Sadly, Bamse himself passed away in 2011.

The Wimmer Space presentation I gave at the Innovation Forum at the Scandinavia Radisson turned out to be very memorable – for the wrong reasons!

HR and marketing representatives from many of Denmark's largest companies were in the audience, to get inspired and possibly find speakers to book for internal corporate events. Dina Al-Erhayem, a Danish TV presenter most famous for *Dina's Dates*, was the moderator. The speaker before me was Jens Arentzen, an actor known for the likes of cult TV show *Een gang strømer* ... ("Once a Cop ..."), who has become a successful public speaker. And what a performance he gave on that day. He was lively, engaging, constantly surprising. He really knew how to hold an audience. A tough act to follow, quite frankly!

I was up. I got off to a good start but just as I was getting into my stride, the fire alarm went off. It was so loud it was impossible to hear anything. It seemed to go on forever and was only interrupted occasionally by a robotic voice saying, "This is only a fire drill. No need to panic." Well, that depends if you're in the middle of a presentation or not, I guess! I had to think of a way to get things back on track, so I tried to 'integrate' the alarm into my presentation by talking about the alarms that sound before every rocket launch. The audience laughed, and I managed to bring them back into the spirit of things. It ended well, but it was not the best timing for a fire drill!

That year, I bought my own flat in central Copenhagen. I would miss the Hotel D'Angleterre, but it would be nice to have a base of my own. The apartment started off as a bit of an ugly duckling, but I enjoyed turning it into a beautiful swan.

I had to take my mind off flat renovation to visit Carnegie Asset Management, one of my financial clients. I was delivering another presentation on nuclear energy and uranium. It was a wide-ranging presentation that covered the historical, political, geopolitical and economic trends of nuclear power generation. I was pleased with my efforts.

Early that afternoon I treated myself to a spree in Bang & Olufsen's amazing showroom in Copenhagen. I picked out a 10-speaker sound system and a flatscreen TV. I even indulged in electronically controlled curtains and lighting. For lunch, I stopped at one of my favourite sandwich places on Strøget, where I enjoyed some traditional-style open sandwiches and a Danish muffin – must-have home comforts whenever I'm in Copenhagen.

The next stop of the day was another, very different presentation at an IT security conference sponsored by C-Cure. Most of the early speakers that day had been talking about very 'techy' issues, so a video- and photo-filled presentation about an exciting space project was a refreshing break. The audience was very engaged, and I was pleased with how it went. I even got a couple of further bookings.

The most out-of-the-box question I was asked that day was from a woman who asked whether astronauts travel with magnets in their pockets to enhance their wellbeing. She told me she sleeps with magnets in her bedding, and even showed me a magnet she wears inside her shoe. I told her I would have to get back to her on that one! That evening I jumped on the last flight to London. Even though I didn't arrive until after midnight, I still had emails to respond to. I was up at 6.15 the next morning to catch up with the markets.

The next couple of days went by in a flurry of meetings, on everything from medtech to real estate, before I was back in the airport, flying back to Denmark for my mother's birthday.

My sister, her boyfriend and I drove to Slagelse for my mother's 65th birthday celebration. I had been looking forward to it as much as she had! We enjoyed delicious food, the fine company of family, and some quality playtime with Filippa. Before returning to Copenhagen, I managed to fit in a visit to my aunt Aase and uncle Ejnar, too. On Monday morning I had an early meeting with a TV production company to discuss the possibility of making a documentary about my space project. After a few more meetings, I headed over to the planetarium, where I gave another space presentation. It went so well that afterwards I was overwhelmed by questions, invitations and even requests for my autograph. The organizers invited me to dinner after the presentation, and when I finally returned to the Hotel d'Angleterre (the flat was still being renovated and wasn't ready to move into), I was exhausted. But I still had to fill in a 17-page business document to be sent out that evening. I slept well that night.

I was up again early the next morning and straight to the hotel's fitness centre for a run, swim and steam to set me up for the day. Then straight to the airport in a taxi for a flight to Dusseldorf, where I was picked up in a black Mercedes S-class by the vice president of a German medtech company. After greeting a few of the company's staff, I had an excellent lunch with the CEO, who was hoping to get my advice and assistance in raising $40 million for his plans to expand the company.

Straight back to the airport and on a flight to Lyon, where, after a couple of phone calls and losing and then finding my luggage, I boarded a plane to Toulouse. A taxi took me to one of the best hotels in town, the Grand Hotel de l'Opera, a palatial building in the centre of town with a history dating back to medieval days. I was there for dinner with the head of corporate and investor relations at British Aerospace Systems. Four courses and a few glasses of good wine later, my hotel bed was an overwhelmingly pleasant sight.

The next day I visited Airbus. The morning was primarily made up of corporate presentations about opportunities in the airplane market in the next five to 10 years, which did, indeed, look promising, not least because of economic growth in Asia. Low-cost carrier growth in China, Russia and the Arabian Peninsula strengthened the case for strong structural growth in the airline industry, which Airbus and Boeing looked well-placed to benefit from.

After digesting the numbers, it was time for digestion of another kind: an experience of French cuisine, this time at the award-winning in-house Airbus restaurant. But it was after lunch that was the highlight of the visit: a factory and site tour. It is always fascinating for people in finance to see real value creation happening on the factory floor – but I must admit the real fascination for me was being up close with big things that fly in the sky close to space!

The Airbus site is impressive. It is, frankly, enormous; €13 billion does buy you a few acres and facilities! In Toulouse alone, Airbus has around 50,000 employees. The A380 was particularly impressive, almost like two planes in one. We visited models of both the A380 and the A340, a luxury version that included sleeping cabins for the staff. The assembly areas were as clean as a dental practice. No spills, no dirt. Even the workers' overalls looked like they had been freshly ironed. And what I saw was only the Toulouse assembly plant – there are other factories across Europe. All in all, it was a fascinating visit. When I made it back to London, I fell asleep as soon as my head hit the pillow. I slept all night ... until my alarm woke me up for work the next morning at 6.00.

My visit to Airbus was a warmup for the biggest aerospace event in my calendar that year: the International Space Development Conference (ISDC) in Los Angeles. The few days before were spent between London and Copenhagen for meetings for my then-employer, Man Securities. One meeting with our client, Sampension, was also about a speaker engagement for me at their upcoming conference to address their two-year strategic and core value review process. My task was to kick off proceedings with a 'trip to space' and to share stories about the execution of high-flying projects. Between flying back from Copenhagen and flying to LA, I had precisely 14 hours and 55 minutes in London. Just long enough to remember where I lived!

The ISDC conference in 2006 had a very positive buzz to it. The then-recent arrival of space tourism had given the space industry renewed energy and renewed media interest and was creating increasing interest in science and space in schools. Robert Bigelow, owner of the hotel chain Budget Suites of America, was attending. Another entrepreneur with a passion for space and someone with more at stake in space tourism than most was also attending: he was planning to create a 'space hotel' and had put up a $50 million prize for the first successful low-cost private orbital space vehicle. Elon Musk, who had become a multimillionaire from the sale of PayPal only a few years before, gave a presentation about his new venture, SpaceX, launched in 2002, and his plans to send low-cost rockets into space. Later that year, SpaceX would be able to announce its first contract with NASA to supply the ISS with crew and cargo – the first time that NASA had looked to the private sector to supply flights into space. There were talks from Rick Homans, then the secretary of economic development in New Mexico, who was building a spaceport in the state; XCOR test pilot Rick Searfoss; Will Whitehorn, president and CEO of Virgin Galactic; and Shana Dale, deputy administrator at NASA. Attending the conference gave me an opportunity to talk to some of the most exciting and respected figures in the community, from X-prize founder Peter Diamandis to Apollo 9 astronaut Rusty Schweickart.

The conference would cover all possible topics relating to space, from technical scientific discussions – such as "Advances in Autonomous Orbital Rendezvous Technology"; "Utilizing Solar Power Technology for On-Orbital Propellant Production"; and "The Physics and Metaphysics of a Black Hole" – to, on a lighter note, "Sex in Space" and "The Art of Star Trek." I was particularly looking forward to the seminar on astronaut training for the moon and Mars surface. It was enlightening and, I hope, will come in useful one day.

We were given updates on the latest scientific findings from Venus and Mars, plus the latest solar sail and space elevator technologies. The legal implications of the private use of space were discussed by expert panels while artists exhibited their latest work in the corridors. There were representatives from venture financing as well as contractors such as Boeing, Lockheed Martin and Northrop Grumman. But NASA was the main sponsor of the conference. One of the key presentations had been "Back to the Moon; on to Mars," exploring NASA's vision of establishing a moon base that would offer a platform for further exploration of the solar system. Which made it especially exciting that, during this conference, I first met living legend and Apollo 11 moonwalker, Buzz Aldrin (the second man on the moon together with Neil Armstrong). Funnily enough, the first conversation I had with Buzz was while we were waiting in line for the restrooms and got chatting. Since then, we have met many times and have become firm friends.

Buzz is a great character, incredibly smart and well-informed. He still has very strong opinions on the future of space travel. Just don't ask him whether the moon landings were real! There is a crazy conspiracy theory that NASA never did land astronauts on the moon and that all of the video and other evidence was mocked up using training facilities on Earth. Which is all very amusing, if conspiracy theories are your bag – unless you happen to be one of the 12 people in history who have actually stood on the moon's surface. A fellow space enthusiast warned me that a few years earlier, Buzz had liter-ally punched one particular conspiracy theorist who was hounding him. A prominent moon-landing denier called Bart Sibrel was fol-lowing Buzz with a camera crew as they made a 'documentary' about the 'fake' lunar missions. He asked Buzz to swear on the Bible that he had walked on the moon. As Buzz tried hard to get away, Sibrel pushed his luck too far. "You're the one who said you walked on the moon when you didn't!" he said to Buzz. "You're a coward and a liar!" he shouted, "And ..."

He didn't get any further. Buzz landed a very neat right hook that sent the much taller and heavier Sibrel staggering back against the entrance of the building Buzz was trying to enter. You can believe any nonsense you like, but nobody gets to call Buzz Aldrin a coward and a liar and say that he never went to the moon!

In 2006, Buzz was 76 years old, but his energy levels were sky high. He was still travelling all over the world for speaking engagements and book signings. He really is space royalty. In spite of the glamour,

Buzz does not shy away from talking about his troubles with alcohol after the moon landing. In fact, he talks about that period as an opportunity to rebuild and re-emerge as a stronger, better person.

In recent years, one of his main focuses has been on inspiring children to learn about science, a value we shared and bonded over. He is also a great supporter of private space tourism and a board member of Space Adventures. As we stand on the verge of a new space age, one of private enterprise, we all thank Buzz for showing us the way.

Buzz and I met again at a party hosted by Dennis Tito, the world's first private astronaut (as we saw earlier, I was on the Baikonur launchpad 15 minutes before Dennis took off to the International Space Station as the first private astronaut in March 2001). Dennis's house is more like a palace: it's a 30,000 square-foot hilltop mansion in Pacific Palisades, overlooking everything from the Santa Monica Bay to the San Bernardino Mountains. It's castle-like, with a long winding driveway and an impressive collection of art and paintings, plus a lot of discreet high-tech gadgets.

Tito's fellow private space traveller Greg Olsen – the third private astronaut (after Tito in 2001 and the South African/British entrepreneur Mark Shuttleworth in 2002) – gave a short presentation about his flight to the International Space Station in 2005, which included lots of interesting little details about life in space. How to drink water, how to shower, how to sleep, email and move in a weightless environment ... even how to use the toilet, the perennial question asked at school presentations!

Another interesting figure I had the opportunity to speak to was Amir Ansari, a softly spoken, eloquent man whose family was having a major impact on private space travel. The Ansaris not only sponsored the X Prize – the $10 million competition that ignited a new era of commercial spaceflight – they were in a joint venture providing funding for Space Adventures' efforts to work with Russia to develop a suborbital spaceplane – the Cosmopolis XX1 (C-21). With Russian scientific talent and Ansari money, my planned trip to space with Space Adventures felt more unstoppable than ever.

I also caught up with another space celebrity at the conference: Burt Rutan, the Einstein of rocket design. I had first spoken to him at his workshop at Scaled Composites in Mojave, right after his team won the Ansari X prize in 2004 with SpaceShipOne. Burt is easily recognizable, with his piercing blue eyes and distinctive sideburns. One half of Burt's mission for the future of space travel is to show the government how things can be done more cheaply and efficiently in the private sector. The other, to use his words, is to "reach the moon in my own lifetime." Those are his main drivers. "We're not here to make money," he said. "We're here to fly humans into space."

He has a very strong anti-government stance. His thoughts on government involvement were a big part of his eloquent, witty speech at the Orbit awards evening (the Oscars of space development). His biggest issue is with how the private space industry is regulated. The Federal Aviation Administration (FAA), he said, seemed disproportionately concerned with the slim chance of debris hitting people on the ground, rather than protecting the space travellers themselves. He had a point. Obviously, every space traveller is aware of the risks and willing to take them on, but as incidents are far more likely to affect travellers rather than people on the ground, legislation should reflect that.

I got to have a brief conversation during the conference with FAA official Patti Grace Smith. The FAA was trying to cater to both concerned groups, she told me. She seemed genuinely excited to help this new industry get off to a good start. Through the development of new regulations, Patti was a key facilitator of private space travel; the space community owes a lot to her. Both parties are incentivized to work hard on making flights safe. If too many accidents occur, the FAA will be under fire from Washington, the space tourism industry will grind to a halt, commercial rocket builders will go out of business and private space travellers' feet will remain planted firmly on the ground.

The conference led to some interesting invitations for me, including an opportunity to speak at the Las Vegas Space Conference later that year, and a visit to the Cannes Film Festival, extended by two nice Hollywood producers. I was introduced to them by a space-loving journalist from New York who writes for *The Wall Street Journal*. Going to space doesn't just take you out of this world, but around it, too.

I had originally signed up for lots of tours and excursions, but in the end, there were so many interesting presentations and people to catch up with I didn't have the time. Not to mention a few fun parties, including Peter Diamandis' birthday party. One party – the New Space Frontier Organization party – was so noisy that someone called the police, who arrived and shut it down for an hour. Who said geeky space enthusiasts don't know how to have fun?

June was characterized by record levels of business at Man Securities, as well as lots of media interest and TV filming. I had decided to press on with making a documentary about my space project. It was decided that a Danish TV-production crew would shadow me for a few days to capture my life in London. One afternoon, the crew came to the Man building to discuss our filming schedule for the coming days. Our quiet lunch was interrupted by my colleague, who came storming over, shouting, "Per, Per, can you come to the desk? We have an emergency situation! One of your Scandi clients just called in with a massive order and I'm not certain I got it all right. I'm not sure if the order is as big as I think I heard. Can you come up quickly and call the client to confirm?!"

I apologized to the TV crew and rushed upstairs to call the client. My colleague hadn't heard wrong. I had received a massive single stock high-margin transaction, the largest order our department had ever received. I gave word to get the trade executed immediately. The traders' jaws dropped. Once they had regained their senses, they also double checked with me that the size of the order was correct. It was true, I assured them. I returned to the TV crew but stayed much closer to my desk. Mistakes are not an option with orders of that size. Not only would it be incredibly costly but would lead to a serious loss of confidence from the client. Once word had spread, colleague after colleague came over to my desk to congratulate me on a beautiful piece of business. We were all excited. The only person who didn't share the joy was the previous holder of the total daily business record!

That night, instead of celebrating with champagne, I spent the evening walking around Bond Street and Knightsbridge to get some shots for the documentary. We didn't finish until around 11pm and picked up where we left off early the following morning.

We spent the day visiting London-based hedge fund clients with the camera crew in tow. In the evening, we took a river cruise down the Thames to get some shots of the city from the river. During the boat cruise dinner, we happened to be sat next to some journalists from various Norwegian media. Naturally, they were intrigued to find fellow Scandinavians on a Thames River cruiser and curious to know what we were filming. We told them about the documentary and my space project. The atmosphere around the table completely changed: our small talk about London was replaced by intense questioning about my trip to space. A casual dinner seemed to have turned into an informal press briefing for the Norwegian media! The documentary crew left me to it and went outside to shoot the city skyline at sunset.

It was interesting to see how the Norwegian journalists, despite emphasizing how eager they were to work together, each wanted to get the 'scoop.' It became a competitive situation along the lines of "We are all good friends and fellow journalists – just so long as I get the story first!" In the end, it was agreed that two outlets would run the story: NRK, Norway's equivalent to the BBC, and *Aftenposten*, a national daily newspaper.

The documentary crew took a few last shots as darkness fell over the city; the river cruiser returned to its pier, and we headed off to a bar for a nightcap. Documentary filming continued the next day. The crew were at my door at 6.15am, ready to film me eating my cornflakes and watching *Bloomberg News*. They wanted to capture a normal working day in the life of Per Wimmer, so they filmed as I took a taxi to work and chaired the morning meeting, giving updates on the US and Asian markets and introducing various company-specific updates from our analysts. Then back to my desk, talking on the phone with clients and carrying out live stock transactions with the cameras rolling. One of the crew said it felt as if they had been filming for a whole morning – and it was still only 10.00am!

It soon became clear that my intense lifestyle was too much for one member of the crew. After our rather late night and my usual early start, he was starting to feel the pressure, complaining of nausea and a massive headache. We packed him off back to the hotel to get some sleep. He clearly hadn't been quite prepared for what was in store for him on this shoot. I live my life to the max: I get up early, manage my time to the minute, and I thrive on it. I've built up a capacity to perform under pressure and with little sleep. But I also know my limits. Our fallen crew member finally re-emerged in the evening, having slept all day. A cocktail at Nobu in Berkeley Street – the 'in' place at the time – was followed by dinner in an Italian restaurant in Mayfair, where we bumped into Kelly Osbourne.

Saturday was our last day of filming, when we captured everything from me jogging through Hyde Park, to an interview aboard the London Eye with the Palace of Westminster and Big Ben in the background, to brunch in Wimbledon with two Danish friends of mine. The crew took the opportunity to take some shots of Wimbledon tennis club, where I would be watching the ladies' final later that summer.

Just two days later, filming began again – this time with a crew from NRK, arranged by one of the journalists I had met on the Thames cruise. It was the same procedure: at my door at 6.15am to film breakfast, taxi to work, morning meeting and so on. The day was so intense that by the time there was a moment for lunch, it was 4.30pm! But in that time the crew had managed to get a range of shots that really captured my life at the time. It had been a very busy day at the office, and I was constantly on the phone to clients and colleagues in between filming shots and interviews. The highlight of that busy day was another huge order, which ended up being worth the equivalent of about 1% of the market value of a very large, well-known UK company. Again, lots of excitement and applause from the office while I was too busy to celebrate.

The next afternoon was given over to journalists from *Aftenposten* for the other story agreed on the cruise. We did an interview about the motivation behind the space project and a photoshoot near Tower Bridge. It was a challenge to juggle this with keeping an eye on the markets and transacting big business, but it was a lot of fun. The rest of the week I could 'relax' by just focusing on my main markets business. Thursday was the Man Securities summer party: a big event at a venue on a jetty right by Tower Bridge, with an MTV DJ, games and a huge pistol-shaped ice sculpture that dispensed shots of chilled vodka. It was a seriously good party. The next day at the office was, unsurprisingly, a quiet one. My social calendar is always full over the summer: Henley Regatta, then Wimbledon, then the China White Cartier Polo Party at Windsor. I had also been personally invited to a cocktail party by the Danish ambassador at the embassy, to mark the end of his term in London. And that's before the Monaco Grand Prix and a trip to St Tropez – something that would become a regular fixture of my summers, where I would catch up with fellow members of what they used to call 'the jet set' for a week or two of sunshine, yacht-hopping and serious partying.

July brought another interesting aerospace event: Farnborough Airshow, a key event in the industry, where contracts were signed, and deals done in civil and military aerospace. It is a huge display of technical might, from fighter jets, helicopters, jumbo jets, satellite rockets and unmanned flying vehicles to sophisticated reconnaissance equipment and even airplane ball bearings. I was attending during the week as a trade participant and would have the opportunity to see an extraordinary range of gadgets available at prices that only states can afford to pay. No expense is spared when it comes to multimillion dollar deals on defence contracts and this was reflected at the air show.

My first meeting, joined by a colleague and a client, was with the chief financial officer of Cobham, a UK-based technology innovator whose business includes supplying to the Eurofighter programme, to discuss the performance of various business units and long-term strategic plans. After the meeting, I immediately disappeared into the space exhibition and studied the exhibitions on the European Space Agency and the Russian and Chinese equivalents. Then I spoke with someone from the Space Foundation to offer my services in helping educate children about space and science.

On leaving the exhibition, I spotted a familiar face: Buzz Aldrin! What an unexpected pleasure. It was great to see him again. We had a catch up, where I discovered his drive to get British enterprise more involved in private space travel to push space exploration further and faster. Another meeting followed, with the chief financial officer of British Aerospace Systems. Finally, I had been invited to lunch with a group of city competitors by the head of investor relations at Rolls Royce. Coincidentally, I looked across the table to see an old colleague from Goldman Sachs, Sash Tusa, who was then an aerospace and defence analyst there. The company had just announced new orders worth $600 million, so their air show had got off to a flying start, as did the real air show after lunch.

The new A380 Airbus jumbo jet was flying over UK soil for only the second time. The MiG-29 brought back happy memories from my space training in Russia. The Saab Gripen fighter jet proved that Scandinavians can also manufacture military hardware of a high calibre. The US showed the F-16 and F-18 fighter jets, and the Eurofighter Typhoon fighter jets were also very impressive – and exceptionally loud. Watching these magnificent feats of engineering from the ground, I only wished I could have been on board. Impressive as they are to watch, nothing compares to actually flying.

Back in London, my day ended with a cocktail party bidding farewell to the outgoing Danish ambassador, Tom Risdahl, where I caught up with a number of leading Danish businesspeople living in the UK. I even arranged a few more space presentations, in the Danish consulates in Liverpool and Manchester. It was a shame that London was losing Tom. He was such an enthusiastic, eloquent ambassador; Stockholm was lucky to be getting him.

THE SECRET MILLIONAIRE

"How did I end up here?"

I was sitting on an uncomfortable sofa, looking around my drab council estate apartment on the rough side of Nakskov, in Lolland. My hands and feet were freezing. It was -3°C outside and felt like -15°C with the windchill factor, and I was struggling to warm up, even inside. The hourly rate from my job as an unskilled factory worker meant that I was living on the tightest of budgets. My credit cards had been taken away; I had traded my favourite London restaurants for a bowl of soup every night, with a piece of fruit if I was lucky. I felt as if I was in the movie *Trading Places*.

My new situation was courtesy of Denmark's TV 2, and I was the focus of an episode of *Den hemmelige millionær* (*The Secret Millionaire*), a documentary that follows entrepreneurs as they go undercover in impoverished areas. I would be spending 10 days experiencing the lifestyle of ordinary people in one of Denmark's poorer regions, while identifying charities and social entrepreneurs working with some of the most disadvantaged members of the community. At the end of the week, I would reveal my true identity and make a financial contribution to the charities and social entrepreneurs I felt could most benefit, helping them continue with their invaluable work. The opportunity to take part in the documentary appealed to me as a way of making a financial contribution to those who need it most, and as a learning experience. It is always good to remind yourself how fortunate you are and to get out of your comfort zone. At this precise moment, I was a long way out of my comfort zone!

Once a centre of trade, Nakskov had been devastated by the closure of the shipyard in the 1980s. Twenty years later, it was still recovering from that economic shock. When the three-person film crew and I arrived at the estate where I'd be staying, my heart sank: rows of identical, sterile blocks of flats, grey under the overcast sky. But suddenly, it burst into life. A group of children bounded downstairs to play football. Their laughter and fun were so infectious, I couldn't resist joining in!

In retrospect, my experience had started as it was to go on: Nakskov could look bleak to an outsider looking on, but it was full of people with warm hearts and resilient spirits.

My first port of call was to get some food. My budget for the 10 days was 620 kroner (£70). To make the most of my money, I headed to Aldi for some basics. I rarely pay attention to how much food items cost – I simply buy whatever I need without thinking – so even this first task was a wake-up call. I'm used to thinking about finance on a macro scale, but found I'd have to invest some serious time into my daily budgeting to make sure I could live within my very limited means. At the supermarket I settled on soup, pasta, bread and pâté. That's it. Even that simple fare cost me almost one seventh of my entire 10-day allowance. After leaving Aldi with my very limited bounty, I headed back to the apartment and got an early night. Knowing what was in store the next day, I would need it.

At 5.30am the next morning, my alarm forced me out of a deep sleep. It took me some time to remember where I was and collect my wits. I dragged myself out of bed in my freezing bedroom to get ready to leave at 6am for the factory where I would be working. It was still pitch dark by the time we arrived, and the cold got into my bones as we waited outside. Thankfully, I was soon greeted by Kim, my coworker for the morning, a friendly man who was clearly dealing with the early start better than I was!

The factory manufactured insulation material used in flooring during housing construction. I was familiar with the construction industry, but from the 'top down' vantage point of my Bloomberg screen and large cap stocks. I was fascinated to get a glimpse of the industry from the 'bottom up.' My role was as an all-rounder on the factory floor: sweeping up and helping the other workers wherever needed. It was physically tough – I couldn't help but wonder how Kim did it! It wasn't long before my muscles were aching and, by our first scheduled break at 8am, my ankle hurt where a metal part had fallen on it earlier. I imagined the strain of doing a monotonous, low-wage job like this every day for the foreseeable future. But the kindness and openness of my colleagues made up for a lot. There was a real sense of camaraderie with my fellow workers.

I was amused at how Kim's stomach was set like an alarm clock to the factory's 15-minute breaks at 8.00 and 10.00 – and the all-important half hour break for lunch at 11.45. Kim and I chatted while we ate our lunch. Kim was suffering from osteoporosis, which made it difficult for him to work for more than short bursts before his knees became painful. His illness meant that it wouldn't be long before he was unable to work at all, at which point he would have to go on social welfare. The financier in me wondered if he was able to save up for that time, but with a low hourly wage and a family to support, I doubted he was able to put much away for a rainy day.

In the afternoons, Kim helped his son by driving him to distribute newspapers. His son was saving up to buy a motocross motorbike. "Even if I had the 20,000 kroner to give him, I wouldn't," Kim explained. He was the proud father of a daughter and a son and was teaching them the value of hard work: that rewards must be earned. His son would earn the bulk of the money for the motorbike, with Kim making up the difference.

I had a lot of respect for Kim. He stuck to his principles, and the way he treated me like an old friend from the moment he met me warmed my heart on that chilly morning. I really wanted to be able to help Kim in some way, but giving his son the money for the bike would undermine Kim's efforts to teach his son to be self-sufficient. I also knew that Kim would not want a handout from me. His greatest wish was for his osteoporosis to be cured so that he could keep working, but the doctors had told him there was nothing they could do. I was frustrated to find that there was no obvious way I could help.

It struck me that businesspeople like myself are often quick to praise companies for 'restructuring' and laying off thousands of people. We talk about business leaders having to make 'tough decisions.' Jobs in Nakskov were few and far between; losing one can have a devastating effect on workers and their families. Kim's employer had been through a difficult phase of its own and talking to Kim and others about former colleagues and about the devastating impact of unemployment on people and families was a sobering reminder of the human consequences of those 'tough decisions' – essential though they sometimes are.

But there was a lot of brightness in my morning at the factory: the team spirit was warm and palpable, as was the kindness of the people who welcomed me without question.

After my morning at the factory, I was ready to get started on my main mission: scoping out potential charities. I had drawn up a mental checklist: I was looking for organizations with a clear need for financial and nonfinancial assistance that would have a maximal and sustainable impact, run by competent social entrepreneurs who knew where the greatest needs were and could put any money to the best use. I couldn't help but approach the search like an entrepreneur – I wanted a big return on my investment: a lot of bang for my bucks. My criteria were very similar to those I would use when looking for companies I want to work with, but with the return on investment measured not in money but in the improvement to people's quality of life.

We went to meet Marie Nielsen from the Frivilligcenter Lolland, a volunteer organization that promoted social work in the region. I was hoping that Marie's knowledge of local charities would help me identify some potential beneficiaries. Indeed, from Marie's fantastic database, one charity caught my eye: Kontakten, an organization that aims to improve the quality of life of elderly and vulnerable people, run by 75-year-old social entrepreneur Inge Ehli. The following morning, I went to meet Inge at the Kontakten office, posing as an enthusiastic volunteer new to Nakskov – which wasn't entirely untrue!

Inge was hugely impressive. In 10 years, she had built an organization of 154 volunteers who carried out more than 3,000 acts of service every year, visiting elderly people: helping them with shopping; providing activities for vulnerable children; creating networks for those who had lost a significant other. Remarkably, hardly any of the volunteers she recruited had ever left Kontakten, a testament to her outstanding leadership. She always takes the time to talk, I was told, and the love she spreads through her warm hugs and words must have an unimaginable impact on the lonely and vulnerable.

I was impressed with the way Kontakten's work was filling in the 'gaps' in the existing social welfare system. The charity's dependency on Inge was my only worry. But, at the end of the day, you invest in people. Most successful startups are driven by the energy and vision of one person, and it was clear that Inge was a sufficiently savvy entrepreneur not to let things fall apart without her. My gut told me: stick with Inge. We arranged for me to do a few home visits with Kontakten throughout the week.

Our first excursion out of Nakskov was to Rødby, a quaint town set back a little way from the coast, to visit *Skomagerens Hus*, or Shoemaker's House, a drop-in centre for people who are suffering from mental illness. It was clear that it was a wonderful sanctuary, a safe space where their struggles would be understood, both by the wonderful, supportive staff and by the people they met at the centre who were in the same situation as themselves. The centre had been raising money for some time to create a new workshed, which a nice lady called Rita assured me would add greatly to the services the house could offer.

Fortunately for them – if unfortunately for me! – they had recently reached their funding target. The next thing on their list was a sensory garden, an interesting project designed to soothe the mind, make people more mindful of their surroundings and reawaken the senses of people who have been on high doses of medication. However, they had already raised some money toward this, and the rest of the house looked well equipped. I enjoyed the conversations I had at the Shoemaker's House, but I felt that a donation might be needed more urgently elsewhere.

We headed back to Nakskov and straight to another charity called Locomotion, a project that organized local sports teams and exercise classes, run by a very accomplished social entrepreneur called Jack. Jack immediately struck me as someone who goes beyond the call of duty and doesn't stop until he makes things happen: he carefully managed everything from budgets to equipment to booking sports centres and organizing teams. His passion for sport was obvious, and I could see he had a keen eye for finance. When he told me he had raised 36,000 kroner (£4,300) from sponsorship branding for 10 exercise bikes, I couldn't help but be impressed! That was real initiative. In another life, Jack would have made a fantastic businessman. I loved the spirit of Locomotion and found myself wanting to be a part of it in some way. But Jack had every angle covered. It's no wonder he wasn't wanting for cash: he really delivers. Within 10 minutes of being there, I could tell what a difference he was making.

Of the three charities I'd visited so far, it was Kontakten I couldn't get off my mind. I was excited to see the work they were doing firsthand and had volunteered to make some home visits with the charity's volunteers, to provide what practical help I could and a bit of company.

The next day, after taking a walk through the winding streets of Nakskov with the camera crew for some shots of me walking past the beautifully-painted old buildings – splashes of yellow, blue and orange in the charming crooked lanes – I met a Kontakten volunteer, Bente, who took me to visit Irene Nakskov, a 95-year-old woman living in sheltered housing. What a woman! Irene was full of life: she welcomed us with a beaming smile, a hug and delicious homemade biscuits and chocolate, as if she was greeting a favourite grandchild. Eating happily (I was very hungry!), we settled in for a chat about her life.

Irene was born in 1912, the same year, incidentally, that Danish powered flight pioneer Jacob Ellehammer got airborne in his rudimentary coaxial helicopter, having previously experimented with a monoplane and a 'semi-biplane.' I found it incredible to think that in the course of this woman's life, air travel had developed from primitive flying machines to space tourism. Irene had lived through World War I and the Nazi occupation of Denmark. By the time I met her, she had seen more than 20 prime ministers take office. For a while, she worked as a cashier in the School of Agriculture and talked proudly about how wonderful it was. She was also very fond of her summer house 11 km away – a place where she still spends five months a year. She started suffering with osteoporosis in the 1960s and had been walking with crutches for many years.

Some simple practical things we could do for Irene emerged from our conversation. The cleaning service provided by the council was only 45 minutes every two weeks and didn't include the bathroom or the kitchen. Naturally, Irene's osteoporosis was also bothering her. I was shocked to hear that she had been to a specialist osteoporosis hospital just once in the 44 years since her first operation, and that was six years ago! She positively lit up when she was explaining how much relief the treatment to her spine provided – something that was not available to my fellow worker Kim with his osteoporosis of the knees. The only reason she had not had further treatment was because it was too expensive.

There was also one fun thing I thought I could do for Irene: during our conversation, I learned that she was passionate about the theatre. I thought about how she would love the Royal Danish Theatre in Copenhagen, the grandeur of the old building, with its velvet seats and ornate golden décor. I could see her there, watching an opera perhaps. My aim was to donate my money for sustainable purposes ... but how could I resist sending Irene and her friends on the trip of a lifetime to the Royal Danish Theatre?!

But before that, there was something more immediate I could fix, not with a donation but with a moment of my time – and a bit of muscle. She was having an issue with her hearing aid. She told me it made her voice sound tinny, as if she was talking into a barrel. Awful! When I asked why she hadn't got it checked out, the problem was straightforward: the ear doctor's office was on the first floor, and she couldn't walk up the stairs. As soon as she explained this to me, I thought, "I'll carry her up there myself if I have to!"

A couple of days later, I returned with a colleague, Bente, to see Irene. We lifted Irene carefully into Bente's car and drove her to the audiologist. It was there I swept Irene off her feet and carried her up the stairs. After 15 minutes with the doctor, she emerged smiling. Her hearing aid was fixed – which would be all the better for the opera, I thought to myself! I carried her back down to the waiting car, feeling happy. The whole experience taught me a valuable lesson: simply understanding what is important to people and making a bit of an effort can make an immeasurable difference to someone's life.

I left Irene feeling excited, hardly able to wait to surprise her with a donation. It was such a pleasure being with her. Irene was an absolute treat, a fabulous personality. Despite her physical challenges, she had such a positive spirit and got so much pleasure from the small things in life. What an inspiration! I've never forgotten the time I spent with Irene.

After leaving Irene, the film crew and I went back to their hotel to talk about our plan of action for the next day. When we got there, we struck up a conversation with an easy-going man called Alan, who worked at a local youth centre. He told us to stop by anytime, so we did – the following morning. When we arrived, Alan immediately put his work to one side to show us around. It was a well-run institution with a lot of facilities: a swimming pool, a music room, games consoles, televisions, and plenty of outdoor equipment. The seven-strong staff were doing a great job. They had even put on concerts to raise money and had bought a popcorn machine that made money to fund trips for the kids. It was all very entrepreneurial – a great source of inspiration. The most useful thing I could offer were some kind words of encouragement. They were already doing a great job.

Our next stop was Ørnen, a boxing club run by retired mechanic Jan, who had a passion for supporting troubled young people through sport. I'd heard about Jan from a social worker called Bjarne, who positively sang his praises: we had to check this guy out. Most of the kids at the boxing club had had an uphill struggle in life, Jan told me: boxing allowed them to blow off steam in the ring and bond with their clubmates outside of it. It was great to see that it wasn't just boys – there were plenty of girls, too; some of them the toughest of the lot!

Jan raised his annual budget almost exclusively through membership revenues, which amounted only to around 35,000 kroner (£4,200) a year, so it would not be difficult to make a big financial impact to his work. "You invest in people," echoed in my mind. I was enthusiastic about investing in Jan but wasn't yet convinced by boxing as the sport of choice. It seemed such a violent sport to me. Was a violent sport really what these troubled kids needed?

The only way to put my doubts to rest was to give it a try.

Jan started the session with a warmup of stretching, running and skipping. After 30 minutes, I was certainly warm: my T-shirt was wet through, and my muscles were feeling tired but invigorated. I was ready for the ring. As Jan strapped on my gloves, I thought to myself, "Just keep moving." Honestly, I was reluctant to hit anyone.

The match mostly consisted of getting punched as I tried to move away! Thankfully, my opponent was a good sport and didn't go too hard on me.

Jan said he was impressed with how I coped for a beginner. That was kind of him. I think I may have given a whole new meaning to fight or *flight*! But I began to see why people might love boxing: it was intensive and gave every part of your body a full workout. And it was great fun. I wasn't keen on a sport that encouraged people to hit others but, in the ring, I discovered it was more tactical, more athletic, than I had given it credit for. I also realized that Jan was providing a safe outlet for troubled kids, who might otherwise have played out their anger on the streets. So whereas I had thought that boxing was just about hitting people, Jan's club was in many ways about exactly the opposite – blowing off steam in a controlled environment and not hitting people in real life!

Jan commanded the respect of the boys and girls in his club. He had an instinct for teaching: when to discipline, when to encourage. He was not only helping these kids develop healthy physical habits, but having a clear social impact, too. His support for them went far beyond the training room, as he made himself available whenever they needed, empowering them to be their best selves. He was more than a coach – he was a mentor. I felt I had found my next beneficiary.

Tuesday started with another good deed with Kontakten. We drove to a simple apartment block in town to pick up a lady named Tina Hansen, who had difficulty walking, to take her to SuperBest for some groceries. Another big character, she kept wagging her finger at the cameramen. I carried her shopping basket while she went searching for her favourite bread and soup, as well as other essentials – and at such a good price. With my new focus on household budgeting, I could see why Mrs Hansen liked SuperBest so much! It was heartbreaking for someone with such a warm personality to spend so much time alone. But, like Irene, Mrs Hansen made the best out of what she had. I could see what a huge impact Kontakten had on her quality of life.

After dropping Mrs Hansen back at her apartment, we made our way to Havnen, to a Salvation Army house run by a kind couple named Magnus and Petura. It started snowing when we were on our way there. The white blanket of snow made even the bleaker parts of Nakskov look beautiful.

Magnus and Petura devoted their lives to taking care of people with nowhere else to go: convicted criminals, people with drug and alcohol problems and other troubled souls. They provided three meals a day, space to relax and a bed for the night for 60 kroner (£7) and were kind enough to let me, as an interested volunteer, stay for a night.

At check-in, Petura made the rules clear: no drugs, no alcohol, no aggressive behaviour. I thought I could manage that! Unfortunately, I'd arrived 15 minutes late for dinner. It was a lesson – be on time for meals, or you might not eat at all! The staff were kind enough to give me some potatoes, which were enough to satisfy my rumbling stomach for the time being. I thought about Mrs Hansen, who would be enjoying her bread and piping hot soup right about now. It's funny how bread and soup can seem like the best meal in the world when you are hungry and dining on cold potatoes.

At the dinner table, a volunteer named Jørgen introduced himself. He was very open in telling me about his journey. He was the kind of man who had lived many lives: one as a purser on a ship; another as a restaurateur in Papua New Guinea. He had been happy, with a wife and children he clearly loved very much ... until he fell ill and took to the bottle, and slowly his family life broke down. Eventually, his wife threw him out, and he relied on the Salvation Army for food and shelter. While staying there, he fell into a dark depression and attempted suicide by taking a drug overdose.

A staff member from the house found him in the nick of time and got him to hospital. That was a turning point. He got sober and began to put his life back together. He started work as a 'soldier' at the hostel. If someone was short of cash, he would give it to them; if they tried to reimburse him later, he would ask them to give the money to someone else in more need than him. It seems that was typical of Jørgen. His life had been a bumpy ride, but he was a testament to the fact that it is never too late to turn your life around. At 71, he was a bright, happy, kind man, weathered by his journey but with a lot of wisdom to share. I was very sad to hear that shortly after we filmed with him, Jørgen passed away.

Jørgen's story is just one example of the good the Salvation Army dormitories do for people who have nowhere else to turn. No one should have to sleep on the street, especially on a freezing November night like the one I spent in the house. No one is beyond saving. When people think of the Salvation Army, they usually think of the groups of singers rattling tins for donations. But the amazing work done by staff, as I saw in Nakskov, really deserves more attention. Their work is driven by compassion. The next time I see one of their donation tins, I'll be reminded of the great efforts of people like Magnus and Petura.

I spent the rest of the evening chatting with my fellow residents before Frank, my roommate for the night, joined us. Frank had the gaunt look of an addict: his cheeks were hollow, his teeth rotten, his face expressionless. He told me that he had a history of aggressive behaviour and would easily explode into a violent rage. He had killed two people, and had many convictions for violent behaviour, including beating someone with an iron bar and stamping on somebody else's head. He became more unpredictable when he drank, he said.

I mentally thanked Magnus and Petura for the no alcohol policy of the house. As we were watching TV, he left the Salvation Army premises to get a drug fix somewhere in town, which only added to my level of discomfort. My previous reservations about sleeping in the dormitory – sharing a bathroom with strangers, an uncomfortable bed – faded into insignificance. How could I be disturbed by that heavy, uneasy smell in the room when I'd be sleeping next to a convicted criminal with anger management problems? I lay in bed, stock still, eyes wide. Frank returned to the room sometime after midnight. I did eventually fall into an uneasy sleep but was woken many times during the night by noises from the bathroom and the corridors. It wasn't the most relaxed night of my life, to put it mildly, but I survived. When the wake-up knock came at 8am, the camera crew came in to film me talking about how my night in the hostel had gone. I was still a bit bleary-eyed, but they got a cup of coffee into my system, and we went on our way.

I livened up on the drive to Riddersborgparken, a visit by Kontakten to help a couple with some chores. Both Preben and Susanne struggled with their health. Problems with their knees and hips meant that it was almost impossible for them to climb stairs, so they rarely left their second-floor apartment. Susanne had lost the use of her arms in a car accident and was hugely overweight. Preben had a medical condition that required a colostomy bag. Even something as simple as taking the rubbish out was too much for Preben and Susanne. Someone came to collect it once a week, which was not enough, especially when Preben's full colostomy bags would stay in the household rubbish until the bin was emptied. The apartment smelled appalling. Kontakten volunteers would pop in to take down the rubbish, do what they could to keep the place tidy and – perhaps most importantly – stay and chat. It was heartening to see how much of a difference my own insignificant efforts made during our visit.

I couldn't help but think of Preben and Susanne, stuck in their apartment, as we set off for one last adventure the next day. Kontakten invited us to accompany a nice man called Hans Gotfredsen and a few of his friends on a bus drive through the beautiful landscape of Lolland. It was lovely to take a break from the town. Even in winter, Lolland showed the Danish landscape at its best: trees silhouetted against the bright blue sky, golden in the sunlight, casting long shadows across the crisp snow, like a scene painted by Mønsted.

We stopped for coffee at Blans Marina, a beautiful, remote spot, with boats of all shapes and sizes rocking gently in the harbour and gazed toward the tiny island of Lindholm. Local legend has it that this is the Lindholm where Ellehammer took flight in his semi-biplane in 1906, considered by some to be the first powered flight in Europe. Ellehammer's pioneering aircraft, featuring two triangular wings joined at the corners with a motor of his design fitted beneath, managed a short, sustained, tethered flight. I imagined how he must have felt on that day, to make that breakthrough from being Earth-bound to airborne and wondered what that pioneering Dane would have made of my flight into space.

I closed my eyes and took a deep breath of the fresh sea air, clearing my mind for the exciting reveal to come tomorrow.

"You look very dressed up today – are you getting married?" asked Inge with a smile when she saw me in my suit and tie. I laughed and assured her I wasn't. She clearly wondered what on Earth was going on.

I sat down with her and praised her for the wonderful work she was doing for so many people. I told her she was making a huge difference and that leadership and commitment like hers are hard to find. Just a few words of appreciation brought tears to her eyes. Then I pulled the cheque out of my pocket and handed it to her. Seeing the shock on her face – I couldn't help but laugh! Kontakten's current funding was almost spent, and here was a cheque for 150,000 kroner (£18,000) in her hand. Once she was over the shock, she jumped up and gave me a massive hug. She couldn't believe it. I explained to her who I was – not an eager volunteer new to town, but an undercover entrepreneur. She had to sit back down; it was all too much. Her reaction was a joy: so surprised, so grateful. I almost cried myself.

It was a similar story at Jan's boxing club. Jan greeted me like an old friend, so I couldn't resist giving him a few kind words, too, about how his work goes far beyond the training room.

I was surprised and moved when Jan, a very tough guy, burst into tears when I handed over a cheque. He was embarrassed but, to me, it was a testament to his commitment to the kids and how much he deserved the money. As with Kontakten, the boxing club budget was almost gone; being handed a cheque that covered an entire year of operations was overwhelming for him. He hugged me and showered me with thanks. There are not many better feelings than that.

I also gave money to the Salvation Army 'Havnen' hostel run by Magnus and Petura, to the lovely Irene Nakskov and to Hans Gotfredson, the gentleman Kontakten had introduced me to on the bus ride through the Lolland countryside.

Seeing the faces of everyone I gave money to – Inge, Jan, Magnus and Petura, Irene, Hans – made every bin I had emptied, every sleepless moment in the hostel in Havnen, every soup dinner, more than worth it. I knew from my activities with Wimmer Space how rewarding charity work could be, but when you are face-to-face with the recipients of a charitable donation, it is so much more powerful. It really feels as if you are making a difference – not just to budgets or statistics, but to people's lives.

There was a moment in the week when we went to the top of the DLG building by the harbour in Nakskov for photos. We watched the sun rise: it was incredibly beautiful on a bright, cold, windy morning. While we were up there, overlooking a view of the whole town, I had time to reflect on the week.

Firstly, it had been hugely rewarding at a personal level to make some small contribution to improving people's lives. Secondly, I think and hope that it had made me a better listener: just taking a moment to hear Irene's story properly got us halfway to the solution. Thirdly, it had been a privilege to meet so many of the everyday heroes of our communities – unselfish social entrepreneurs who organize and execute very meaningful acts of charity with a significant impact on disadvantaged people's lives. It was a reminder that small acts of human kindness can have a huge impact. Finally, I was struck by the inflexibility of life for so many people in Nakskov: most people's lives were controlled by external factors such as bus schedules, timed work breaks and short opening hours for various facilities, apart from the obvious financial constraints. It gave me a renewed appreciation for the level of freedom I enjoy as an entrepreneur.

When *Den hemmelige millionær* was broadcast on TV 2, it clearly had a big impact on viewers. I received over 100 moving emails from people who had felt the need to reach out and thank me and tell me how the programme had touched and inspired them. It was both humbling and deeply gratifying. I stayed in touch with Irene after filming. Her trip to the opera with her friends was clearly a memory she would treasure for always. And every year thereafter, I would give her a call on her birthday to give her my best wishes and catch up with her. Unfortunately, Irene has now passed away – but at the ripe old age of 104. Shortly after her death, I got an email from her children, all these years later. They were thanking me again for the donation, but mainly for staying in touch. The money had been useful and had made Irene's life better, but the simple human contact had been more important.

A LIFE-CHANGING YEAR

To a visitor, Black Tom's restaurant and bar in Perth, Western Australia looks much like any other, with a welcoming terrace at the front in the welcome shade of two large gum trees, a spacious and airy dining area with a long, well-stocked bar. The bistro-style menu is varied but unpretentious – pizza, pasta, steak with prawns, various salads.

But Black Tom's is not just any old restaurant and bar. It is the centre of Perth's thriving mining community – the place where Perth's mining entrepreneurs get together to talk about prospecting over a beer and maybe a bite to eat. The place where multimillion- and even billion-dollar mining ventures are born, if the entrepreneurs are lucky.

There are many mining businesses based within a few blocks of Black Tom's, and people in the mining business all seem to know each other. When someone is surveying an area that may have promise and thinking of starting a new venture, a group of people will get together over a beer at Black Tom's and decide if they are 'in' or not, typically putting up a few hundred thousand dollars each – maybe even half a million or a million dollars – to start exploring the site for mineral or metal resources. This is the highly speculative end of the business, raising seed capital for explorations that might, or might not, 'hit gold' – or iron or aluminium or copper or uranium or agricultural phosphates. Western Australia has vast deposits of metal ores and minerals buried beneath its rugged terrain. The seemingly casual meetings over a drink on the restaurant's shaded terrace are the beating heart of the region's mining industry, worth billions of dollars.

When I found myself in Black Tom's in April 2007, the industry was in the middle of the biggest boom since the gold rush of the 1800s. Little did I know the life-changing role that Perth's mining industry would play in my career.

The story starts a month earlier in another bar on the other side of the world – a British pub in the city of London. I had heard that an Australian oil and gas company was in town looking to finance a US$10 million oil deal, and through mutual contacts I arranged a meeting with the senior manager, Tom, in the Fox and Anchor near Smithfield Market, an archetypal London pub with wooden panelling, dark brown leather benches and chairs and walls covered with prints of 18th and 19th-century cartoons and paintings. Over a plate of steak and chips and a pint of beer, Tom told me that the brokerage house they were working with had gone weeks without making significant progress toward finding investors. I had looked into the deal carefully; the potential was immense.

I was still working at Man Securities, but, whereas at Goldman Sachs the focus had been on launching new companies onto the stock market or making secondary placements of new shares, Man Securities was an old-fashioned stockbroking business, researching markets, presenting opportunities and charging a fee for buying and selling shares (typically 0.1–0.2% of the trading value). The Goldman Sachs business was more exciting and much more profitable (typically 3–6% of the placement value), but it was also more cyclical: there were boom times and lean times. Man Securities' business was less glamorous, but it was steady: people buy and sell shares in good and bad markets.

There was no conflict of interest if I wanted to work on Tom's deal in a private capacity, because Man Securities didn't do those kinds of deals. I had contacts in various hedge funds who might be interested in Tom's opportunity; I also had high quality contacts at larger institutions from my days in institutional equity sales at Goldman Sachs – I knew some fund managers who wouldn't normally consider a deal like Tom's but who might nevertheless be prepared to take a punt at the very fringes of their fund on something interesting, particularly at my recommendation. Tom gave me three weeks to get the job done. I came back to him with full financing in three days.

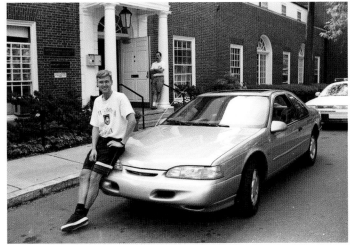

Top: Arriving at Harvard, August 1995.

Second row left: Participating in Community Teamwork landscaping at the retirement home.

Second row right: Cycling on the banks of the Charles River.

Bottom: Playing tennis with fellow Danish Harvard students.

Top: Lessons at Harvard Business School with Axel Wulff and Dutch Jan.

Second row: With Crown Prince Frederik of Denmark, who also studied at Harvard's JF Kennedy School.

Third row: On the winning team of Harvard Leadership and Ethics Debate Forum competition.

Bottom: Harvard in winter.

Opposite page
Top: George W Bush visiting Harvard.

Second row left: Community Teamwork at Harvard.

Second row right: In the computer room at Harvard exploring the new digital world.

Thrd row left: Procession at the Vienna ball.

Bottom right: Dancing with Dorte at the Vienna ball in Feb 1997.

Bottom left: Taking a break from studies to explore America.

HARVARD UNIVERSITY

Opposite page
In between years one and two at Harvard, I set off on a round-the-world trip, visiting many countries in South America, Easter Island, the Galápagos Islands, Fiji, Hawaii, Thailand, Vietnam and Australia.

Top to bottom, left to right:
Hang gliding over Rio de Janeiro.

Taking the helicopter down off Sugarloaf Mountain in Rio de Janeiro.

The famous statue of Christ the Redeemer.

In the Amazon rainforest, where I lived with a local family.

This page
Top row: Brasilia, capital of Brazil.

Rappelling down a waterfall in Brazil.

Others: At the Iguaçu Falls on the border of Brazil and Argentina.

Opposite page
Top: The Perito Moreno glacier in Argentine Patagonia. Minerals in the ice give the glacier its stunning blue colour.

Below: Visiting an island off Puerto Montt, Chile, after an eventful 3-day ferry trip from Puerto Natales, 1,490km to the south.

This page
Top: Exploring Rapa Nui (Easter Island) on horseback.

Others: Rapa Nui's famous mo'ai statues.

Bottom right: Sculptures in various stages of completion on the slopes of Rano Raraku – a volcanic crater filled with solidified volcanic ash or 'tuff' from which the mo'ai were carved.

This page
Lake Titicaca in the Andes, on the border of Bolivia and Peru.

Top: Villagers display their wares on one of the man-made floating islands of Lake Titicaca, created from the waterproof roots and reeds of a local plant.

Bottom right: With Danish friend Bab, who lived in Santiago, Chile, skiing the world's highest ski resort at Chacaltaya in Bolivia. The resort closed in 2009 when the glacier on which it stood finally melted.

Opposite page
In Southern Peru, hiking the Inca Trail with Bab.

Top left: Catching the early morning train to Cuzco, once the capital of the Inca Empire.

Third row right: The end of the trail – sunrise at the world-famous ruins of Machu Picchu, the 15th century Incan citadel.

This page
Top: With giant tortoises in the Galapágos.

Middle: Learning to scuba dive in Galapágos.

Below: Taking the PADI scuba diving license in less than 2.5 days in Fiji Islands, July 1997.

Opposite page
Riding Harley Davidsons coast to coast across America and back again with friend Axel Wulff, 1988

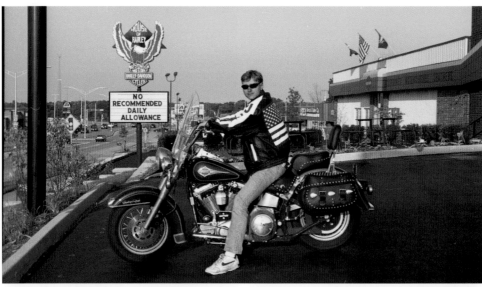

Opposite page
Top left: Interviewing at the White House, Washington DC, before becoming the only non-American offered a place as Presidential Management Intern under President Bill Clinton, 1998.

Top right: At my apartment in Harvard, Spring 1998.

Middle: Visiting JFK presidential library, Boston.

Bottom: Receiving the Don K. Price Award, Harvard, for academic excellence, community contributions and potential leadership in June 1998.

This page
Top left: Family arriving at Boston Logan Airport ahead of Harvard graduation in June 1988.

Top right: With my parents and sister at the John Harvard statue.

Second & third row: Mum, Dad and Dorte at Harvard for my graduation in June 1988.

Bottom: Graduating from Harvard with a Master of Public Administration (MPA) 1998.

Top left: At Harvard Faculty Club with my parents, sister, roommate Bob Crane and girlfriend Nikki Gordon in June 1998.

Top right: Harvard graduation.

Middle: Celebrating graduation with a Plymouth Prowler.

Bottom: Another fancy ride.

Completing this deal gave me confidence in my ability to execute deals from start to finish, single handed. Tom was so surprised and impressed that he invited me to visit him in Perth for Easter to celebrate. Good food, boating, diving, plenty of beer ... it sounded pretty appealing. But the trip ended up being so much more than a celebratory holiday. In retrospect, that meeting in the city pub was the catalyst for the launch of my own investment bank before the year was out. That deal with Tom was like the first spark of life that would lead to the successful birth of Wimmer Financial.

Perth is the centre of the Australian mining industry. The whole mining sector had huge potential at that time. I was convinced there was a super-cycle coming, particularly in metals. At that time, China accounted for around 10% of the world's consumption of metals. The Chinese economy was growing like crazy, and it was clear that demand was going to grow. Today, China accounts for around 40% of all metals. You didn't have to be Einstein to see that coming. India was also starting to become a major consumer.

The global uranium market was even easier to predict. You know how many nuclear power stations there are in the world, and you get about 10 years' notice if a new plant is being constructed. You know how much uranium is needed per reactor, so then it is just a matter of doing the maths. On the supply side, it takes about seven years to get a permit for a uranium mine, so it is easy to assess where supply will be in years to come. Funnily enough, there was one complication in supply at that time: a large quantity of highly enriched uranium (HEU) was coming onto the market from the decommissioning of Russian nuclear warheads, so you had to factor that in also. But you could still do the sums. You could build a portfolio for investors, wait for the price to jump from $40 a pound to $140 a pound and advise them on when to sell.

The early stages of mining exploration are highly speculative. Entrepreneurs in Black Tom's will set the wheels in motion: once an area has been identified as being of geological interest, a new venture might commission an aeromagnetic survey to confirm the site's potential and finally start some exploratory drilling. Sample cores are taken and sent to a lab. This begins to give you a feel for what could be there – but it is all still very speculative. It is only when you have drilled enough holes with a certain spacing between them that you have reached what is called 'JORC' standard, from the Australian Joint Ore Reserves Commission code (or 43-101 code in Canadian terms). There are three levels of JORC classification. If your exploratory holes are still quite far apart, you might be given 'inferred' status, because it seems that there might be a good resource there, but no one can be sure. With more holes drilled, a resource might be classified as 'indicated,' and after further sampling you get to 'measured,' which, as it sounds, gives an assessment of the grade, quantity, etc. of the minerals or metals underground, to a high degree of confidence.

Each stage of this process needs financing. The early studies are called 'scoping' studies and they try to determine whether it is worth funding the further investigations needed to be sure that the resources will support a viable mine. The next stage is a 'prefeasibility' study to try to estimate how much it will cost to develop the mine. This might cost several million dollars, so at this point you need to raise more money: you might be able to call on more personal contacts for a couple of million dollars, or perhaps float the new company on the Australian stock market with an IPO of around AU\$5–10 million.

The Australian stock market has a long tradition of raising capital for mining ventures, with ordinary Australians – the 'mom and pop' market as it is known – buying shares and hoping for a good return. But there is a limit to how much can be raised on the Australian stock market, and moms' and pops' appetite for new share issues varies, depending on the economic climate.

The final stage of launching a new mine is a full 'feasibility study,' which produces a 'bankable' or 'definitive" feasibility report, an extremely detailed (and expensive) geological road map of the contents of the resource and how it would be extracted, which often requires another round of financing, to raise perhaps AU\$10–20 million.

One of the things you need to know, of course, is how much metal ore or other resource is estimated to be there. If a mine looks as if it has only three years of life, that would be harder to finance. A mine with 10 years' of life would be considered 'bankable' – a commercial bank and/or a mining hedge fund would be likely to put up the necessary money. For smaller or riskier mines, you need more private finance, or you can turn to the stock market.

Once the bankable feasibility study is produced, you can look for the serious money needed to construct and operate a mine – perhaps AU\$100 –150 million, which you could look to raise through stock markets or from banks and/or mining credit funds. For a launch of that magnitude, you would normally reach out beyond the Australian market. Hopefully your new company's market capitalization has been rerated because of the potential your project is showing, and it can be much easier to raise these larger amounts of capital than it is to raise the AU\$10–20 million for a banking feasibility study.

The hardest part of financing tends to be finding AU\$3–5 million for the prefeasibility study: too much for the guys at Black Tom's, too speculative for the big players. This was where I came in: with my contacts, I could offer a kind of bridge between Perth and the money markets of London for this sort of early-stage investment.

I had planned on my trip to Australia being primarily a relaxed diving holiday, but I had a few important meetings lined up during my stay. I arrived in Perth on the Thursday; the following day was Good Friday, a business holiday in Australia, as in the UK. The plan was to meet up with my host Tom from the oil and gas company whose deal I had helped to close, spend the day with Tom and his family and then drive down to fashionable Margaret River (about a three hour drive from Perth) to meet a group from another Australian mining company, Uranium Equities, which I recently successfully assisted. Then back to Perth for the planned diving expedition with Tom.

But it seemed my reputation as the 'mystery rainmaker from Denmark' – the man who could make deals happen – had preceded me and continued to grow while I was in Perth. I ended up getting so many calls and requests for company meetings, in spite of the Easter holiday, from expansion-hungry junior mining companies keen to meet the deal-making Dane, that my diving trip ended up being seriously shortened. I had meetings lined up with corporates from 7.30 in the morning, and I was still getting calls at 9 in the evening asking if I had a few minutes to learn about an exciting mining opportunity. Some of the ventures I was told about were too early stage and too speculative, though I was able to advise people on where the appetite might be from a capital perspective, but many of the ventures I heard about were very exciting. Some of the first equity deals I eventually executed with Wimmer Financial involved companies I met on this trip, including the uranium mining firm Bannerman Resources and other companies that became corporate clients further down the line, such as clean power innovators Carnegie Wave Energy.

The days leading up to my flight to Perth were hectic. I had just concluded a challenging deal in Peru and had spent the previous weekend working on an interesting Canadian deal that had fallen through the night before. On top of that, I had been working with one of the Wimmer Space charities, The Hospice Foundation, and had the founder and CEO of a Malaysian portable battery company roadshowing in London on the morning of my departure. Consequently, I turned up to the airport having entirely forgotten to acquire an Australian visa. Thankfully, I was issued a visa electronically at the check-in desk for just £25 – the ease of it was brilliant.

My first impression of the Australian authorities when I got to Perth was friendly but unusually interfering. They did several checks after I went through passport control, including a long list of detailed questions and a demand to see my extensive travel schedule. I'm not sure whether it was my last-minute visa or 19 hours without a shower that made them so suspicious.

While I was waiting for my luggage, I got my camera out to record my first impressions of Perth. A security officer came running up to me, told me to stop filming and insisted I erase the content. I seemed to get my fair share of a post-9/11 traveller's hassle that day, but I guess they were just diligently doing their job.

I picked up my rental car and drove 20 minutes to pick up Paul, whose brother was a contact of mine in London. It was Paul who first took me to Black Tom's. We had a quick coffee, then it was right into my first meeting, with gas exploration company Nova Energy. For almost two hours, we discussed everything from the company structure and the bid the company had received from mining firm, Oxiana, to the sector's outlook and its political and economic background.

Then, at nearly seven in the evening, after almost a day of flying, I went straight into another meeting to discuss various projects including a Croatian steel mill, a titanium processing plant and a base metal operation. The CEO of the organization was incredibly entrepreneurial, making the most of the Australian mining boom. I later discovered that many people in the industry were involved in two or three companies at one time. There was a lot of crossover, with mining entrepreneurs sitting on each other's boards. Perth is a very small town in that sense.

I finished my first day in Australia with a wonderful Italian dinner courtesy of Paul's parents, Peter and Judith, followed by a few drinks with Paul. Western Australian culture is exceptionally welcoming to visitors. People are kind and go out of their way to be helpful – always going above and beyond. Everyone is a 'mate.' There is a strong sense of community spirit and support, possibly dating back to the earliest days of settlement by the British, when people had to help each other to survive in a challenging environment.

I paid for my long first day in Australia the next morning when I fell fast asleep on the beach after an excellent brunch. Though it was technically autumn in Perth, the temperature was still in the mid-twenties celsius, but the sea breezes made it feel deceptively cooler and the lack of ozone in that part of the world means the sun rays are very strong. The result: quite bad sunburn.

The next morning, Tom picked me up, and we drove down to Fremantle Harbour with his four-year-old son, Finnegan. The three of us climbed into a twin 115hp speedboat and jetted off to join Tom's friend Gus on his boat for a freshly caught lobster lunch. It seemed we just could not go fast enough for the excitable Finnegan!

Eating, chatting and drinking wine on the deck gave me a taste of the Western Australian emphasis on quality of life. People here have a great work-life balance. Work doesn't completely take control. Even business dealings are more informal: the dress code for a meeting is quite casual, the tone very friendly and the location more likely to be a local bar like Black Tom's than a boardroom. Weekends are spent outdoors – camping, boating, biking, preferably with good food and good company. Judging from the number of boats around us, Gus wasn't the only one who enjoyed relaxing in this way. It also turned up another business opportunity, with Gus's uranium exploration company, Peninsula Energy. I was getting the hang of doing business in Perth!

After a delightful long lunch, we returned to Perth exhausted from the fresh sea air. An early night was on the cards – but not before Tom's kids could watch the videos of my space training, which they insisted on seeing.

The next morning, I did the three-hour drive down South to Margaret River, a small town near the coast on the southwestern tip of Western Australia, famous for its beautiful scenery and delicious wines. It seemed like there wasn't a mining executive in Western Australia without a summer property down there. The average property at Margaret River costs about AU$500,000, but luxury places could easily set you back AU$1 million.

Australians drive on the left, like in the UK, but the road systems and signs are very much like the US highway system. There are parts of Australian culture that seem, unsurprisingly, very British – from the popularity of cricket to bacon and eggs for breakfast – but the future looks to have more American and Asian influence. Most of the cars are automatic, as in the US, but they are typically manufactured in Japan or Korea; holidays are likely spent in Bali, but the Australian beach and surfing culture feels very Californian.

In my eagerness to see this place everyone had been raving about, I managed to pick up a speeding ticket. Road safety is policed very strictly in Australia, particularly over Easter; there were not only speed cameras but police officers everywhere. I have never seen such unforgiving enforcement of a speed limit, which means hardly any drivers ever dare to break it. But I took my ticket on the chin and made my apologies to the officers of the law.

Perhaps Margaret River was never going to be able to live up to its reputation as a famous beauty spot. It might be an unpopular opinion, but I found it to be a bit of a tourist trap, complete with generic "I was here!" souvenirs, and a slightly boring village high street. I ended up leaving not long after I arrived and drove on to the beautiful coastal town of Dunsborough to visit Tim Goyder of Uranium Equities. I had recently helped one of Tim's companies with a AU$23 million capital injection.

Tim's place was absolutely stunning: an AU$6.5 million beach house, which led right down to the water. He had also recently acquired another AU$6 million house, he told me – there was a property in front of his main residence in Perth that was 'spoiling' his view, so he bought it. The mining boom had been very kind to Tim.

The wealth effect of the mining boom in Perth is quite astonishing. The property market had been appreciating at around 30% annually over the previous 4–5 years. This newfound wealth created a curious contrast between the straight-talking, hands-on culture of what was previously primarily a farming community, and a newly acquired taste for the finer things in life. The Aussies are not afraid to spend their money on property and expensive luxuries, maybe even more so than Russian and Arab millionaires with their reputation for extravagance and 'bling.' I enjoyed my evening at Tim's immensely. He is a wonderful guy, so down to Earth, full of life and laughter, always telling stories. Tim's colleague Richard, when his taxi arrived, gave the driver AU$50 to come back later, as we were having too much fun.

We couldn't resist discussing a bit of business. I could see the impact of the booming economy here. The biggest complaint at the dinner table was how impossible it was to hire a gardener – even at AU$40–50/hour. In fact, labour was so hard to find then that, apparently, at the local supermarket, cashiers were paid AU$50 per hour. Drilling engineers saw their average salary skyrocket from AU$65,000 to AU$200,000. Another of Tim's guests had taken a serious punt on a promising mining stock – and had paid off his entire mortgage with the profits.

Tim could clearly have retired long ago but he was in no rush to do so. He had a few exceptionally interesting opportunities at hand in the mining dot.com age, and relished being at the centre of it all in Perth. I stayed over at Tim's and had breakfast before driving – slowly! – back to Perth.

On Easter Monday, I had dinner with a couple of people – one of whom I knew from London – from Scimitar Resources, a gold company turned uranium explorer. The meeting was Aussie-style, wearing jeans and T-shirts, at the popular Ocean Beach Hotel, which, as the name suggests, has spectacular views over Cottesloe Beach. Their excitement about the potential wealth creation and their confidence in their assets was palpable. While I was in Perth, the uranium spot price hit $113 per pound. Five years before, it was around $10 per pound. They were right to be excited.

My phone had been ringing nonstop all weekend with people from the mining community who had "heard I was in town" and wondered if we could have "a quick chat". The next couple of days were filled with back-to-back meetings. It became clear that the mining industry was undergoing a period of consolidation: many companies were considering bids, or were in strategic partnership discussions or contemplating buying another company.

As an example, at my first meeting with Alan Eggers from uranium explorer Summit Resources, we were unable to discuss much in detail as the company's stock had been suspended from the Australian stock exchange that morning pending an announcement. Two days later I found out that Areva, a French nuclear power and renewable energy company, had taken an 18% stake in Summit. But another uranium miner, Paladin, had already bid for Summit, and immediately made a counterbid. Coincidentally, I met with Paladin CEO John Borschoff the night before the counterbid was announced. John is one of the most knowledgeable people I have ever met when it comes to the uranium industry. He bought the Langer Heinreich uranium mine in Namibia for about AU$50,000. When we met, Paladin was worth several billions in market capitalization. Despite the evolving situation on the evening we met, we spent almost two hours discussing the economics of the uranium industry, supply and demand, his company – and my upcoming space adventures.

A late night was followed by an early morning. Only a couple of hours after retiring for the night, my alarm went off at 4.45am. I picked up Tom and we drove to a small aerodrome to take a private hire prop jet to the Abrolhos Islands, an archipelago off the west coast about 400 km north of Perth, famous for its coral reefs. The plane ride gave us beautiful views of the coast – but I was so tired that I slept for most of the journey. The landing strip on the island was 200 m of gravel; a good landing in those conditions is hard to achieve, but our pilot did a great job and landed us very smoothly. I assumed he had flown to the island many times before, but he told us it was only his second landing on this strip. I guess light aircraft pilots in Western Australia are used to landing in some pretty unusual conditions.

A friend picked us up and took us to Tom's boat: a converted crayfish boat that had been kitted out with all the amenities of a tourist motorboat, including state-of-the-art navigation systems, high-spec sound and light systems, a barbecue and plenty of space to party. Quite a transformation. Tom's true passion soon became clear: fishing. After a quick breakfast, we all jumped into the small diving boat and went spearfishing – although my headache still hadn't cleared up and the beating sun wasn't helping. The lack of sleep was getting too much for my body to handle.

I had never done freediving before, nor spearfishing. Spearfishing in Australia is highly regulated to protect fish stocks. In most places only freediving ('breath-holding') spearfishing is legal. A lot of time is spent snorkelling on the surface looking for fish – and when the hunt is on you have only as much time as you can hold your breath to catch your fish and spear it. I was amazed by how long the other guys could stay under water. Tom was quite literally like a fish. He could stay under for minutes at a time and swam incredibly fast with his huge 'fins' – or flippers, as I would call them. The fins really did help you power through the water, but I struggled to stay under for more than a minute. I saw some beautiful fish but never got close enough to take a shot, though the others caught quite a few coral trout and groupers.

I have to say that I was getting increasingly nervous about sharks. There had been a well-reported fatal attack by a Great White in this area the previous year. As I snorkelled around on the surface, I felt very exposed and found myself less concerned with spotting a fish to chase than I was with peering into the depths for any approaching sharks and scouring the horizon for a glimpse of a shark's fin speeding through the water toward me. We've all seen the movie, *Jaws*, after all.

Spearfishing attracts sharks. They can smell the blood of the fish from hundreds of yards away, and the guys were carrying their catch strapped to their waists. I assumed the dead fishes' blood was like a giant underwater neon advertising sign saying, "Shark Food Here!" I felt we were like a kind of welcoming roadside diner in the Australian outback – but the customers were sharks, and we were potentially on the menu.

I wish I could say that I was being paranoid, but I was not. A shark suddenly appeared among the divers. It swam right up to Tom and made a sudden jerking movement with its head, its razor-sharp white teeth flashing. I thought Tom was done for – but then I realized that the shark had taken one of the fish from his belt and all that was left was the fish's head, still attached to his belt. It's hard to scream with a snorkel in your mouth, but I tried. One of our party had stayed on the diving boat, and I assume he could hear something like "hnnnnnngg-gggg!" coming out from the top of my snorkel. If the shark could take a sizeable fish in one bite, I couldn't see why it would not take my foot, for example, or a larger part of my leg, with equal ease.

The guys under water seemed incredibly calm and collected. As more sharks arrived on the scene, Tom poked one in the nose with his spear, but it didn't seem to have any effect. The group decided to head back to the boat. I happily joined them. Safely back on board, the Aussies all seemed unphased by the incident, which I would have described as "a shark attack." I asked Tom – calmly, I believe – if we had been in serious danger. "Nah – they're grey nurse sharks, mate. Pretty harmless." I wondered how harmless 'pretty harmless' was on a scale of one to 10.

It was decided that we should relocate and carry on fishing some-where else, so we did, and I am happy to report that there were no further shark attacks, since we only had a broom for defence, which the guys had brought from the boat, probably to reassure me. Back on the big boat at the end of the dive, we got our catch cleaned up and started to prepare our supper. As darkness fell, after the most beau-tiful sunset, the boat's underwater lights attracted a squid, which we caught for an unparalleled fresh sushi calamari starter for our meal. I've eaten the most wonderful fish in some of the best restaurants in the world, but that fresh fish supper on the deck of Tom's boat under the stars of the southern sky was hard to beat.

The next morning, we were up bright and early and back on the diving boat. We did a beautiful wreck dive of the Dutch ship *Batavia*: its huge cannons were slowly becoming integrated with the vegeta-tion on the seabed, as were the anchors. We swam past some beauti-ful brain coral – shaped like a miniature planet. As I swam around it, I felt like I was quietly doing a fly-by in a weightless state around some distant world. We saw many shoals of beautiful brightly-coloured fish swim – but, fortunately, no sharks.

We did one more spear dive, and Tom made the catch of the trip: a 1.6-metre Spanish mackerel. A Spanish mackerel has the same iridescent blue-grey skin as an ordinary mackerel, but it is about 30 times the size and looks more like a barracuda. It is a big, powerful game fish. Tom was using a reel gun. When he speared the fish, it took off at high speed. He let the fish run and take out the line from the reel while he headed back to the surface and then back to the diving boat where he was able to play the fish in, after a long fight. What a catch! We took photos of Tom proudly holding the monster in his arms. We sailed back to the small island with the airstrip, where a charter plane arrived to pick us up. Once back at the aerodrome in Perth, I drove the others to 'the big airport' and then went back into town, only to return later that evening to begin the longest airplane journey I have ever done in (almost) one stretch.

I was setting a few personal records or 'firsts' on this trip: the longest nonstop flight I had ever done: Sydney to Los Angeles, my longest journey on Earth within 24 hours – Perth to Sydney, Sydney to LA, LA to New York; a total of 19,308 km in 23 hours. Given that the around-the-world distance is approximately 44,000 km, this means that I was travelling almost half the globe in one trip within one day. En route to Sydney, I crossed the date line travelling West to East for the first time ever. I had boarded the plane in Perth Friday evening at midnight and tried to get as much sleep as possible. The journey only lasted five hours but the two-hour time zone difference took me straight to breakfast in Sydney. My very last meeting, on my stopover in Sydney, was with Neill Arthur, the chairman of Uranium Exploration Australia, for whom I later did some work, even becoming a board member of a Northern Irish gold exploration company that was eventually sold to US-based Focus Gold in 2011.

The whole trip had taken me round the world in just 20 days – from London to Australia, on to LA, across the US to the East Coast for some business in New York and a walk down memory lane at Harvard, and back across the Atlantic. My brief trip to Cambridge, Massachusetts, to visit my alma mater, Harvard University, was like stepping back in time: as I arrived at Logan Airport and took a cab along the beautiful Charles River, it felt like I had never left. Checking in to the Charles Hotel was a first: I knew it well from recruitment events where corporations set out their stalls in the hope of recruiting Harvard's top talent, but I had never stayed there. I took a walk down Brattle Street, past our old haunts – our regular Indian restaurant had been replaced by a dental clinic, which jarred – and on to my old dorm in the Cronkhite Centre. I spotted the window to my room and was glad the light was off. It would have felt wrong for someone else to be there. Standing outside, I could imagine my old friends Philip and Carsten, standing right where I was standing now on the lawn, shouting up at me to join them for my first game of softball. I peered into the common room where we used to hold parties and events and was sad to see the big wooden-floored room with its huge fireplace now divided up into soulless, glass-walled seminar rooms. Sometimes it's best to let memories remain memories.

The round-the-world trip I took in 1997 had needed meticulous planning – visas ordered far in advance, meeting points carefully arranged with friends months before, numerous reassurances to my mother that I would return in one piece after five months of adventuring. Travelling around the world was a big deal back then. Now, almost 10 years to the day, I had set off again, but just for my Easter break. The world had grown remarkably smaller in those 10 years. It's no wonder we are now looking to carry on our adventures beyond Earth.

———————————

The following month was another milestone, a 'giant leap.' It was one of the busiest months I had ever experienced – which is saying something. It was also my most financially successful period to date: 'deal mania' indeed. There was a £12 million wind farm deal in Denmark, Poland and Italy; an AU$10 million deal in Australia and Namibia; another AU$2 million deal in Western Australia, with a 7% new company cornerstone investor; a couple of great mining deals in Canada; a 250,000-tonne iron ore deal. And on top of all of that, a US$700 million cement deal that was ongoing. It was crazy, especially considering, at this stage, I was still working for Man Securities. My contact network was thriving and growing fast with each new deal. There is no better advertisement than successful execution; finish one quality deal successfully and three others appear like magic.

It was in May 2007 that my dream of starting my own investment bank really began to seem as if it could become a reality.

The Danish production company Strålfors had invited me to make a presentation, "Failure is Not an Option" about my space project to 150 of their top clients who were spending half a day visiting their facilities in Copenhagen. When I arrived, the event organizers seemed to have everything in hand. It was great to see everyone in an upbeat mood, but there was pressure on me for everything to go smoothly. My introduction was very complimentary. My presentation outlined my space projects, including video clips from my training, which were very well-received by the audience. The latter included representatives from some of Denmark's biggest corporations, including IBM. I got some great feedback, including a couple of thank-you emails with invitations to deliver the presentation at their own companies. Presentations like this require a build-up of energy and adrenaline ... followed by a collapse on the other side. It is thrilling but draining.

The following day, I had arranged a roadshow in Copenhagen for Bannerman Resources – an outcome of my meeting in Perth with the company's impressive CEO, Clive. I had another hugely important meeting arranged, introducing a potential investor to another very attractive deal, an investment in an alternative energy company. A successful roadshow for Bannerman, and a successful deal with the energy company could lift me into a different league and make the launch of Wimmer Financial a real possibility.

Bannerman's uranium asset in Namibia was right next to Paladin's and had huge potential. I had pulled together a great collection of potential investors: I was confident I had found the perfect investors for Bannerman and the perfect opportunity for the investors. I went back to the Hotel d'Angleterre in central Copenhagen for an early night. But the early night did not happen; Clive and I ended up going out to dinner.

I had really taken to Clive when we met in Perth. With more than 20 years' experience in the mining sector, he is very direct – the type of person who calls a spade a spade. He is loyal and reliable, as well as commercially driven and, most importantly, is the type of person who does what he says. He is as passionate about mining as I am about space. We spent the evening talking about our common interests and the time flew by. When I eventually made it to bed, I knew that the next day was going to be one to remember, a day that could catapult me into the next league, financially and in terms of business contacts. I was raring to go.

I woke up early the next morning, fresh, well-rested and eager to get started. I met Clive at 8am, and we drove to our first meeting. Clive's presentation was polished and well-prepared and went brilliantly. Danish pastries were served. Clive's personality and experience, together with the company's mining assets and its strategic positioning, proved a winning combination. While we were on our way to the next meeting, 15 minutes after leaving, I got a call from our first potential investor: "We would like to do the entire deal right now, if possible." Now that's what you call a fantastic start to the day. The previous week, I had finished the first tranche of the financing, but the second part was moving more slowly. Now, after one meeting, it was, in principle, closed and done. If this was the music industry, we probably would have celebrated immediately with a bottle of champagne. But this is banking. The show must go on. We quietly bumped fists together and moved on to our next meeting. For this one, I had flown in an investor from Sweden. He was already a significant investor in Clive's business, and he was interested in more exposure. The investor trusted my word that the meeting would be worthwhile – and it was. Another brilliant presentation from Clive; the same eager reaction from the investor.

Demand was already starting to outstrip supply. Things could get difficult – and I always wanted to deliver and leave good clients happy. We took note of the client's interest and said we would get back to them. 'Deal mania' went into overdrive when we got back to the Hotel d'Angleterre. I had reserved tables in different corners of the hotel's excellent restaurant, to be able to juggle simultaneous investor lunches. In one corner, Clive was presenting over lunch to three investors. In another corner, I had a colleague presenting to two other clients about the sector, after I had made introductions and set the wheels in motion. Meanwhile, I left for the lunch meeting with the CEO of the alternative energy company and the potential investor.

It was a rocky start: I was 15 minutes late, which was not clever because the investor had a flight to catch immediately after our meeting. Thankfully, we still opened on a good note, and lunch was already served, which meant we could get straight down to business.

The CEO outlined the company's excellent situation and the compelling nature of the investment. He had a clear focus on what his company had to offer and a thorough understanding of his industry. I liked what he had to say. Potential growth, low capital expenditure, high investment returns, reduced risk, strong management team, industry experience, clarity of communication ... it was all very impressive. In the end, we ran out of time. We had many more questions to discuss and agreed to talk again. I had a cab to the airport on standby; as soon as the investor was in the car, I returned to the hotel restaurant at the perfect moment.

One of the meetings was just wrapping up, and I could tell from the body language that it had been a success. I said my goodbyes to that group while taking the other group of investors across the restaurant for another meeting so that my colleague could get off to his next meeting. It was all happening so fast. The restaurant staff could hardly keep up, but I reassured them that everything was on my tab and just to keep going and we would sort it all out later!

The roadshow had been a huge success; demand was outstripping supply by three to four times. It would be a challenging job to manage allocation expectations diplomatically without jeopardizing good relationships, but that is the nature of the business. Finally, we left the hotel restaurant and caught a cab to our final meeting. At that point, the time pressure was off; it was late afternoon on a Friday and Copenhagen was beginning to wind down for the weekend. As a result, our last meeting was much less intense, more relaxed and very enjoyable. The institutional investor, in the end, however, did not participate although he really found the story compelling. We didn't mind, as we were scrambling for stock anyway and we felt we had made another potentially useful connection. As we were on our way out, we bumped into a senior figure from the same institution whom I knew, and we had a brief chat. "It seems like you know everyone in the finance industry in Copenhagen," said Clive. I pulled a face and smiled in a self-deprecatory sort of way. But, actually, I probably did!

Tired but happy, Clive and I headed back to the Hotel d'Angleterre for a beer, served in the hotel's trademark tall slim glasses. It had been a fantastic day; intense but focused. It was finally time for my last meeting, this time with the banker involved in the alternative energy deal. We had a very business-like banker-to-banker discussion and got the final details of the potential deal agreed to in no time.

The deals were nearly done. It seemed that Wimmer Financial had passed its own feasibility test. I took Clive out for dinner at one of Copenhagen's 'hot' restaurants, the Grill Bar. He was very appreciative of our collaboration and the day's efforts, and we spent an excellent evening together before heading off, exhausted, for bed.

The next morning, I had a brunch meeting scheduled with a client who was also a personal friend, so I joined Clive at the breakfast table for just a quick coffee, and he introduced me to a new potential gold deal. It was only 8.30am on a Saturday morning and the next deal was already on the table! He took me through the assets, details and terms, and I liked the sound of it. We agreed to talk further when I was back in London.

While in Copenhagen, I was able to have a meeting with a member of my Wimmer Space team, to discuss everything from speaking engagements and media initiatives to a collaboration with the Copenhagen Planetarium. Luckily, the meeting wasn't far from my sister's place: I swung by to say hello to her, Jesper and the kids. From there, I went to visit my wonderful mother for Mother's Day. I've eaten in some lovely restaurants, but nothing can beat a traditional, home-cooked Danish dinner. On Sunday morning, I got up early and went for a jog in the forest near Slagelse, along one of my favourite old routes from the days when I would run several times a week to keep fit for badminton and handball. The route seemed easier than it did then. It was a beautiful, mild spring morning. As I ran through the forest in the pine-scented air, I felt good; I knew I had passed an important milestone in my life.

The deals didn't let up as May went on. Just a week later, an exciting opportunity came to my attention: a listed Canadian company with mining assets in Sweden had come under severe pressure from the stock market. Market capitalization was around CA$130 million and, with CA$34 million in the bank, the assets were priced at sub-CA$100 million. That looked exceptionally cheap. As I learned more about the company's poor management, a great investment turned into an even bigger opportunity: a potential takeover. By sheer luck, Clive would be in Toronto later that week. I organized for him to meet with the company and lined up CA$300 million of financing, should it be needed.

We found out that the insider directors only controlled 10% of the company, so they had no power to prevent a takeover even if they wanted to. But we learned another business was also interested. We would have to move fast.

A couple of days in London were absorbed by a copper deal, a coal deal, two property deals and stock market trading. Then I flew to St Tropez to join my friend Sophie and her parents for the Cannes Film Festival. Though I was in St Tropez, my mind was still on work. Sophie's father, Claude, is passionate about his trading business and, within 10 minutes of my arrival, we were talking about a big cement trade he was involved in. Soon enough I was on the phone to contacts, trying to help him execute this great piece of business. The total value of the deal was around $700 million. What was supposed to be a quiet afternoon in the sun turned into a mad frenzy of cement prices. This was a taste of life as an entrepreneur.

————————

4 October 2007 is an historic day to me – for two reasons.

Fifty years before, to the day, the USSR had launched *Sputnik* – the world's first artificial satellite. Launched into orbit from the Tyuratam base in the Kazakh Republic, the shiny metal sphere with its four spindly trailing antennae circled the Earth once every 96 minutes for months until it slowly fell back toward Earth and burned up in the atmosphere. The space age had begun.

It was also the day I chose to launch my own investment bank, Wimmer Financial.

Just as the Soviets had no way of knowing the impact of *Sputnik*, I had no idea how far the Wimmer Financial adventure would take me. In many ways, Wimmer Financial was the natural extension of my entrepreneurial efforts with Wimmer Space. That adventure started with me buying my ticket to space and flying to Russia for my first space training. The scope widened to include other adventures, such as an Everest skydive and an attempt at the world's land speed record. In time, I became involved in numerous charity efforts, book publishing deals, documentary-making, international motivational speaking and regular media work, including my monthly slot on BBC World.

But alongside Wimmer Space, I had kept my full-time job. With Wimmer Financial, it was a full-time commitment and there was no safety net. A good part of my net worth was on the line. But, in the words of André Gide, "Man cannot discover new oceans unless you have the courage to lose sight of the shore." For me, high stakes equal high focus. Failure was not an option. By the time I launched Wimmer Financial, I already had quite a few corporate clients, institutional investor relationships and a number of deals in the pipeline, many from my time in Australia and the roadshow in Copenhagen.

The support and praise I received for branching out on my own blew me away. The initial challenge would be the administrative elements, from getting the essential Financial Services Agency licence, to recruiting the best available talent, to buying equipment for the office and choosing the best ergonomic office chairs for my new colleagues. There were also vital meetings with counterparty suppliers like Goldman Sachs and my accountants at PricewaterhouseCoopers (PwC) – I had decided from the outset that I would work only with the best; we were truly 'punching above our weight.' In those early, heady days, I found myself flipping between doing multimillion-dollar deals and ordering a few pounds' worth of paper clips.

On Tuesday, five days after the launch of Wimmer Financial, I had a sandwich lunch with a Canadian company that resulted in the first mandate to the new company: selling a $200 million property with mining rights. An excellent start. But starting a business comes, of course, with some sacrifices: when November arrived, I mourned the loss of my base salary. Being employed, you hardly think about it; money just shows up in your bank account. As an entrepreneur, you have to go out and make your money – and, in the meantime, there are a surprisingly long list of bills to pay. I remember looking at my bank account that month and thinking, "What's gone wrong? Where's my salary?" Until of course I remembered: no more salary. On top of that, Man Securities had recently completed the IPO of what was to become MF Global, in which I acquired some shares as an employee. There was a vesting schedule of a couple of years attached, and leaving the company meant that I would leave some of those shares behind. They were quite valuable; walking away comes at a cost.

But with the increased responsibility of running your own business – ensuring that there is always 'money in the till' – comes a tremendous amount of freedom. I felt so optimistic and impatient to progress. I love doing deals. It gives me a big adrenaline kick. When I have a big day ahead of me, I wake up early, eager to get going. Working with other highly-driven entrepreneurs trying to get a deal together is great. In a way, it is like climbing a mountain every time. You take it step by step. In the beginning, things move slowly ... then a challenging incline appears. You climb that, and on up to the next section to conquer. Eventually, you reach the point of no return; you have to make the final push to the summit – you have to close the deal. The triumphal moment is followed by the climb down – in terms of deal-making, the implementation, technical problems, settlement issues and so on – which can be hard work. But nothing beats the rush of reaching the peak.

While Wimmer Financial was going through its first days and weeks, I was also undergoing medical tests in preparation for a later centrifuge training session with Virgin Galactic in Philadelphia. My ECG showed a small anomaly, so I was sent for extra cardiology tests at the brilliant London Bridge Hospital, the most advanced of which was the injection of a small amount of radioactive material and a treadmill stress test, to monitor my heart at 100% utilization. And I had thought that being in the middle of one of the riskiest moves of my career to date might be stressful enough!

As well as marking a turning point in my career, 2007 included some incredible highlights in my journey to space. During a visit to the Esrange Space Centre in Sweden in January, Will Whitehorn, president of Virgin Galactic, gave a flawless presentation about Virgin Galactic's space plans, complete with a video clip of Sir Richard Branson. A student had asked about the future affordability of tickets to space and Whitehorn spontaneously launched a competition for local students to win a free ticket to space, immediately creating a flurry of press excitement. The first Swedish Virgin Galactic space traveller was presented to the audience to great acclaim. The previous day, Christer Fuglsang, the first Swedish astronaut, who had flown to the International Space Station on the space shuttle in December 2006, had returned to his hometown of Stockholm to be welcomed by huge crowds and a media frenzy. Everyone was going 'space crazy.' At the Spaceport Sweden event, I was interviewed in French by a Belgian TV-crew about my passion for space and my current plans.

The National Space Society (NSS) International Space Development Conference in May planted the seed for many interesting developments, from establishing a private space travel code of conduct – The Wimmer-Whitesides Private Space Travellers' Manifesto (George Whitesides was president of the NSS at the time) – to creating an educational computer game following my trip to space. At a Wimmer Space presentation in the fairy-tale setting of Holckenhavn Castle in Nyborg, I discovered I was a distant relation of Countess Cristina, the castle's chatelaine. In June, I had lunch with Buzz Aldrin in Paris, where we talked about everything from the moon landing to making a cartoon based on his life.

My space year ended on a high, with a trip to Princeton University in the US to meet with Greg Olsen, one of the first private space travellers. Greg gave me a tour of Princeton, which was followed by two days' centrifuge training at the NASTAR centre. I learned various techniques to counter the effects of G-force, when you experience a pressure on the chest equivalent to the weight of six people, from 'trumpet breathing,' where you suck in air through pursed lips and then exhale with lips pressed tightly together, to tensing muscles to minimize blood flow away from the brain, to the 'Hook Manoeuvre,' where you inhale while saying the first part of the word 'hook,' close off your throat, and then exhale on the 'k' sound.

Trying them out in the centrifuge was amazing. The pull of 6 G is incredibly powerful, but I actually enjoyed it. F-16 fighter pilots must be able to pull 7.5 G – not far from astronaut training levels. Having successfully completed my training at 6 G gave me a lot of comfort about going into space since I knew what to do and how much pressure my body could handle.

EVEREST

When mountaineer George Mallory was asked why he wanted to climb Everest in 1923, he famously replied, "Because it's there." Over the years, the world's greatest mountains have challenged adventurers to test their skill, strength and endurance against these forces of nature. Everest, the world's tallest mountain at over 29,000 ft, is the ultimate challenge.

Mallory and his climbing partner Andrew Irvine set off from Advanced Base Camp at 21,330 ft on 4 June 1924 and never returned. They were last seen some 800 ft below the summit. Speculation continues to this day as to whether they reached the summit before they died. Mallory's body was found by an expedition in 1999. Irvine's remains have still not been discovered.

More than 300 people have now died attempting to climb Mount Everest before and after Sir Edmund Hillary's first successful ascent with Tenzing Norgay in 1953. Now I found myself falling under its spell – though not as a mountaineer. In 2008, I was one of a group of ambitious thrill seekers undertaking a world first: skydiving over Mount Everest.

The event was organized by mountaineer, skydiver and adventurer Nigel Gifford, who had been part of the team for Richard Branson's 1998 attempt to fly around the world in a hot air balloon.

In the spring of 2008, Nigel and a team of three other skydivers had successfully completed the first-ever skydive in the Everest region, jumping from an altitude of 16,000 ft. Nigel's UK-based High and Wild adventure travel company was given a permit to run the world's first Everest Skydive that coming autumn.

This adventure would take me to new heights, both literally and figuratively. It was the perfect embodiment of my mantra: *the sky is no limit*.

I spoke on the phone to Nigel soon after his 'proof of concept' expedition, and he told me about this latest and possibly craziest adventure. I was hooked. Thirty-one people from around the globe signed up to take part, including one adventurous Dane, Per Wimmer. I was scheduled to attempt a world-first: a tandem skydive over Everest from a height of 29,500 ft – higher than Everest itself.

In August, together with my video cameraman, Jan Kanstrup, and still photographer and extreme-conditions communication expert, Morten Brandstrup, we flew to Geneva Airport. We were picked up in a Breitling-sponsored Hummer H1 to drive two hours to the village of Biel, close to Bern and Mont Blanc, to test and prepare for the world's first Everest Skydive. The weather conditions were improving, with scattered clouds but some sunshine. I had brought my new red jumpsuit with a big white cross on the back and front to emulate the Danish 'Dannebrog' flag.

I met Nigel and our pilot. After a long conversation and a couple of coffees (as if the adrenaline would not ensure sufficiently high heart rates during the skydive!), we began putting on our parachute harnesses. Then followed some basic skydiving instructions. We took some amazing photos in the bright sunshine with the team's airplane in the background. I later made a photo edit to produce a sepia version of the image, which reminded me strongly of the classic photograph of Charles Lindbergh standing in front of his record-breaking aircraft, the *Spirit of St Louis*, before attempting the world's first solo nonstop transatlantic flight.

We boarded the plane and took off. It was an incredibly beautiful flight through layers of clouds with the Swiss lakes and green fields on one side and Mont Blanc and its surrounding mountains towering over us on the other. As we kept climbing, a funny feeling took hold in my stomach as I began thinking about 'the opening of the door.' It is one thing to plan to go into space in a spaceship, but it suddenly struck me that opening the door of a small aircraft at a great height and actually jumping out was a whole different proposition. I had made one parachute jump before, but that was at least 15 years previously. The realization that I would be skydiving over Mount Everest in just a few weeks' time suddenly felt ambitious, to say the least. Meantime, in the very near future, one of our instructors was about to open the plane door. It seemed like a bad idea.

Cold air came flooding into the cabin. The plane door was open. This was real. Not a dream. Very real! My heart rate went up significantly; my mind was incredibly and exclusively focused on the procedures. This was my last chance to bail out. Not going to do that. Everything went very quickly from that point. No more time to think about going or not going. Nigel sat himself on the floor of the doorway in the strange banana-shaped position we had been taught back on the ground: legs bent backwards, chest and belly forward, arms close to the chest. Then he was gone, in a flash. Only a few seconds later, I found myself sitting in the same position with effectively my entire body outside the airplane and my feet dangling loose while we were racing through the air and the strong wind was pulling me out and down.

"Go!"

The next thing was a split-second whirlwind experience as I fell through the air, accelerating to a speed of approximately 150 km per hour. The fall was so fast I could hardly breathe.

I was able to 'play superman,' with one arm stretched out, and to carry out some other manoeuvres we had been taught. Freefall really is like being able to fly. After an amazing 50 seconds, the ripcord was pulled, the parachute deployed and my speed dropped from 150 km per hour to only a few, within seconds. Everything suddenly became very quiet. I drifted slowly but surely toward the ground and carried out a couple of 360 degree turns. Wow!

Now I could see the drop zone, hidden among the surrounding multicoloured fields. We steered toward it. Nearly there. Suddenly, the ground came closer very quickly ... preparation for landing ... "Bang!"... on the ground again, right in front of the photographers. Big smiles from everyone. Loud laughter replaced the silence. What a jump and what a thrill!

The parachutes were repacked, ready for the next jumps and a new group of experts and test organizers arrived from the UK. Unfortunately, the weather turned to rain, and we had to abandon any more jumping for the day, including our anticipated sunset jump. Later, we all went to a local village restaurant for a meal. Everyone was in high spirits. Suddenly, all the lights went out and the restaurant staff brought in a huge birthday cake – it had been my 40th birthday the day before. To my embarrassment, the whole table started singing "Happy birthday to you!" But it was truly thoughtful of everybody, and I joined in the fun.

The adrenaline and the fresh air from the skydive were beginning to take their toll, and I was feeling very tired. Still, I had a drink with Nigel until midnight to discuss various logistics and initiatives as part of the Everest Skydive. I had intended to check my emails before going to sleep, but the minute I got into bed I absolutely crashed and slept like a log.

The next morning, we jumped again, this time from a higher altitude – around 16,000 ft. We had a full load of jumpers this time, so the cabin was very crowded. Again, my heart rate went up several notches when the door opened. Yes, again, this was very real. Out the team went, one by one. As they left the plane and the wind caught their jumpsuits, there was a little flutter of noise ... fuhh! fuhh! fuhh! ... as each person disappeared into the sky.

Then came my turn: Outside the airplane in the banana position; 3-2-1 ... GO! and off into the strong cold wind. Again, turning, twisting and manoeuvring during freefall until ... pfft! ... the chute was successfully deployed. Another smooth glide down while I tried to equalize the air pressure in my ears. The ground rushed toward me. Again, huge smiles and laughter once I was safely down.

I grabbed a quick lunch with the others while checking a seemingly neverending stream of incoming messages and voicemails, trying to catch up with business back in London and with an ongoing deal in the Middle East. I had so much going on that my mobile phone battery went flat several times. Then followed the big skydive test: a 'High Altitude Low Opening' (HALO) jump from over 30,000 ft, using oxygen. My first HALO jump was to be only my fourth skydive ever! It seemed like I had skipped several classes, to say the least. When I looked at my skydiving colleagues and the instructors, who included ex-military high altitude experts with literally thousands of skydives under their belt, I felt as if I had been thrown into the middle of a special forces unit. The jump was scary but exhilarating, and it gave me confidence in my abilities.

---

15 September 2008: 'Black Monday.'

Whoa ... what happened?!

The global financial world was experiencing a seismic shift. Lehman Brothers, the leading global investment bank, had gone bankrupt. Unbelievable! Wall Street was in turmoil and the shock quickly ricocheted around the world's financial markets.

A number of my ex-Goldman Sachs colleagues had joined Lehman Brothers. Now the media were broadcasting images of Lehman staff around the world walking out of the door of their offices carrying small cardboard boxes containing their few personal belongings. No one was allowed to return to the office. It was unlikely they would get paid next payday as Lehman Brothers could not meet their global monthly payroll. Most people at Lehman had also paid a good portion of their bonuses in stocks and options; these were now worthless.

Then came the news that investment bank Merrill Lynch had been bought by Bank of America. The company had suffered the same loss of confidence in its solvency as Lehman Brothers. Fearing that the approaching collapse of Lehman Brothers would bring them down as well, Merrill Lynch had negotiated a deal with Bank of America over the weekend, at an impressive 70% over its current depressed stock valuation but nevertheless at a 60% discount on its valuation one year previously. Astonishing! The following evening, I met with a Merrill Lynch employee. He told me the news of the sale had sent shockwaves through the trading floor on Monday morning, but he said staff soon realized that they could have gone down the same route as Lehman and could consider themselves 'lucky.'

I was shocked and stunned at these dramatic events. Mid-tier banks run into trouble from time to time – but not these well-managed giants. The next day, we woke up to hear that AIG, the world's largest insurer, was also on the brink of bankruptcy. Absolutely incredible! During the day, it became clear that they might be able to sell assets and attract around $20 billion, but a minimum of $40 billion was needed and, ideally, quite a bit more. JP Morgan and Goldman Sachs desperately tried to raise $75 billion to shore up the AIG balance sheet to ensure their vital credit rating, but they failed. The end result was announced the following day: a near nationalization of the world's largest insurance company by the US government. AIG had been deemed 'too big to fail.'

Another gut-wrenching shift in the tectonic plates of global finance! Where was the world heading? A global stock market crash like in 1929? What would be next?

These dramatic global financial events obviously affected me hugely. I had started Wimmer Financial less than 12 months earlier. We had done pretty well during the first half of 2008 in the face of quite adverse market conditions – another global investment bank, Bear Stearns, had been rescued and bought out by JP Morgan during the spring of that year. We had been quick and agile in executing good quality deals in the few short windows when markets were friendly and risk appetite was 'on.' Up until Black Monday, and in spite of the huge challenges, I had loved every minute of it.

The summer had been a really great summer. I had been working hard but also partying hard in St Tropez twice during the season – I had thrown a wonderful and extravagant birthday party there for me (turning 40) and my sister (turning 35). We had a wonderful time with events spread over two days, a Sunseeker yacht on hire for guests; a helicopter arrival for my sister and me; a private room in St Tropez with special lighting and our own DJ; an endless stream of champagne. Then, just six days before I was due to leave for my historic skydive over Mount Everest, Black Monday ushered in what we now know as the Great Recession. Talk about 'boom and bust'! It was a good reminder that you cannot take anything for granted; you never know what might be just around the corner.

For the first time since I had taken the dramatic step of starting my own business, I was seriously worried. The market had gone from not great to complete chaos: panicked, dramatic, irrational. The worst part of it all was the lack of visibility. Nobody could predict what would happen next or how long the consequences would last. Then ... another day, another drama! On 17 September, the largest UK mortgage bank, HBOS, saw its share price collapse during the early morning trading session. The BBC broke a story about a possible buy-out by Lloyds TSB. The Financial Services Authority made reassuring noises ... but by Wednesday evening, that merger was a reality. These were truly transformational and historically volatile times.

Why did it all go so badly wrong?

In the world of finance, individual and organizational compensation structures and incentives are typically built around success fees: the more deals, the larger the deals, the greater the financial pay-out. As an individual, there is very little downside risk to doing a deal – even a low-quality deal. If the deal closes, you get paid. When money is cheap, as it had been the past few years, there is plenty of room and appetite for both high- and low-quality deals. In the US mortgage market – where the problems began – the big mortgage banks were aggressively lending out money for property purchases to people who were extremely unlikely to be able to keep up their payments. Banks and bankers made very good money; poor people who had always dreamt about owning a property suddenly realized their dreams. Property prices rose because of the strong demand. Speculators entered the market, adding fuel to the fire; prices rose even further. Everybody was a winner. The people who probably couldn't afford to repay the mortgages they had taken out saw the value of their property rise and remortgaged to release some of the increase in value. People started using the housing market like a giant cash machine. The only problem was that nobody really had the money to pay in the long term. The whole system was a house of cards. The party had been paid for by the global credit circus, which had become more and more sophisticated with various derivative structures: swaps, options, exotic collaterals, 'packaging' of many mortgages in various tranches of perceived risk without anyone really knowing the exact content and true risk assessment of each tranche, etc., etc. Many of these had now become toxic – and no one could be quite sure which institutions were holding what bits of paper and to what terrifying debts they might now be exposed. Every institution became scared of lending to every other institution because no one was sure who was truly creditworthy. The 'credit house' had been built on very weak fundamentals and, predictably, it all came crashing down on Black Monday. Now, the ordinary US and European taxpayer had to foot a bill of gigantic proportions to bail out institutions deemed too big to fail and to reboot stalling economies. These are the hard facts of the global credit circus facts – but is the result morally right? Should the average tax-paying employee pick up the tab for such a disastrous collapse?

At Wimmer Financial, the challenges we faced in a collapsing market were made even more difficult when our external share execution institution, Instinet (backed and owned by Japanese investment bank Nomura) suddenly cut its ties with all third parties like ourselves. Other institutions that we approached either dragged their feet or rejected us outright. We were too junior and too new. Nobody wanted to enter into new counterparty relationships during this period of time, when even the titans of Wall Street had proven to be untrustworthy counterparties.

Part of our earnings stream was cut off at a stroke. No execution capability means no trading income. Corporate finance, which had been another significant part of our income, also dried up because of a lack of appetite for risk. An oil rig deal we had been near to closing after much hard work collapsed, as did a promising hotel transaction in the Middle East and a shipping deal involving a Korean bank. Our revenues had slumped to zero within one week, with no immediate prospect of recovering anytime soon.

In the midst of these problems and anxieties, one of my greatest disappointments was actually at a personal level. Six months earlier I had appointed a friend, Lars Krøjer, from my Harvard days, to the board of Wimmer Financial – someone I had great respect for, both personally and professionally. The plan was to make use of his extremely strong network of professional contacts to help the company and for me to be able to turn to him for valuable advice. In fact, neither of those things came about. He showed up at the office on a grand total of two occasions. On every other occasion when I asked for a meeting, he suggested we meet at his summer house, where he was enjoying time off from the financial markets and writing a book. I never made it there. I didn't have time. I had been planning to ask him to step down from the board because he was not making any useful contribution.

Just after Black Monday, with the financial world and potentially my business collapsing all around me, my old friend emailed me to say that he was not really adding any value to Wimmer Financial – how true! – but also attaching a sizeable invoice for his 'services' to date, in full!

I was absolutely shocked. I had expected us to reach a reasonable agreement about some recompense for the small amount of time he had committed to Wimmer Financial. Instead, he had sent me an invoice for his full salary for the whole period – a few days after Black Monday. I suspected he was expecting us to go under and was getting his invoice in before we went bust. I should add that my friend – or ex-friend – is a multimillionaire with a hedge fund background. His invoice, though painful for me to pay at a time when I was slashing every possible cost to try to keep the business alive, represented an insignificant amount of money relative to his considerable fortune. The person I thought was a dear and trusted friend was prepared to add to my misery in historically unprecedented times for the sole purpose of adding a completely insignificant amount of wealth to his swollen bank account. I can't describe the level of shock and disappointment I felt. When the champagne corks are popping it is very easy to be friends; when the music stops, the true colours of friends and foes really come out. I paid him in full because I honour my commitments, but he lost my friendship in the process.

During the early part of the Black Monday week, I seriously considered cancelling my historic Mount Everest Skydive. Then I realized that, with the current paralysis in the markets and investors holding on grimly to their cash, there would be no deals to be

215

missed over that period and the 'opportunity cost' of my trip would be nil. I decided to go ahead. I was incredibly excited, but my occasional feelings of nervousness about the trip and my focus on the details of the preparations were now overwhelmed by a feeling of deep anxiety about the state of the financial markets – and, to put it bluntly, about the survival of Wimmer Financial. I was in uncharted emotional territory. On the eve of one of my most ambitious adventures to date, I felt that my professional dreams were about to come crashing down at about the same speed as my coming skydive!

The one heart-warming consolation in these anxious times was the support of my team at Wimmer Financial. Despite my having had to ask everyone to accept a cut in pay earlier in the week – hopefully temporarily – they all showed increased dedication to the task, working late and doing everything they could to be ready to get back to business when – if! – the markets picked up. My assistant Louisa even brought me the perfect gift just as I was leaving the office on Friday: a T-shirt with the words "The First-Ever Everest Skydive: I DID IT ... !" with a collage of images of me parachuting. How sweet was that? What fantastic staff I have!

I arrived in Kathmandu on Saturday 21 September 2008, to find an airport in chaos. Luggage was strewn around the baggage belt, while everyone competed for the services of the local porters, who were being run ragged. Nonpermanent Nepalese passport holders had to pay a $40 fee, the processing of which was excruciatingly slow. The mayhem continued in the pickup area outside the airport, so much so that I was unable to find the person who was meeting me. I hailed a taxi to the hotel, where our production team for the trip would be assembling.

The Yak and Yeti in Kathmandu was a grand, 'old colonial' style hotel, an imposing red-brick building with a sweeping central staircase in the spacious lobby. It had once clearly been a fine hotel, but by 2008 it had seen better days – a characteristic that was to become familiar by the end of our trip. The only thing that was truly up to date was the price list!

The Everest Skydive team had arranged our flight, two days later, up to Lukla (9,380 ft), where we would begin our four-day trek through Namche Bazaar, Tengboche and Pheriche to Syangboche (12,400 ft), the departure point and the drop zone for the skydive. Our trek would immerse us in the beautiful Himalayan landscape on the way up; a helicopter would take us back to Lukla, before a flight back to Kathmandu, after the dive.

Kathmandu itself is a really buzzing place. Motorbikes weave around cars, buses and rickshaws. People and street vendors crowd the streets. Ramshackle old buildings stand side by side with ornate Nepalese architecture. It can be overwhelming and exhausting – but I loved it.

Nepal is one of the poorest countries in the world, but the people I encountered in Nepal were so accommodating and helpful. From a visitor's point of view, it has an original, unspoilt charm, unaffected by the trappings of Western life.

The production team for the trip was five strong: journalist, blog- and book-writer Lars Vestergaard; Morten Brandstrup, our photographer and communications and satellite broadcast expert; young Danish documentary producer Kenneth Andreasen; cinematographer Peter Laursen; and British documentary maker Stephen Slater. We began by spending several hours to plan the media operation for the trip, from coordinating the filming of two documentaries and the technical challenges of uploading photos and videos to our FTP server, to organizing our visit to a local orphanage on behalf of the Global Angels Foundation, an international charity the Everest Skydive operation had linked to that helps disadvantaged communities grow sustainably. We ended up funding two orphanages in Nepal, hoping this would help local children live out their dreams, just as we were living out our adventures. Prior to the skydive, I had also agreed to support UNICEF. The Everest adventure was truly historic, and it was global; I wanted to do something that would contribute to children's wellbeing and education on a global level, and we became one of UNICEF's corporate partners. That evening I had an interview with Reuters that would go worldwide the next day, and a live interview for Danish radio. There was a lot of media buzz around the dive.

That evening, we kicked off the trip with dinner at the Rum Doodle, a famous Everest mountaineering restaurant decorated with paper footprints bearing messages from past travellers. Anyone who successfully reaches the summit of Everest – the number currently stands at only 4,000 people – can eat there for free for the rest of their life. The atmosphere at dinner was one of great excitement: there was a lot of fun and laughter, but also a real sense of the historic adventure we were about to undertake. I have no doubt that many groups of adventurers have eaten at the Rum Doodle with the same feeling.

The team spirit was superb. We were ready for adventure, but also quite jet-lagged, so we took rickshaws through Kathmandu's characterful old town back to the hotel. There was still a lot of work to get through, so the laptops came out during the Wimmer team's after-dinner drinks – and were not packed away until 4am.

A safety briefing the following day brought an unwelcome surprise. We were talked through the trekking route and shown how to use the oxygen bottles, which are needed in high-altitude areas where the air is very thin. The last thing we did was to lay out the jumpsuits for the dive, including my red jumpsuit with a white cross, the only possible colours for the first Dane to skydive over Everest. But when we laid them out, there was one missing – mine. Only my name tag was there. I tried to imagine the mental processes that would allow someone to pack a name tag without being concerned that there was not a suit attached to it. We were at panic stations, with less than 24 hours before our departure to Lukla.

We tracked down a local tailor and rushed straight over to his shop to give him my measurements and instructions as to the placing of various logos on the jumpsuit. I was astonished by the tailor's calm competence. It was as if making emergency jumpsuits was an everyday occurrence for him! He assured us that a new jumpsuit would be ready by 10 o'clock that evening. We went back to the hotel to get some work done – for me, that meant helping try to keep five deals alive across four continents in the face of the ongoing financial crisis. At the same time, I was trying to help Stephen acquire some extra camera equipment while also getting content up on the website. Annoyingly, Stephen seemed to have arrived seriously underequipped. He had been a last-minute replacement for a very experienced BBC producer who had been forced to cancel in the last weeks leading up to the first Everest Skydive. Tracking down the necessary additional camera equipment was proving very time consuming. I worried that Stephen lacked the necessary experience for the task. We had to leave for the airport at 5am the next morning, so things were getting intense.

I fell asleep at midnight, only to be woken up half an hour later by the tailor, who had missed his deadline by a couple of hours but had still delivered, as promised. The jumpsuit fit perfectly, and the Wimmer team bags I had also ordered looked great. The tailor's efforts had been critical. Crisis averted.

The next morning, the hotel lobby was in a state of disarray comparable to Kathmandu Airport, with daypacks, backpacks and camera equipment piled up around sleepy skydivers. We had been told to arrive in the mountains well rested for the demanding trek ahead, but I had only managed three hours of sleep.

The domestic airport security was very light. "Do you have any knives or bombs in your possession?" We said we did not, and they let us through without searching our baggage. It had been a long time since I had an airport experience like that.

We climbed into the 16-seater airplane and started our 45-minute flight up to Lukla, a small town high in the mountains. Arriving at Lukla is a unique experience: the airport – also known as Tenzing-Hillary Airport – is often described as the most dangerous in the world. The landing strip is just 200 m long and begins at the edge of some steeply sloping, rough and wooded ground; landing too early would be a disaster. After 200 m of (relatively) flat tarmac, the airstrip comes to an abrupt end in front of a building. It doesn't feel like the best place to have a building. Behind the building is a sheer mountain face. There is literally no room for error.

It is not just the sharp landing that makes Lukla dangerous. Heavy fog often appears suddenly and unpredictably. A plane can be approaching to land when, out of nowhere, the visibility drops to zero. Only a few days after we completed our skydive, a plane crashed just short of the runway when clouds suddenly came down and burst into flames, killing all 18 mainly German passengers. The pilot survived.

After our own successful landing at Lukla, we were greeted by what seemed to be the entire village who had come out of curiosity and potentially to earn some extra cash as porters for our luggage to the Shangri-La Hotel. We spent some time acclimatizing to the altitude before setting off on the first leg of our trek, which would take us from Lukla to the village of Phakding. As we left, we were distracted by the charming scenes in Lukla itself: yaks wandering around the village, young kids playing, workers digging up the 'road,' quaint houses, many with bright blue roofs. It was an hour before we were out of Lukla. Our pace hardly improved from there, as we were captivated by the beauty of the landscape: wooded mountains, dramatic waterfalls, hanging bridges, deep valleys, tumbling rivers. The trek was only supposed to last three hours, but after three and a half hours we were only halfway. We stopped for lunch and, after our break, rainy weather kept us moving. We arrived at Phakding (8,560 ft) just before sunset, finishing the day with a beer and some local food before a much-needed 9pm bedtime.

I could very easily have stayed in bed when my alarm went off at 6am the next morning ... but we had to stay on schedule. After a quick breakfast, we set off on the hardest leg of the trek so far, to our next acclimatization stop at Namche Bazaar. It started with a casual – and wet and rainy – stroll along the river. We saw some workmen chiselling stones for a new house, carving each one individually.

Later, the weather improved, but the incline did not. We stopped for lunch at 9,180 ft, and had to reach 11,300 ft by the end of the afternoon. We climbed up stony 'stairs' cut into the mountainside. One of the team kept singing "The Only Way Is Up" – and they were not wrong. I started to feel the weight of my legs. The thin air was having an effect, too: I had to take short breaks and breathe much more frequently, but the beauty of the mountains made up for it.

Near the end of the afternoon, we finally reached the base camp for our jump. Namche Bazaar is an old trading village, built like an amphitheatre on terracing cut into the half-moon mountain. Arriving from the path, you get a great view of the village, with houses that seemed to crawl up the mountain. Bright green seemed to be a favoured roof colour, along with the blues we had seen in Lukla and the more 'usual' (to Western eyes) reds. We passed the city gate stupa and went up to the hotel. Stupas often contain sacred relics linked to the Buddha or to other Buddhist saints. The stupa in Namche Bazaar has a classic white hemispheric roof on top of a stepped white stone base, with a short gold steeple with brightly painted Buddha's eyes – 'Wisdom Eyes' – painted on all four sides.

The trekking and the altitude were very energy draining. I had a headache and felt very tired. That evening we ate a simple meal and, after checking my emails, I slept very heavily. After a quick breakfast the next morning, I went back to bed for a few hours to rest before our 10.00 media production meeting to coordinate our next efforts and initiatives. The rest of the day was spent sorting out practical things in Namche – giving interviews, filming and editing news clips for a Danish TV-station.

Saturday brought my first real sight of Mount Everest. We got up early to watch the sun rise over the awe-inspiring mountain. The weather was perfect: crystal clear, crisply cold, with not a cloud in sight once the sun was up. The Himalayas looked magnificent; Everest itself, flanked by Lhotse, Ama Dablam and others. Trekking uphill with sore feet before sunrise had been painful and tiring – but that unforgettable image of the sun rising over the world's highest mountain made everything worthwhile.

After a quick local coffee, we went to check out the drop zone at nearby Syangboche (12,350 ft). For the first time, the prospect of the Everest Skydive started to feel real. This small strip of grass, surrounded by some of the world's tallest mountains, was where we would take off in our plane for the jump and where we would be landing after the skydive. The scale of the mountains towering around the tiny landing strip was awe-inspiring – and also intimidating.

That night, the Wimmer team spent hours editing video clips for Danish TV-2, and uploading the final edit via BGAN satellite, working till 3am. I couldn't have brought a more committed team with me to Nepal. The next morning, we continued our exploration, heading out early for a five-hour trek to Tengboche, where we would be visiting one of the oldest monasteries in the region.

Again, it was a steep climb the entire way, but we were treated to some of the most breathtaking views I have ever seen. We arrived at Tengboche (12,680 ft) mid-afternoon, where, after some soup to keep us going, we climbed on to the monastery.

A brightly painted gateway with an ornate roof led to a steep stone staircase leading up to a tall white building with elaborate wooden windows shaded by canvas awnings. The mountains towering behind the building seemed so close you felt you could reach out and touch them.

We were at the monastery for a puja ceremony, in which the monks meditate, chant and give offerings. After the ceremony, one of the monk students gave me a scarf and a small bag of gifts from the head Lama to bring me good luck for my skydive.

That evening I had a telephone call with Reuters to talk about the expedition. The rain had set in by then, and the only place in Tengboche with mobile coverage was outside, near the entrance to the village. I got soaked. As soon as the call was finished, I rushed back to the dining room and sat next to the fire for a quick dinner, while I warmed up and tried to dry off. Most people had gone to bed at 9pm, so I sat alone, reflecting on where I was: in a village at almost 12,500 ft altitude, just days away from the world's first Everest tandem skydive, with some of our sherpas for the next day stretched out on the dining benches to sleep. I thought I would call it a night too.

———————

The following day, another uphill hike (The Only Way is Up!) took us to Pheriche, one of the last villages before Mount Everest base camp. We had been told it was a beautiful trek and were looking forward to it – but the rain arrived halfway through, and the temperature plummeted. I had packed my raincoat into my luggage, so my fleece was my only protection from the elements.

Finally, we arrived at our accommodation for the night, the Himalayan Hotel (13,940 ft). Our rooms were freezing, and the hotel only had two hot showers, which cost NR350 a time (about $5). We congregated around the fireplace in the dining room, the only warm spot in the hotel, and took the chill off with tea, coffee and hot lemonade, which were quickly served. I happily invested in a hot shower when one became available; one really appreciates the small things in life at 14,000 ft!

The next day, we followed the trail back to Tengboche, which seemed more difficult than we remembered. The last stretch up a hill to Tengboche and the monastery was a challenge for most of us. While Tengboche had some of the most limited facilities on the trip – no shower, no phone service, basic meals, freezing cold nights – it is one of the most beautiful spots I have ever seen, with views across Everest and Lhotse. To wake up surrounded by the highest mountains in the world is moving and memorable.

At 7am the next morning we said goodbye to Tengboche to hike the last stretch back to Syangboche, where we would check in at the Hotel Everest View Hotel, our home until the dive. At this point, most people had had their fill of trekking and were ready for the dive. In many ways, the last stretch was the hardest – we were used to the scenery, our muscles were tired, and everyone was pining for a long, hot shower.

As the name suggests, the Hotel Everest View is in one of the best locations for uninterrupted views over Mount Everest. Opened in 1971, it was originally a luxury hotel built by the Japanese. A luxury hotel in the mountains is a great idea in theory, but the owners forgot about altitude acclimatization. Tourists were flown straight into an altitude of 12,800 ft, and many of them fell ill. The altitude sickness was so severe that two people died, which did not make for very positive PR.

Since that disaster, there had been little new investment and the condition of the hotel could no longer be described as luxurious. Hot water for showers is provided in buckets, and any meal had to be prebooked. There were no laundry facilities, so I had to trek 45 minutes to Namche Bazaar to clean my clothes. I had stayed in several former Soviet hotels in the course of my astronaut training, and my stay at the Hotel Everest View made me think back to those experiences with fond nostalgia.

After lunch on Wednesday afternoon, we hiked down to the drop zone to join the other skydivers in the group, expecting to see our

Pilatus Porter plane there. We were told that it was stuck in Kathmandu. Our permit had been withdrawn.

Our very experienced pilots, Rudy and Henri, had also been asked to complete an 11-hour flight-test programme, complete with a written exam. No one had been informed about these requirements beforehand, but there was nothing for it; our pilots dutifully went back to school. Meanwhile, Nigel, the organizer, had stayed behind in Kathmandu, where he pulled out all the stops to get a new permit. Thankfully, it was granted. What a relief! Apparently, a new bureaucrat had started their job that day, and had no idea about the scale of what we were undertaking – and was presumably keen to show how assiduous he was.

Wednesday was a waiting game for us. We became the highest media station in the world that day, with Kenneth and Peter editing video, Stephen filming, Morten doing the satellite uploads and Lars writing his blog, while Nicolai in Bangkok updated the Wimmer Space web page, Jesper in Denmark moved content to the Copenhagen server, and Louisa and James in London emailed updates and coordinated sponsorship and PR. It was a great achievement to run a sophisticated media operation from our remote and low-tech environment.

The next morning, from our balcony, we saw the Pilatus Porter plane circle the mountains and land in the drop zone. We let out a whoop of excitement and ran down to the drop zone to greet Rudy and Henri, whom I hadn't seen since my training in Switzerland. At that moment, we knew that nothing was going to stop us. The mood at the drop zone was cheerful, excited and full of expectation.

On Friday morning, two staff test jumps brought further excitement. But we could see the clouds blowing in. Before long, the drop zone was completely covered in fog. All operations came to a halt. Frustration was brewing among the other skydivers. The organizers were trying their best to explain the slow progress of the schedule, but people were getting nervous. Most had other commitments back home, and there were complaints about the food, the accommodations and, above all, the lack of communication.

I was told that I would be the first-ever skydiver to carry out a tandem jump from over 29,500 ft, and I was over the moon –

my excitement about being written into the history books over-shadowed any concerns. I was ready.

On Saturday, we awoke to clear blue skies. The first flight took off at 6am with two successful test jumps and then two familiar-ization jumps; it looked as if we would be jumping later that day. But soon clouds were gathering at a surprisingly fast pace and by 10am, the drop zone was once again covered in fog. It was hugely disap-pointing. Saturday was the first anniversary of the launch of Wim-mer Financial: 4 October 2007. It would have been wonderful to have made the historic jump on that day. But you can't argue with nature. We waited for a few hours until, at around 3pm, the skydive master, Dave Wood, called it a day. It wasn't meant to be.

On Sunday, we hoped that an early start could give us the edge. We got up at 4am and walked down the tiny mountain paths to the drop zone in complete darkness. We arrived to find the drop zone once again completely covered in fog. We couldn't believe it. It was 8am before the first flight could take off. Because of the weather conditions, three divers did a low-altitude familiarization jump. My dive would have to wait.

By that time, many of the skydivers were getting agitated, and there was a disturbance at the drop zone. A big row had broken out between some of the spoiled millionaires in the group and the organizers about the jumping order. Some very self-important peo-ple who were used to getting their own way were shouting about their other commitments, schedules, flights to catch ... it was all very disappointing. Words were exchanged with strong language and raised voices. Things were getting ugly. It raised tensions in the drop zone and made for a very uncomfortable atmosphere.

Still, I got fully suited up, with oxygen mask, helmet and jump-suit, and went through the final instructions with Ralph. My jump would be next. The mood in the team was high. A group of local children waved Wimmer flags and cheered me on. I was ready to go. Out of nowhere, a carpet of clouds blew in, completely covering the drop zone at 10am once again. Within 10 minutes, we had gone from clear skies to thick cloud. We waited for things to clear, but to no avail. Other divers continued to argue with the organizers, with some begrudgingly having to throw in the towel and make arrangements to leave Nepal without having made their jump. We stayed at the drop zone for as long as possible until, once again, Dave called it a day. We went back to the hotel feeling very low.

Monday did not get off to a smooth start. We were supposed to be at the drop zone at 5.30am. We all got up very early, but by the time we had organized our luggage and navigated the dark path, it was 5.50am. Drop zone HQ was already buzzing. The race to get ready for the 6am departure was intense. Jumpsuit on, oxygen bottles attached, safety procedures explained. The sky was clear, the sun barely up. I was on the plane. It was happening.

There were two people on board with me and Ralph: Naseer, an envoy of the Sheikh of Dubai whose solo jump would make him the first Arab to skydive from 29,500 ft, and Wendy, the photographer. Our oxygen masks made it hard to communicate; we all sounded like Darth Vader. The only way I could communicate was with an occasional thumbs up to show that I was fine and in good spirits.

It was the most amazing flight of my life. I have never seen such stunning views. I couldn't believe my eyes. One beautiful white-topped mountain after another. The landscape was vast. From the plane, it was impossible to tell which of the mountains was Everest itself, the landscape was simply too vast and overwhelming. I found it hard to comprehend how ordinary humans could actually reach the summit of these mountains.

At one point during the ascent, I was looking at a most beautiful snow-covered mountain ridge below us. I remember I was incredibly impressed by its beauty and by its sheer size and height. Then the plane flew past a mountain that reached way up beyond the altitude the plane was flying at: a huge rocky structure that looked like it was growing into the sky. It was surreal. Here I was, being impressed by a mountain ridge that was not even half the height of the mountain we were passing. The sheer scale of the Himalayas throws everything out of kilter.

As Rudy took us higher and higher, we got further away from the drop zone. I experienced a moment of real fear. What would happen if I got stuck on the side of one of these mountains? How would I survive? We had been flying for 40 minutes, and we were travelling at almost double our land speed because of the thinness of the air – by now, the drop zone was miles away. Would we be able to find our way back to the drop zone over this terrain if we landed in the wrong place? It seemed like mission impossible. The time of exit, freefall calculations and windspeed must all be exactly right. Previously, I thought the probability of failure was low; suddenly, the probability of success felt equally small. What if Ralph and I crash landed somewhere in the mountains after our jump? Would we survive? We were wearing radio transmitters, but how could a rescue team reach us among all the ridges and peaks?

Only in that moment did it truly occur to me that there was a reason we were the first to do this. I realized how dangerous this adventure could turn out if things went badly wrong. Our Pilatus Porter plane was not even technically approved to fly to 30,000 ft, and it was not a given that its hard-working engine would get us to the required altitude.

The atmosphere in the cabin was one of quiet excitement. We gave each other more reassuring thumbs ups. We were all OK now, simply sitting in the plane enjoying the beautiful views of the Himalayas. Would we still be OK when the doors opened, and it was time to jump?

Wendy looked tired. She was the only camera flyer on duty, so would be covering many lower jumps that day. Naseer kept checking his altitude metre, banging his hand against it as it stopped working past 26,000 ft. We were definitely out of the normal bounds of skydiving.

I don't know how many civilians have skydived from almost 30,000 ft, but it can't be many. Jumping from that height alone is an extreme undertaking, let alone adding the unforgiving conditions of the Himalayas. I was glad to have done my training in the same plane, with Rudy as the pilot and Ralph as my tandem instructor. Those familiar factors were reassuring. I knew that Rudy was an excellent pilot. I knew Ralph's procedures and his reactions. I knew that Henri, who owned the plane, would ensure it was properly maintained. At no point could I have wished for a more talented team. But jumping from such heights in the incredibly hostile environment of the Himalayas is an extreme undertaking.

Rudy held up a message: "Standby."

Ralph opened the plane door. The wind swept in and the wind-chill factor made the temperature in the cabin feel like -60°C. I knew we were long past the point of no return. In my subsequent Wimmer Space presentations, when I talked about 'Focus and Execution' – taking a decision to do something and sticking to it – I would always think and refer back to this exact moment. With us skydivers on board, we would not have been able to abort and land back at the drop zone: our extra weight made the risk of a crash too high in the thin air. If I am ever in doubt about following through with a decision, I think back to the moment I boarded the Pilatus Porter. That was truly the point of no return. The same applies to all other important decisions: consider the pros and cons, but once a decision has been taken, it must be the point of no return. After that, the only focus is execution, execution, execution. No second thoughts. No wavering.

Ralph asked me to move toward the edge. This is what we had trained for. The cold, the wind and the altitude sent my heart rate into overdrive. Two minutes to go.

I moved to the door and sat with my legs hanging out of the plane. Ralph joined me. I suppressed all feelings of fear and focused 100% on the procedures. I have never been so focused in my life. These are levels you can only reach when your life is at stake.

Rudy counted us down.

"3-2-1 ... GO!"

We were in freefall at a speed in excess of 170 km per hour, shooting through the thin air. Wendy was falling with us, filming. When we had stabilized, Ralph and I were having a ball, going through various formations.

Suddenly, the speed of our fall ripped my goggles from my face. They flew into Ralph above me. We struggled with the wind for a while to get them back on. I looked down so the force of the air rushing past us would keep them on.

Our freefall lasted for about 60 seconds – 60 intense and beautiful seconds that I will never forget. Looking down on Everest and the Himalayas and the top of the world – what an adventure!

Ralph pulled the ripcord and the parachute canopy opened. Our speed slowed abruptly. The thin air required an extra-large parachute.

If we had tried to land in the drop zone at 12,000 ft with a normal parachute, we could have broken our legs.

Drifting down to the drop zone was an unforgettable 10 minutes. When we jumped, the drop zone was nowhere in sight. We steered ourselves in the right direction. It was a great relief when we eventually spotted it, a small strip of green amid the rock and snow. As we touched down, the team on the ground came running toward us. All of my suppressed emotions burst out, like champagne from a shaken bottle, expressed in huge excitement and shouts of joy. We did it! On 6 October 2008, Ralph Mitchel and Per Wimmer completed the world's first tandem skydive from above Mount Everest. Wow! My first 'world first'!

Ralph, Wendy and I were so happy and relieved to be back on terra firma again after a historic skydive. Some of the press at the drop zone came over for instant reactions and interviews. I think it was probably one of my less-coherent interviews, but nothing could hide my joy and excitement!

I lay down and relaxed. Another mission went up and the skydivers came down successfully. Then another. Soon afterwards, a fog began to set in. The organizers radioed Rudy: "Don't jump! Don't jump!" But it was too late. The skydivers had already jumped.

It was hard enough to see the drop zone in clear skies, and the fog made it almost impossible. Two of the three divers managed to land successfully in a field not far from the drop zone but the third, an American woman, crashed into a small stone stupa on the mountainside and broke her leg. The team located her via her transmitter, gave her a shot of morphine and carried her across the difficult terrain on a stretcher back to the drop zone. Once she had stabilized, a helicopter took her to hospital in Kathmandu. She fully recovered and had no regrets. In fact, she said she would do it again if she got the opportunity!

Before I left the drop zone, I put in a call to my parents. My mother was so happy to hear my voice. They were on a cruise ship near South Africa at the time, and another Danish guest had asked them if they had heard about a Danish adventurer who was about to skydive over Mount Everest. "Yes, we know only too well," my dad told him. "That's our son!"

I left later that same day, taking a helicopter to Lukla and a small plane to Kathmandu. Back in London Gatwick Airport, I picked up a copy of London's daily newspaper, *The Evening Standard*. The headline read "FTSE in freefall." With the Everest dive successfully executed, I had another freefall to worry about – a freefall in the financial markets that could spell the end of Wimmer Financial and my dreams of running my own business.

LOVE

Everything is upside down.

I am on a flight to London from Copenhagen. I picked up about six newspapers as I always do. Normally I would have scanned through two of them before take-off, but today I cannot concentrate. Everything is different. I have this strange feeling in the pit of my stomach. It hurts a little, but it is also a sweet feeling – the feeling of having something, or rather, someone, under my skin.

I am in love. Truly in love.

It has been a very long time since I have felt that way. I was not used to the feeling at all. I have had many girlfriends and – I guess because I am seen as a wealthy man and I have quite a high profile in some circles – I get quite a lot of approaches from women, some of whom I have never even met! It's nice to meet people; it's nice to go on dates. But dating and romantic evenings out always took second place to my business concerns. Now, for the first time in a very long time, I was no longer in control. All I wanted to do was be with her, all the time. I could not get enough of her – and the more I had, the more I wanted. It was like a drug, and I was completely hooked.

Thank God the feeling was mutual. I would have gone out of my mind if not. When we said goodbye in Copenhagen's Kastrup Airport, there were tears in her eyes. That was the most difficult goodbye

I had experienced in years. I missed her so badly – yet it had only been half an hour since that fond farewell.

———————

I had been invited to an awards ceremony at the Hilton in Copenhagen Airport. It was typical for that type of affair: lots of glamorous people mingling in a large, soulless room, chatting and sipping champagne. I arrived early and spotted a Danish TV-2 talk show host I had worked with before. While we were catching up, a group came over to the bar table where we were standing to say hello. Suddenly, I saw her. An absolutely gorgeous young Swedish woman who looked like a supermodel who had stepped straight off the cover of *Vogue* magazine. I noticed she didn't have a glass of champagne. I was breathless but, fortunately, not quite speechless, and I generously offered to rectify that state of affairs. She accepted. I quickly grabbed a glass of champagne for her from a waiter's tray, and we started to chat. Her name was Vicky. She was, indeed, a model and, in fact, one of Sweden's top models. It turned out she wasn't very keen to be at this party, but she was presenting one of the awards. Our conversation felt very natural; effortless. It was as if we were the only two people in the room. Then dinner was announced, and everyone was asked to kindly take their seats. I knew that I was not at the same table as Vicky and the other awards presenters. I would have paid a lot of money just to delay the start of the dinner and keep chatting. I asked for her phone number and was lucky enough to be given it, which was some sort of compensation.

I looked around for her during dinner but could not see where she was sitting. When she suddenly appeared on stage to present the award, I couldn't take my eyes off her. When she handed over the award after making the announcement, I applauded wildly. The award winner herself must have thought I was her biggest fan.

The dinner and award ceremony felt endless. At the party afterwards, I briefly hooked up with her again, but we were interrupted by people who I knew wanted to talk to me, and a stream of men who seemed unreasonably keen to get Vicky's attention. We didn't even get to dance. But at the after-party in the hotel's VIP suite, we finally managed to talk – and we went on and on and on.

"Did you always want to be a model?" I asked her. She looked sheepish. "Actually, I wanted to be an astronaut."

What were the chances?! She was absolutely passionate about science and space – it was her dream to fly into space to study what is 'out there.' I listened carefully and asked lots of questions. I couldn't believe what I was hearing, but I loved every syllable of it.

Eventually, I told her about my training and upcoming space travels. She was absolutely speechless. She was so excited and touched that her eyes filled up with tears, and she started to cry. Her friend came over to make sure she was all right and looked at me suspiciously. It took Vicky a while before she could get her speech back, and then she reassured her friend that everything was OK – and more than OK; her tears were tears of happiness and pure emotion.

We started to talk again, brushing off the various admirers trying to get Vicky's attention. As the party began to wind down, we went downstairs to the breakfast area and shared two glasses of water. I wanted that night – which had turned into morning, since it was now 6am – to go on forever. In the end, we were so tired we simply had to stop. I walked her to her room and went home. It felt like the start of something.

The next day she was flying to Barcelona for a photoshoot – I had hoped to see her, but time didn't allow it. We started arranging our next meeting: at first it was meant to be Stockholm, then changed to London, but ended up being in Copenhagen, where she came to stay with me for a long weekend.

When she arrived at my place, she was a bit nervous. She told me she had been getting cold feet about the trip and was thinking of cancelling. Four days later, she couldn't be happier that she had not. We had been together 24/7 the whole time, and it wasn't enough. We must have looked like silly teenagers falling in love for the first time – we couldn't stop staring at each other. But the feelings were very real.

On Thursday, we drove to Nakskov to pay a visit to some of the people I had met while filming *The Secret Millionaire*. We had a big gathering for 100 local charity volunteers and elderly people in need, with coffee, cake and live music. I made a speech to thank them for their wonderful hospitality and for the consideration they had shown me while I was a humble 'volunteer' working alongside them.

Vicky loved it. The three-hour drive to and from Nakskov with her at my side passed by in a flash. I could have kept driving all night, but when we finally got back to my apartment in Copenhagen, it was even better: just the two of us, free to do whatever we liked.

The next morning, I was due to give a presentation about space to a school in Malmö. I had spent nine months planning it, so I was excited to finally deliver it. The kids' love of space was clear: they had so many questions, and every answer inspired another question. At the end, everyone wanted autographs and business cards. I felt like a rock star for a few hours! One girl started to cry – all of the signed postcards from my Everest expedition had been grabbed before she could get one. But Vicky took good care of her: she brought the girl over to me and made sure she got a specially signed business card.

When we were finally allowed to leave, we drove across Øresund back to Copenhagen, where I had a business lunch and an interview with a tech magazine lined up. Later that night, we went to a sushi restaurant, followed by a visit to a gallery and then to a fashion party, where there was a great deal of very superficial chat. We escaped as soon as we could to a local bar where we had our own little party, dancing together while others celebrated J-Day – the release of Tuborg's classic *Julebryg* or Christmas beer, which marks the start of the *Juletid* season in Denmark. It was a wonderful time spent with a uniquely lovely woman. I was so much in love. Before we knew it, the weekend was over. After another painful separation at Copenhagen airport, Vicky flew back to Stockholm, and I got on my plane to London. We agreed to meet up again in London, three days later. Three days! It felt like an age. Every time I checked my phone to see a text from her – or, better still, a call – I felt a rush of teenage excitement. It was a bit silly, at my age, but it was absolutely wonderful and beyond my reasonable control!

The three days passed in a flurry of calls, emails and meetings. Vicky showed up with her beautiful smile and positive attitude; in love, as I was. Over the first two days, she was busy with meetings with her London-based modelling agency. I was thrilled to see it seemed she had every intention of spending more time in London.

On Thursday, I did something unheard of for me at the time: I cooked dinner for us both in the apartment. On Friday, we ate out at a trendy but intimate Soho restaurant and then we went partying at the Cuckoo Club in Mayfair until the early hours. The rest of the weekend went by in a flash. Before I knew it, she was flying back to Stockholm. We both missed each other terribly. I felt like part of me was going with her and she felt like part of her was staying with me.

I couldn't believe how lucky we were to have found each other. A beautiful woman with a thriving modelling career who was likely to have a copy of *Science Illustrated* magazine in her handbag rather than the latest copy of *Vogue*! Although her past had involved some of the usual excesses of the top model lifestyle, she was well-balanced and grounded, loving, caring and passionate.

I absolutely loved her. I couldn't wait to see her again.

This wonderful thing was happening to me in the otherwise dire context of the worst financial crash since 1929.

When I landed at Gatwick from Kathmandu and saw those newspaper headlines – FTSE in Freefall – my first thought was simply: "Oh no!" But I hoped and prayed Black Monday would only be a short disruption. Soon, we will be able to get on with business as usual, I thought.

Not so! The freefall continued and a really bad situation only got worse. The financial market was in complete meltdown. Overnight, the UK banking sector was effectively nationalized. The worst hit was the Royal Bank of Scotland (RBS): after the government bailout, two thirds of its equity was state-owned. Lloyds Bank followed suit. Within a year of launching, Wimmer Financial would have to navigate a continuing global financial crisis. I knew that to survive, I had to devote my full attention to my investment bank.

The first option was to cut back on costs as much as I could. The revenue outlook was completely uncertain: many investor clients, especially hedge funds, were going to go bust – or, at the very least, close many of their funds. Many funds were scrambling to meet investor redemptions – investors demanding the immediate return of their investment capital. A good example was RAB Capital, one of London's largest and well-known hedge funds: it nearly went down after a run of redemptions, but was saved in the 11th hour by giving up future fees in exchange for a three-year asset lock-in.

To make matters worse for Wimmer Financial, I had returned from Everest to discover that our regulatory 'umbrella company' had given us notice. Wimmer Financial would be without regulatory cover from 1 January 2009. And the lease on our office was coming to an end and was not up for renewal.

They say bad luck comes in threes. To sort out any one of these challenges would be hard enough, but an investment bank without a banking license, no premises and in the most difficult market conditions in almost a century ... all three of these issues are pretty fundamental to the business! These were truly challenges of Everest proportions!

If the challenges were obvious, the solutions were not. One issue compounded another. After Black Monday, everyone was worried about counterparty risk and was pulling back: credit lines, partnerships, agreements.

Risk. That four-letter word can tell you so much about both the financial collapse and its slow repair. During the three to four years prior to Black Monday, money was cheap. You could borrow in Swiss francs or Japanese yen at 2–3% interest. As a result, almost any project was financially lucrative: any business manager who couldn't make a healthy return when the cost of capital was in the low single digits deserved to be sacked. As a result, credit analysis became sloppy and superficial and – importantly – it was in the interest of bank staff to encourage more borrowing. Lend, lend, lend: that was the rule. I remember we were working on a $100 million deal, and the lender asked whether we would like $200 million instead. "Sure; why not?!" Our corporate client gets more capital to build a bigger business, faster. Intermediaries get paid more as their charge is a percentage of the size of the deal. The staff member gets paid more as a bonus. It was a win-win-win. It seemed so easy.

What was forgotten, however, was the fact that these arrangements were not risk free. The first projects that were funded were sound and reliable. But then, in their insatiable thirst for growth, banks went after riskier and riskier business, with less collateral and a worse outlook for repayment. Though the more sensible banks finally refused to lend to the riskiest projects, there was always someone who was willing to lend – the banks whose staff were most incentivized to increase their loan book. In many of those cases, the bank would become part owner or a profit beneficiary in the project, taking a share of the potential future success of the business. But that is exactly when incentives and banking priorities get mixed up.

The business plan and credit analysis that banks carry out serve a very good purpose, especially where overenthusiastic entrepreneurs are concerned. Entrepreneurs tend to see opportunity but are blind to risk. Serious banks serve as a good health check and stress test for any new proposal, particularly when they are putting money at risk with modest fixed-income returns. But when banks are offered a sizeable equity stake, they become just like any other equity investor – they have a vested interest in the new project doing well, and they develop an entrepreneur's blindness to risk.

The first sign of overenthusiastic borrowing had been the slowing of the short-term credit markets – of which the collapse of Northern Rock should have been a warning. The former building society had 'demutualized' in 1997 (that is to say, it was no longer owned by its members) and had become a bank, launching on the London Stock Exchange. It performed incredibly well at first, becoming one of the top 100 most highly valued companies on the exchange by the year 2000.

But their business model relied heavily on short-term rolling of wholesale funding, instead of borrowing money at long-term fixed rates like most other banks, or on their previous building society model of relying on members' deposits. When the markets got 'spooked' and banks would not lend to other banks because of credit risk, short-term funding dried up and Northern Rock was doomed. There were queues outside branches as people tried to take out their savings – the first run on a UK bank in 150 years. The bank struggled on for a few months and was then nationalized in February 2008.

Risk appetite around the world had fallen close to zero. A number of hedge funds lost up to 75% of their assets, either through the 50% fall in equity markets or through investor redemptions. One hedge fund I know went from having $4 billion assets under management to $1 billion in a very short time frame. Such a fall makes a huge difference to their revenue line, profitability and ability to invest at all.

Credit lines from banks were virtually nonexistent. I distinctly remember a conversation I had with the managing director of debt and credit at BNP, one of France's largest banks. Even though French banks were among those least affected by the financial crisis, proposals had to meet a long list of strict criteria to even be considered: the deal had to be French, the borrower had to be an existing corporate client (so no new business), interest rates had to be double-digit, there had to be lots of collateral provided, and the corporate had to pledge lots of other business to the bank (corporate finance business, foreign exchange and so on). Lending was so strict, it was hard to believe.

The debt market was divided into those banks that could not, under any circumstances, do anything but repair their own balance sheet, and those who could consider lending, but on strict terms. The latter could pick and choose from an abundance of deals. Even then, their lending power was seriously reduced. Liquidity had dried up in the capital markets, which was bad news for those of us in the business of transacting. It was the banking equivalent of an engine trying to run without oil. Oil is what makes the engine run smoothly; starved of oil, an engine will break down and require some serious repair. That's what happened to the capital markets: capital dried up and the markets broke down. Confidence had been seriously hurt. This is an important truth: all markets are ultimately run by humans. When 'soft' factors like confidence and sentiment change, it has a big influence on the direction and sound functioning of markets. Without investor confidence, without investor risk appetite, there is no capital.

The whole situation was a wake-up call for an entrepreneur. When revenues and profits are good, you benefit as the company owner. When the whole world is collapsing around you, you realize the responsibility for finding solutions lies with you. I felt that reality knocking on my door, every minute, every hour. I had many sleepless nights. It required complete focus and dedication. Careful thinking was essential. Mistakes could be very costly. It was difficult – but, also, in many ways, thrilling. There's a scene in one of my favourite films, *The World Is Not Enough*, where Sophie Marceau's Bond girl Elektra King tells Pierce Brosnan, "There's no point living if you can't feel alive." I felt very much alive when running, managing and trying to grow my investment bank in such challenging times.

I had a moment of light relief in November, when I flew over to Los Angeles for a press conference with XCOR Aerospace. Within Wimmer Space, my planned third trip into space with XCOR has been kept relatively secret; we wanted to keep things 'under wraps' until significant progress had been made on the Lynx rocketplane. Now we were ready to announce that I had signed up to be the very first passenger. The programme of tests and flights had been announced in March 2008, with the intention of being fully operational within two years. Ever since XCOR announced that the first named astronaut was 'a European,' I had been getting emails asking if it was me. The space community is really quite small, and people are quick to put two and two together. I was very excited to be able to confirm their suspicions at last.

By the time I flew home for Christmas two months later, I was utterly exhausted. As I sat on the plane, I listened to Chris Rea's song, "Driving Home for Christmas," and looked forward to spending some quality time with my family.

The year 2008 had been a year of extremes. It had seen huge stock market volatility, with global equity markets ending down 40% on average. And the world was a different place after Black Monday. When I arrived in Denmark, I tried to leave the latest reverberations of the financial crash behind me. The historically low pound sterling. The lowest level of property transactions the UK had seen in decades. The never-before-seen near-zero US Federal Reserve System (FED) interest rate levels in the US and also in Japan – a reflection of how seriously central banks took this crisis. The unorthodox resort of the FED buying long-duration bonds and setting up the Troubled Asset Relief Programme (TARP), the $700 billion fund to buy distressed assets. A $13 billion bailout short-term lending facility to save the US auto industry (which I believed was absurd and irrational, unlike the essential rescue of the financial system). And – as a kind of surreal final flourish – the exposure of the largest financial fraud in history: Bernard Madoff Investment Securities' pyramid scheme, which lost investors up to $50 billion in 2008. The world was at panic stations. Everything seemed crazy.

Investors were effectively paying the US government to look after their money, rather than getting a return on their investment. Certain small- and mid-cap stocks were trading at 0.5 times their cash-on-balance-sheet valuations, despite being truly good companies with great prospects. Even big and normally very creditworthy companies had to pay equity-like returns, such as 10–20% yields, on their corporate bonds. The big irony was that the solution – lower interest rates, large government packages, enhanced lending to SMEs – could be creating another credit-fuelled bubble 12–18 months in the future. "Time will tell," I thought. I reassured myself that the world would not end tomorrow – though the markets seemed to think otherwise.

And, for me, 2008 had also been a year of personal landmarks: my 40th birthday, with wonderful parties in St Tropez, in Geneva and in Copenhagen to celebrate my own and my sister's birthday; the historic Everest adventure; my third space trip announcement. I had started to become well-known in Denmark after *The Secret Millionaire* became the third most-viewed TV-2 programme in history, watched by more than 20% of the Danish population. The programme had helped make the Wimmer name synonymous with philanthropy, and I had spent three entire days responding to many heart-warming emails from people who had been moved by the programme.

And then I had fallen in love.

In spite of the financial crash, I ended the year happy.

————

Before Christmas, the investment climate and the markets had been in a state of complete paralysis. After Christmas, investors and corporates were much more positive.

The awful fundamentals of the credit-crunched global economy had not actually improved – if anything, they had deteriorated even further. But, as I said earlier, attitudes and sentiment have a big impact on how markets function, and a newfound determination to leave the *annus horribilis* of 2008 behind and start afresh in 2009 meant that Wimmer Financial quickly became very busy with a high-quality deal flow and interesting corporate opportunities – though successful closing was still a challenge.

As a result, I didn't see Vicky for the whole of January. She was busy with work herself, modelling in Spain, Miami and LA. We were constantly in touch via our mobiles, but it was a poor substitute for being together. On the plane from Copenhagen to Stockholm, I was so excited to see her.

But this wasn't just another weekend trip; I would be taking Vicky back to London with me. We were moving in together.

It should have been a scary thought – we had only known each other for three months. Yet everything felt so right, so simple.

Just a year before, I would typically have left work in the evening and gone on to a cocktail party, an exhibition, an event or a dinner. After we met, I found myself rushing home to call her. Now, I would get to wake up beside her. I couldn't wait for our future to begin.

By May, the worst of the downturn seemed to be finally in sight. Business activity started to pick up again, dramatically.

The morning of 6 May was a case in point. Here's how it went:

6am.	Wake up early for a conference call to discuss a mandate proposal for an Australian mining company with assets in Africa. My contact is on another call, so I ring a different Australian mining company to discuss another mandate. Then I rush to the office, grabbing a coffee on the way.
8am.	In the office. Another phone call with Australia, before quickly replying to my most urgent emails.
8.30am.	Corporate client (also from Australia but this time physically present in London!) shows up early while I am printing out presentations for the first morning meeting with investors. We leave as soon as I am finished to walk to the meeting.
9am.	Investor meeting. An interesting presentation, which gives me a few strategic ideas for the client to consider as part of their medium-term strategy.

10.30am. Straight into a Mergers and Acquisitions (M&A) meeting to discuss combining two mining companies in different countries – one in Australia, one in Kyrgyzstan. Great discussion on details relating to exploration potential, compliant resource level, current ownership structure, infrastructure, mill, financing structure, deal structure and terms, management set-up and so on. I had flown in one negotiating party from Australia and another from Germany.

That meeting lasted more than the 1.5 hours I had allocated, making me late for another meeting. The coowner of a large New York-based hedge fund who had flown in to see me was waiting. I suggested we take a break from the M&A meeting.

12.30pm. Meeting with the 'big guy' from New York. He only has half an hour, so I quickly run through some business and cobranding opportunities. He likes the ideas and suggests his junior colleague should follow up. Excellent!

1pm. Respond to a few more urgent emails. Back to the M&A meeting. The guy from Germany gets called into an investor meeting, so I take the CEO of the Australian company out for a quick lunch to continue our business discussions and get some feedback. He sounds positive and indicates that he would like to give Wimmer Financial the mandate soon. Great!

1.50pm. Rush back to the office and return four phone calls that I missed during lunch. Quick discussion with colleagues about other current deals we were working on.

1.55pm. Candidate shows up for an interview.

2.20pm. Finally start the interview after more incoming calls cause me delays.

2.25pm. Another client turns up unannounced to talk through a few details of a deal we were working on. No problem; business comes first.

2.30pm.	Call Switzerland to tell them about the new details of the deal.
2.35pm.	Back to the interview. A great discussion – I ask for some further information and to have a follow-up meeting next week.
3pm.	Back on the phone to discuss equipment financing for a new coal energy deal in South Africa with some of my US contacts.
3.15pm.	Another phone call to two contacts in New York regarding three different mining deals.
4pm.	A quick email to a Danish client who was flying to London at the end of the week; another email to sort out my flight to Denmark the following week for two space presentations and to Florida at the end of the month, where I was due to speak at a space conference.

All in a day's work, I suppose ... I was certainly looking forward to the weekend – though a film crew would be visiting me to record an interview for the documentary of our Everest Skydive adventure!

LAND SPEED RECORD

I was in need of a break when I arrived in Orlando for the space conference. But I couldn't stop yet: a mining deal I had been working on had just gone live. As soon as we touched down, I was emailing announcements.

I spent the day working, emailing and talking to the CFO of Bannerman, my client from the early days of Wimmer Financial. He was planning to work through the night, coordinating the AU$30 million capital raising between their Australian broker, Argonaut, their Canadian broker, Haywood and their European broker – Wimmer Financial.

It was great to be part of a meaningful global capital equity raise, so I went to bed tired but happy. But at 2.30am EST I had to get up again to start calling European clients about the live deal. I ended up working flat out until 9am. And during any breaks, I worked on a couple of other deals and sorted out some admin.

Because of this, I had no time to refresh the presentation on space financing that I was giving at the conference later that day. Thank goodness my presentation was scheduled for the afternoon; I didn't seem to be able to pull myself away from my hotel room 'office' and, despite all the hours and the efforts, I still had nothing to show for it.

Suddenly, however, orders started flooding in. Within an hour, I had closed Wimmer Financial's part of this global deal. What a relief.

We had needed to demonstrate we had the ability to deliver, and we had. Everyone was happy, including the Bannerman CFO.

At that time in the history of Wimmer Financial, I was personally working on sorting out settlement issues and account opening, effectively running the whole admin side of the business. I was not only the dealmaker, I was also office manager, head of compliance, trading manager and chief bottle washer. A lot of the things I had taken for granted at Goldman Sachs, I had to do for myself. Just as I stepped out of my room, I got a call telling me about a potential settlement issue. Back to the 'office' to phone London. Issue sorted.

I was finally able to join the conference, where an ex-NASA astronaut was giving a presentation about his career. I glanced over the presentation I was about to deliver to some of the space community's brightest minds. I felt more nervous about the presentation than I had about the deal we had just put together!

The presentation went very well. I wasn't sure how many people managed to catch all the finer financial points but, judging by the feedback and the insightful questions people were asking afterwards, I think it was a success. I spiced it up by screening a trailer for my upcoming Everest Skydive documentary, which went down very well. After three hours of discussion and answering questions, I managed to grab a bite to eat. At 9pm I called Australia, where it was 9am the following morning. I was crashing at this point. I fell into bed the moment the call was over and did not stir till my alarm went off the next morning.

The rest of the conference was mostly an intensive networking event. I listened in on a very interesting update on NASA's space activities, including the Commercial Orbital Transportation Services programme, which coordinated private spacecraft delivering crew and cargo to the International Space Station (ISS), and the Constellation programme, which aimed to complete the ISS and return to the moon by 2020. The NASA programmes are impressive – and so are the budgets. That year, the budget was around $15 billion.

In that context, it is even more impressive how much private space companies like XCOR, Virgin Galactic and SpaceX have achieved. The Virgin Galactic budget was $450 million and the XCOR budget was around $25–30 million. The budget for SpaceX was much larger, but still only around 10–15% of the cost of NASA reaching the International Space Station.

I also had a number of meetings with various 'PowerPoint entrepreneurs': people with an idea looking for early-stage angel financing for their projects. I listened and gave them honest, realistic and hopefully constructive feedback. Unfortunately, nothing was solid enough to invest in. There are many great engineers, designers and 'space dreamers' in the space community, but only a small minority are also great businesspeople.

I made time to catch up with the video game entrepreneur and private space traveller Richard Garriott, who had recently flown to the International Space Station with Space Adventures. Richard's father was a NASA astronaut, making Richard the first-ever second-generation American astronaut. (A Russian, Sergey Volkov, was the very first second-generation astronaut.) We discussed everything from recent space activities and business opportunities to alternative energy, point-to-point public transport and gaming. Richard is a very smart guy who is not afraid to think outside the box. (Richard later dived to the deepest point on Earth, the Mariana Trench in the Western Pacific Ocean. Today, he is the president of the New York Explorer's Club, arguably the most prestigious explorers' club in the world (of which, incidentally, I am a fellow.)

I also met with the Odyssey Moon team, who seemed keen to get me on board with their endeavours in some capacity. The Odyssey Moon team are contenders for the Google Lunar XPRIZE, another wonderful initiative encouraging space entrepreneurs. The winning team must soft-land a craft on the moon, move it at least 500 m and successfully transmit data.

Early on Saturday morning, I had breakfast with a Boeing representative, who wanted me to play a key role in the autumn Space Investment Summit in Boston by creating a business plan framework. The Saturday presentation was by Buzz Aldrin. I have seen Buzz deliver many presentations over the years, but this one was the best. Not only was Buzz on top form, but his script was so professional it could have been written by a presidential speech writer. His message was clear: don't redo Apollo by focusing on the moon; work together, internationally, and use the moon as a base for further exploration into deeper space. His speech also shared some specific and personal anecdotes from the Apollo landing. The message, the passion, the conviction: it was all so inspiring. He was preaching to the converted, of course, but even this audience was stunned by his performance – the detail, the delivery, the sharpness of the then-80-year-old moonwalker. After an intense 45-minute journey, he got a standing ovation. But he was only halfway through his speech!

The second half was a very specific and mathematical blueprint for the next two decades of US space policy. In 1961, President John F Kennedy committed the US to landing a man on the moon before the end of the decade. Buzz echoed this historic pledge as he called for a new era of boldness in space policy and explained how this could be achieved. Straight after Buzz's presentation, I jumped into my rental car, which was lined up and ready to go, luggage fully packed, out-side the resort, and drove straight to St Petersburg Airport just out-side Tampa. I was meeting Howard 'Chip' Chipman for a recreational flight in a jet fighter, Chip's own Aero L-39 Albatros, over the coast of Florida. Chip is the owner and chief pilot of a company that offers people of different levels of experience the opportunity to experience aerobatic jet flight, military jet training and periods of weightlessness.

I put on my flight suit, and we got wired up. After a brief expla-nation of the L-39 instruments – I had some familiarity with the jet, having flown one in Russia – we took off. The sky was clear and blue, with a few small clouds. We flew up through the clouds, and the aero-batics started. Five seconds of weightlessness; plane stalling, split S, reverse split S, loops, rolls. I even got to steer and carry out many of the manoeuvres. It was so much fun. Suddenly, I was ace fighter pilot Maverick from the film *Top Gun*!

My space training was a definite bonus. We were pulling 4 to 6 Gs, and there were moments where I almost blacked out. We did so many manoeuvres, twisting and turning so much without stopping, that I was feeling a bit beaten up by the end, and at one point got frighten-ingly close to being sick. It didn't help that my last meal had been the mass catering at the conference. But I made it through – even after two close fly-bys of the control tower. I could almost see the coffee shaking in cups on the desks in the tower!

What an amazing flight, and with a dedicated fellow space enthusiast.

Early the next morning, I scheduled some repairs to my Miami property before heading straight to the airport. I was flying to Houston to meet with the CEO of an oil and gas company. We spent an hour and a half together looking into the company strategy and finance before I jumped on another plane, this time heading back to London, where I would arrive in time to be in the office early Monday morning – and not have to stay up all night to conduct business in a European time zone!

As the year wore on, I was ready for my next adventure: an attempt to break the land speed record.

The record had been set in 1997, when a British team reached a speed of 763 mph, breaking the sound barrier for the first time. The car, Thrust SSC ('Thrust Supersonic Car') was powered by the same Rolls Royce jet engines used to power the British F-4 Phantom II jet fighter. It was driven by an RAF fighter pilot, Wing Commander Andy Green. The Thrust SSC project was a multimillion-dollar effort with substantial sponsor backing. Now an American team headed by a man called Ed Shadle was going to try to beat their record on what in relative terms was a shoestring budget.

A contact had put me in touch with Ed. By chance, he had come across an old Lockheed F-104 Starfighter jet in a junkyard in Massachusetts. And it wasn't just any old F-104 – it had been flown by the legendary USAF flying ace Chuck Yeager, who was the first human to break the sound barrier, flying the experimental Bell X-1 rocket-powered aircraft in 1947.

Ed bought the jet for next to nothing and took it to Seattle, where his team was based, to convert the fighter aircraft into a car. The vehicle was dubbed the North American Eagle and in its finished form it looked exactly like what it was – a jet fighter on wheels with the wings removed. It was 56 ft long, 7 ft wide at the nose and 9 ft wide at the tail, which housed the single General Electric turbojet engine, capable of delivering up to 52,000hp. A lot of Ed's team were engineers from the Boeing factories in Seattle – enthusiasts for whom this was a passion project.

The turbojet engine was easily powerful enough to propel the vehicle beyond the speed of sound. The trick was to keep the North

American Eagle on the ground at those speeds and stop it from trying to take off!

When I heard about the project, I couldn't resist getting involved. So Ed and I became partners in an attempt to beat the land speed record in Black Rock Desert, Nevada – the same place where Andy Green had taken Thrust SSC past the sound barrier in 1997. The deal was that Ed and I would both take turns trying to take the car past the speed of sound – and past Thrust SSC's record-setting 763 mph.

To get to that point, we would need to carry out a number of test runs. The engineers do everything they can with computer modelling, but then you have to test the car in real conditions, in the desert. You take the car up to a certain test speed, feed the data from all the sensors on the car into the computer, tweak the model based on the real data, then drive a bit faster in the next test run ... and so on until you are ready to try for the record.

I flew to LAX from London and headed straight to Reno, from where I drove to Gerlach in Nevada, near to the Black Rock Desert. Getting to Gerlach is like driving into the middle of nowhere and arriving in the Wild West circa 1880. We would be staying at the legendary Bruno's, a family-run motel with a stripped-back bar, a stag's head on the wall and an old-West style sign out front reading "Motel, Café, Casino, Saloon." Gerlach felt like a truly isolated community; a place that cared about what happened locally but really wasn't too bothered about what went on in the rest of the world – it was all just too far away. One sign read: "Gerlach: where the pavement ends." Another said, "There are no services. Little or no water. Your cellphones won't work. You will be on your own."

Thanks ... and welcome to Gerlach!

A final sign read: "Travel at your own risk." That seemed relevant to the reason for our visit!

The desert itself is truly beautiful, with the huge expanse of ancient lakebed and the shadowy mountains visible in the distance. It is also a very forbidding and hostile environment. Ed and the team had carried out several test runs in the Black Rock Desert in July 2009. I had joined the team to watch proceedings, but at that time could only sit in the cockpit and fire up the awesome engine, as I had not yet got my high-speed drivers' license, something I achieved at the famous Bonneville Salt Flats Speedway in Utah in August that year.

On this visit, I was going to drive the North American Eagle for the very first time.

It was great to catch up with the team of speed enthusiasts. Most of them were based in Seattle, and their 14-hour drive south to Nevada wasn't without mishaps. Keith Zanghi, Ed's business partner, set out at 1.30am on Friday, 6 November with two other members of the team in the giant truck that carried the North American Eagle, towing behind it a 24-foot trailer filled with tools, spare parts and all the team's equipment. Before the truck reached the Interstate 5 highway that runs all the way down the US West Coast from Canada to Mexico, it hit a deer, causing about $2,000 dollars' worth of damage to the truck. Ed and other team members had left a little later than Keith, at 2.00am. They caught up with the truck about 30 miles south of Oakridge, Oregon. There had been snow in Oregon and the truck had skidded into the guardrail at the side of the I-5 and was stuck in the snow. Everyone climbed in Ed's van and made the two-hour round trip back to Oakland to buy snow chains for the truck and trailer. They didn't arrive in Gerlach until late Friday, with some other members of the team arriving in the early hours of Saturday.

Saturday dawned clear and bright with no wind. Perfect! The team was out in the desert by 6am laying out a course. It was essential to mark out a 'clean' five miles of good flat space, with no upheavals or loose patches.

After some final checks, the mighty North American Eagle was rolled into position: almost 6,000 kg of bright red jet fighter/car, with a stylized black American Eagle painted on both sides, its white head and golden beak stretching toward the vehicle's own sharply pointed nose cone. There was one new addition that pleased me: a Wimmer logo on the vehicle's tail plane.

Ironically, attempting to travel at the fastest speed on Earth is a very slow process. It requires a lot of patience. By the time the course was marked up and the vehicle finally configured, it was late afternoon. Ed was piloting the first test drive. He was in the cockpit, in his flame-retardant jumpsuit and fighter-pilot's helmet and oxygen mask. We were good to go. The emergency flare went up – a safety precaution to let people know a very fast car was coming their way, even though we were pretty sure no one was wandering around the course. Ed took off, slowly at first, but accelerating rapidly to the target test speed of around 168 mph before running off speed. It was a great run, though the braking parachute malfunctioned (which was a potential worry but not risky on this test) and the ground drag was pretty heavy.

It was now near sundown in the desert on a November evening, and we all packed up and went back to Bruno's for dinner. An inspection had shown that the leading edge of the landing gear doors beneath the Eagle had been damaged by flying dirt. They would have to be fixed in the morning – when it was my turn to do a test run. We were all up at 5.30am, breakfast at 6am, on the lakebed by 7am.

The repairs to the landing gear doors took a few hours, followed by the routine last-minute checks and configurations. It was around midday before we were set to do the run. I was helped into the cockpit, all kitted up in my jumpsuit and helmet. Ed talked me through the instrumentation and dials and emergency procedures one last time, made sure I was buckled up properly and hooked me up to the oxygen. He closed the cockpit top. It was time to go.

I fired up the engine, which screamed into life. The safety flare went up. I eased the Eagle into motion and then opened up the throttle. The power hit me in the small of my back. It was exactly like the acceleration of a jet fighter, but with the huge difference that you were connected to the ground. I had to wrestle with the steering wheel to keep the Eagle in a straight line, and I could feel every tiny bump in the apparently smooth surface of the lakebed. I got to full throttle very quickly. My speed passed 200 mph and kept climbing. Then, around the two-mile mark, I hit what I later learned was some soft ground. All I knew at the time was that the Eagle lurched and seemed to leave the ground. The steering wheel bucked in my hands and then felt unresponsive. I heard and felt a thud as we came back down to Earth with a hard thump and the steering wheel bucked back into life. I shut down the engine, hit the speed brakes and coasted to a stop, concerned about damage to the vehicle.

When the team helped me out of the cockpit, I was ecstatic. The car was in one piece, and I was high on adrenaline. I have driven some fast cars in my life, but always on tarmac. Driving on the Bonneville Salt Flats in the drag racing car in which I had taken my high-speed driving test at Bonneville had been a massive thrill – but the Eagle was something else. Its power was simply off the scale – the GE engine could do Mach 2! You felt the Eagle really belonged in the air. It was a constant struggle to keep it Earth-bound. The inspection showed that the soft ground I had hit had launched the car briefly into the air. As the heavy vehicle crashed back to Earth, the soft ground had snagged the new plate used to repair the damage to the landing gear doors and ripped it off. Someone later found the plate on the test course. The team signed it and gave it to me as a souvenir, as is traditional for all such 'prangs.'

The team was very happy with my test run. I had reached a top speed in the mid-200 mph range, which was good considering the short distance travelled and the heavy ground. But it was decided that the Eagle should not be run again until the areas around the landing gear doors could be reinforced.

Sadly, that was my last run in the North American Eagle. Wimmer Financial kept me fully occupied, and I drifted away from the project. Ed became unwell and was to die of cancer in 2018. Keith continued his quest for the land speed record with the North American Eagle and the team enlisted Jessi Combs, a professional racer known as 'the fastest woman on four wheels,' who had broken the women's four-wheel land speed record in 2013 (399 mph) and 2016 (478 mph).

In August 2019, Combs and the North American Eagle team made an attempt at the land speed record in the Alvord Desert in Oregon. Tragically, one of the front wheels failed and the Eagle crashed. Combs did not survive. She was posthumously awarded the female land speed record the following year, having reached 523 mph.

In light of that accident, I count myself lucky that my journey with North American Eagle stopped where it did. I am happy with taking risks, but I am not foolhardy. I consider my planned flights into space, for example, to carry about the same level of risk as that facing airplane passengers in the early days of aviation, in the 1920s and 30s. The level of risk involved in our Everest Skydive was almost certainly higher.

I am comfortable with levels of risk that I estimate to be in lower single digits – like a 2% chance of something going wrong. When risk gets into double digits, I am less comfortable. Test driving the North American Eagle at higher and higher speeds in order to pass 763 mph and beat the existing land speed record had a higher order of risk – as Jessi Combs' tragic death proved.

I was happy with the way Wimmer Financial was coming out of the financial crisis. Two business strategies had been of critical importance. Number one, on the day after the collapse of Lehman Brothers, I cut costs aggressively to a minimum. Number two, Wimmer Financial had not, thankfully, taken on any external debt.

Those two fairly common-sense moves put us in a situation to get on with business and focus on expansion in the wake of the credit crunch. I had a really good team in place: a senior alternative energy analyst, a senior financial services and insurance analyst, and distribution to Switzerland, France, parts of Germany, the UK and Scandinavia. And I continued to look for good people. I was in the process of solidifying the business, including taking on a long-term office lease to ensure stability on that front. The good news was that it was the best time to negotiate long-term lease agreements. There was a lot of office space available in London, and tenants had the bargaining power. Office rents were down 30–40% from their peak.

People from outside the financial services industry often asked me with concern whether we were doing OK. My answer? "The conditions for a financial services entrepreneur could simply not get any better!"

There was a lot of truly great talent available because of the drastic layoffs of personnel by the larger investment banks, and because many quality staff had simply quit as the outlook for good bonuses looked bleak. The London office space market was exceptionally low, as I say. And, importantly, from May 2009, business opportunities picked up dramatically. Companies around the world were trying to recapitalize their balance sheets and get back to business now that the worst was felt to be over. Investor appetite was returning. I knew, sooner or later, one of those elements was going to have to give. But until then, the fun factor was really high, provided we could manage peak workflow volumes. It was hard work – not in the sense of being any more difficult than usual, simply in terms of the long hours we all had to put in.

In November came one of my highlights of 2009: a trip to Los Angeles for the unveiling of Virgin Galactic's SpaceShipTwo. It was going to be an exciting few days.

After closing an alternative energy deal and completing a global roadshow for an Australian mining company, I boarded my flight to LAX. Richard Branson's mother, Eve, was on the same flight, as was Virgin Galactic CEO Will Whitehorn and a number of fellow Virgin Galactic astronauts. I had never met Eve Branson before; little did I know that we would become close friends.

I was picked up at the airport by Nick Baggarly, an LA-based fellow adventurer with whom I was planning an eco-adventure to the South Pole using biofuel-converted Hummers. Nick drove me straight to SpaceX, which had a site near LA, as well as sites in Texas and Florida. I had been meaning to visit for a while, so I was glad the opportunity arose. We were given an overview presentation about SpaceX's activities and shown video clips of their three locations. I knew from following the news that SpaceX, founded by Elon Musk in 2002, was making good progress, but I was very impressed by what I saw. The size and efficiency of the operation were impressive. Visiting the factory floor where the rocket components are produced and assembled was more like going to a dental clinic than a manufacturing site. Everything was exceptionally clean and tidy, each area carefully marked for its part in the overall production. Overhead, trolley cranes could carry pieces of practically any size and weight to wherever they were needed in the factory. At the entrance, the influence of Elon's dot.com days was evident: free coffee, chocolate, crisps and soft drinks. The office environment is very open, including an open-door policy for Elon's office. SpaceX has been very successful in attracting US government grants, NASA contracts and, most importantly, commercial space business. Elon was clearly heading places with this operation – into orbit, to be precise! In 2009, it looked like he was very much on track to get there. I was then taken from the future of space travel to its past history: Nick and I visited Downey Studios, the famous movie studios that had once been the manufacturing site of the Apollo rockets. We were lucky enough to be given a private tour by John, the operations manager.

He took us first to the hall where the movie, *Indiana Jones and the Kingdom of the Crystal Skull*, was shot. Many other famous movies had been produced there, including scenes featuring Arnold Schwarzenegger in *The Terminator*. Then John took us to the actual manufacturing site of the Apollo rockets. These old buildings suddenly took on a whole new meaning. A nonprofit organization had been formed to preserve as much as possible of the site, and significant amounts of industrial memorabilia had been collected. One of the engineers of the Apollo era treated us to some wonderful stories, told with great pride. We told him about our morning at SpaceX, and he was very keen to highlight how lessons learned from Apollo had influenced the SpaceX Dragon capsule.

My last stop of the day was a Zero South meeting with Nick at Downey Studios, where the main agenda topic was the construction of fuel cell batteries and how to optimize performance. We sat around a lit-up globe table, left behind from a movie shoot. I was impressed by the detailed planning and engineering expertise. However, the vehicle still needed a lot of work and the second vehicle had not yet been built. There was still a way to go before the trip in December 2010. Nick and I went out for sushi in the evening. I was so tired from the excitement of the day that I almost fell asleep eating.

The next morning the weather was terrible. From my room at the Four Seasons in Beverly Hills, all I could see was rain and clouds. Today was the day for future Virgin Galactic astronauts to witness the unveiling of the spaceship that would take us into space: SpaceShipTwo VSS *Enterprise* and its mothership WhiteKnightTwo VMS *Eve*. Richard Branson and the team would be presenting the new spaceship to the world. I talked to fellow astronauts from around the world while we waited for the bus to take us to the spaceport. Among the people milling around were Richard's kids, Holly and Sam, as well as Princess Beatrice and her then-boyfriend, Virgin Galactic's David Clark.

The bus journey to the Mojave Air and Space Port was over two hours long and the weather showed no signs of improving. But the arrival was still spectacular. We arrived in a cortege of five luxury American buses, passing massive Virgin Galactic logos as we cruised down the runway toward a large purpose-built village of inflatable tents. The first tent was kitted out in a space theme. Coffee and canapés were served while we all chatted and caught up. Then we were all ushered outside onto the spaceport's runway, where we joined a crowd of around 800 guests, including 300 journalists. Richard's car arrived on the runway – and the cameras started flashing madly as he stepped out to greet the waiting crowd. Then all 800 heads turned as five black four-by-fours came powering down the runway, like a presidential convoy. It was the 'Governator' himself: California's then-governor, Arnold Schwarzenegger. The photographers went crazy as he and Richard entered the press conference tent with Bill Richardson, Governor of New Mexico. We all followed.

The press conference was underway. Speakers praised the commitment and engineering capabilities of the project in its historic context. This was the world's first privately made rocketship, which would soon be ready to take private passengers to space. Schwarzenegger gave an excellent and funny presentation, emphasizing California's leading role in aerospace, teasing Bill Richardson by claiming that they had "thrown a few crumbs" to New Mexico – because Virgin Galactic would be moving from the Mojave Air and Space Port to the new Spaceport America in New Mexico. He also contrasted his children's excitement with his career as an actor with their boredom at the bureaucratic business of governing – except on days like today, when he was unveiling a California-built spaceship. That was cool! He ended his speech, naturally, with his classic: "I'll be back ..."

There were a series of presentations from Richard, Will Whitehorn, Bill Richardson and Scaled Composites engineer Burt Rutan, designer of SpaceShipOne, as well as Virgin Galactic's commercial director, Stephen Attenborough. Then the big moment arrived: the unveiling of the new spacecraft.

The winds had picked up in the desert. Outside on the runway it was now freezing cold. Luckily, free Virgin Galactic jackets had been thoughtfully provided. Most people, myself included, had arrived dressed for warm desert weather, so we were very grateful when the jackets were handed out!

This was the moment we had all flown in for. SpaceShipTwo, suspended beneath mothership WhiteKnightTwo, came rolling gracefully onto the dark runway. BANG. Giant floodlights burst into life and lit up the runway with dazzling light. Stirring music boomed from loudspeakers. Wow! There was the spaceship! Virgin had really gone all out for this occasion. Many people shed a tear. It was all very emotional and exciting – enough to make us forget the cold. I was overwhelmed by the beauty and presence of the spacecraft.

For me, personally, this moment had particular significance. For almost 10 years – longer than any of my fellow astronauts – I had been signed up for a flight in this spaceship. I had seen endless presentations and computer graphics of spaceship plans and witnessed the test flight of SpaceShipOne. Now, it was real. Houston, we have a spaceship! That moment was truly historic – and brought me one step closer to going into space. I was trained, and we had the ship that would fly me to space. Surely nothing could stop us now. I felt like climbing on board and jetting off to space right then and there.

The wind bit into our bones. My fingers were so cold that after I had taken a few photos, I was having trouble pressing the camera shutter again. It was soon time to get back to the relative warmth of the tent. No Virgin launch would be complete without a party. Buffet-style food, an Absolut vodka ice bar, an ice sculpture of an Apollo astronaut shipped from Sweden's Ice Hotel, a DJ and a great atmosphere. There was lots of excitement about what we had just witnessed. Suddenly, loudspeakers announced that a storm was coming toward us very fast. "Leave the tent *immediately*. Do not stop to collect your belongings."

Panic! We rushed back to the buses. Within two minutes of making it to the warmth and safety of our buses, the entire tent, which moments before contained 800 people, went flying off into the air, torn off its moorings by incredibly strong winds. Steel frames and plastic cloth were swept away in spectacular fashion.

Thankfully they had evacuated everyone. It is rare that the weather in Mojave is as bad as that. It was a dramatic end to an historic day. We all had a lot to reflect on – and look forward to – as we drove slowly back to the Four Seasons in LA.

———————

Before Christmas, everything had been going so right.

Business was thriving. Wimmer Financial was getting good traction with some new corporate clients. An important energy deal had been closed just in time. I had managed to build a strong team, creating a solid platform from which to grow the business. In the office property slump, I had managed to secure an amazing space in Mayfair for a good price, giving us plenty of room without affecting our fixed costs base too much.

The appetite of the global markets had also returned strongly – possibly too soon, in my opinion. The only concern of investors was to get back on the wagon and not miss out.

I had worked very hard to get Wimmer Financial through the crisis and the outlook was very good. On a personal level, Vicky and I had moved from Islington to Knightsbridge SW1X, one of London's most prestigious postcodes. I was actually quite happy in my old Islington apartment, but Vicky was adamant. Islington was not glamorous enough. It had to be Knightsbridge! The move was a formidable effort, given how much stuff I had, so it took a lot of packing, transporting, unpacking and rearranging before everything was finally in place.

I was still head over heels in love with Vicky. Some of her lifestyle and personal issues and challenges had been – to a large degree – sorted out, not at least due to my tireless efforts and encouragements. She seemed more at ease, less on edge. She had stopped smoking and was no longer taking antidepressants. She had restarted her high school studies and seemed happier in herself. For the first time in a very long time, I was seriously contemplating long-term plans and our future together. We had a wonderful Christmas together with my family, followed by a romantic 10-day skiing holiday in a family-run chalet in the French Alps.

Everything was coming together. I thought of myself as one of those super lucky people who had it all. It would have been fun to have more time and energy for socializing, but my business and adventures felt like holidays to me – as did something as simple as feeding the ducks in Hyde Park with Vicky. It all felt so good. In early February, I was on my way back to London from a long day of roadshowing in Denmark, trying to make my way through Gatwick Airport, when my phone rang. It was Vicky, calling from Stockholm.

"We need to talk."

She was thinking about breaking up. It came like lightning from a clear blue sky. I was in a state of shock.

I was so taken aback, I didn't know how to react. All I could do was try to understand her reasoning and find out how deep this feeling was. It wasn't until later that it sunk in. I was devastated. I had planned a romantic early Valentine's Day for the following week, watching Cirque du Soleil at the Royal Albert Hall, followed by a meal in a cosy French restaurant. And now she was talking about breaking up.

I didn't know what to do. I was lost.

That Friday, I got on a plane to Stockholm. I needed to see her. I hadn't told her I was coming. I tried to call her the night before, but she didn't answer. She was due to fly to London the following Wednesday, but I couldn't wait that long to talk things through. I couldn't hold back the tears. I felt like my heart had been cut open and was bleeding all over the plane. It hurt so much, and I couldn't make it stop. My throat was sore. I didn't have a cold or the flu, but my throat hurt whenever I swallowed. I felt awful.

I had lost my passion, my 'mojo.' My excitement for building my business, for getting deals done, just wasn't there. Saving our relationship was all that mattered. Everything else felt unimportant. I couldn't think about anything else but being with Vicky and trying to save our relationship. I couldn't afford to lose her. I didn't want to lose her. I must win her back. Immediately! The plane was too slow getting to Stockholm. If she stays in Stockholm, I thought, it won't be long before she finds someone else. She's a social person and had lots of friends there. Someone as beautiful as Vicky would not stay alone for very long. I knew that if I didn't manage to get her back now, the relationship would be lost forever. And I would never find somebody as perfect for me as her.

I tried to stop crying, but the thought of the breakup was too painful. Love hurts.

I wondered how she would react to my unexpected arrival. If she had other things planned, I would wait. My flight back wasn't until Sunday, so I would have the whole weekend to make my case. I arrived at her place and rang the bell. She was visibly shocked to see me standing at the door. She didn't know what to do. Her friend Louise was on her way over, and they had plans for an evening out together. Vicky seemed annoyed that I had disrupted their plans. But after having flown there from London just to see her, she couldn't exactly throw me out. She invited me in.

Things were a bit awkward when Louise arrived, but I managed to lighten the atmosphere with some friendly chatter about some nonsense or other, and they invited me to join them for the evening: a glass of champagne and then dinner at restaurant Rouge and an after-party at Bern's Hotel in Stockholm until the early hours of the next morning. We managed to have fun. Vicky was animated, but I couldn't read her mood. That night, I slept on the sofa while Vicky and Louise shared the bed. The next day, we travelled to Vicky's father's house in Sollentuna, just north of Stockholm, because he was away and she had promised to look after his cat. The house was surrounded by forests and lakes. It turned out to be the perfect opportunity for a long walk and a chance to talk things through. I needed to understand what had changed.

To the great sadness of my fragile heart, I discovered that she was running away from our more 'normal' life in London. There had been some disagreements, it was true. They had seemed like the kind of minor issues faced by any new couple who have moved in together for the first time. But our lifestyle in London was not making her happy. In Stockholm, she was a top model, a red-carpet celebrity. In London, she felt like a housewife, cooking and waiting for me to come home. She was not ready to give up her glamorous lifestyle in Sweden to be with me in London.

I could feel it and sense it and her words were like a knife cutting through my flesh. It really hurt. I could not believe this was happening. She tried to put on an icy face to communicate her feelings loud and clear. But gradually she started to thaw, as the evening got colder and the long winter's night set in. When we got back to the apartment, I cried again. We had some dinner and cuddled up to watch some movies together. The next morning, we slept in late. It was wonderful and cosy. When we finally got up, we went for a long walk to have lunch with her grandmother, who is such a lovely person. On the surface, everything looked normal. But it felt different. As Vicky petted and hugged her grandmother's cat, I suddenly felt hurt and jealous. I felt she was showing more love and affection to the cat than she was to me, her supposed partner. I returned to London feeling empty and confused. I wasn't sure what would happen next.

Vicky was flying back into London on Wednesday. We agreed to talk further and, bizarrely perhaps, to go ahead with our plans for Valentine's Day on Sunday, with a Cirque du Soleil performance and dinner at a romantic French restaurant afterwards. What had felt so good and seemed so natural before, something looked forward to with such excitement, suddenly felt empty, bland and directionless.

If things were truly finished, then a long road of healing my broken heart was about to begin. When that had happened once before in my life, the process had been a long and painful one. I am slow to give my heart to anyone; it seems I am slow to heal when things go wrong. I kept wondering if we could get back together and try again, but so much emotional damage had already been done and so much emotional trust broken. Could I trust her not to break my heart all over again? All my visions of a happy future together had crumbled into dust. The future looked bleak and meaningless. This was awful!

A month later, Vicky arrived in London with her mum. At the end of a long working week, I took her out for dinner. It was great to see her again: she was full of energy, in good spirits and more confident. We laughed, we joked and, for a moment, the passion seemed to be back. Our chemistry reminded me of that first night we met, at the awards ceremony in the Hilton in Copenhagen. But at the end of dinner, she dealt me one last devastating blow. She was only in London to pack up her things. She was moving back to Stockholm. Our final goodbyes were very painful. It was only once she had left that it really sunk in.

This really was the end. It was over.

———————

In the coming years I would recover from my heartbreak over Vicky, visit Richard Branson on Necker Island and do my share of partying in St Tropez and St Barts. I would launch a new business, live through a family tragedy and go undercover once again as a "secret millionaire"—this time in South Wales. I would fall in love again and get ready for my trip into space.

I hope you will join me for the next rollercoaster ride through my amazing life.

Watch out for *Beyond The Sky*, the next volume of my autobiography, to be published in 2023.

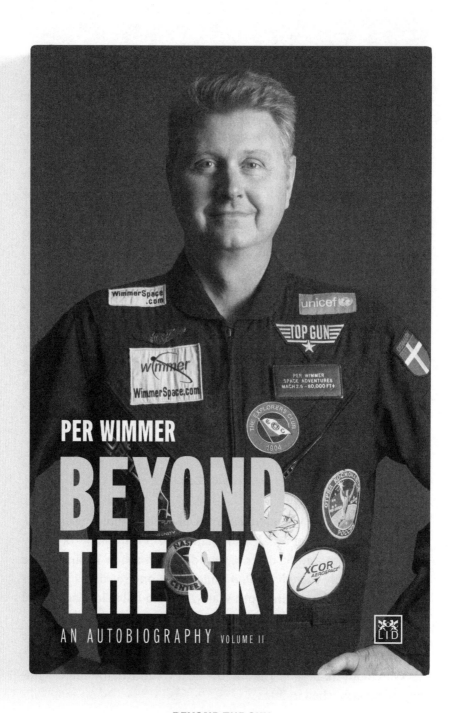

PER WIMMER

BEYOND THE SKY

AN AUTOBIOGRAPHY VOLUME II

BEYOND THE SKY
ISBN: 978-1-911687-72-6
ISBB: 978-1-911687-73-3 (ebook)

ABOUT PER WIMMER

Per Wimmer is an astronaut, adventurer, explorer, philanthropist, entrepreneur, global financier, author and private island owner (WimmerIsland.com). His story is about making dreams a reality – not simply for himself but also to inspire children around the world to live out their dreams, whatever they may be. He is a person who has packed three lives into one: "A true Indiana Jones meets James Bond 007," as one commentator said.

Per has lived with an indigenous family in the Amazonian rainforest; been involved in a world land speed record attempt, driving a modified F-104 Starfighter Jet in the Black Rock Desert, Nevada; visited the remote Easter Islands; been diving in the Galápagos Islands; trekked the Inca Trail to Machu Picchu; skied the highest ski slope in the world in Bolivia; been hang-gliding over the beaches of Rio de Janeiro; ridden across the USA and back on a Harley Davidson motorbike and been diving with sharks in Fiji. In March 2022, Per had his own "Top Gun" experience, flying out into the Pacific Ocean on a C2 Greyhound US Navy plane before landing on and doing a catapult take-off from the aircraft carrier USS Nimitz.

In 2005, Per became a Founding Astronaut for Sir Richard Branson's spaceflight company, Virgin Galactic. He will travel into space on one of the first commercial suborbital rocket space flights following the test voyages of Virgin Galactic's SpaceShipTwo, VSS *Unity*.

Per has successfully completed his space training, flying a Russian MiG-25 over Siberia at an altitude of 80,000 feet and three times the speed of sound, passing medical exams and carrying out space launch simulations in both Russian and American centrifuges. In 2022, Per and Apollo 16 astronaut and Lunar Module pilot, Charlie Duke, became weightless together in a Boing 727 on a zero-G flight out of Kennedy Space Centre as part of his training. Per is a brand ambassador of the Swiss watchmaker Fortis; together they produced the WimmerSpace Fortis Watch – a watch specially designed for Per's trip to space.

Per is passionate about private space travel and is a well-respected member of the international space and adventure community. He is a Fellow of the New York Explorer's Club, a Companion Member of the Royal Aeronautic Society and an Honorary Advisory Board Member of the Scientific Exploration Society. He is a friend of Apollo 11 moonwalker astronaut Buzz Aldrin, and was the first founding member of Aldrin's educational ShareSpace Foundation.

In 2008, Per and Ralph Mitchell successfully completed the world's first tandem sky dive over Mount Everest. After six days of trekking in the Himalayas, Per and Ralph flew to an altitude of around 9,000 metres above Mount Everest. They jumped in temperatures of -50C and free-fell for 60 seconds before opening the parachute and landing at the drop zone near Syangboche Airport, at an altitude of 4,000 metres. Pushing the boundaries, helping to write the manual (as opposed to following one), exploring, discovering, being a pioneer, carrying out first time adventures with fellow adventurers and deploying and acquiring education in a wider sense are what drive Per.

Per owns and runs his own investment bank, Wimmer Financial, which he founded on the 50th anniversary of Sputnik Day, 4 October 2007. The bank specializes in finance for global real estate, natural resources (mining, oil and gas, green energy), industrials and other hard asset areas. In 2020, Wimmer Financial won the Real Estate Investment Bank of the Year at the REFI Awards, ahead of UBS, Credit Suisse and BNP.

Per also owns and runs Wimmer Family Office (WFO), an investment management company. WFO won the Top Hedge Fund Manager award at the 2017 Institutional Asset Management Awards.

In 2019, WFO won the Best Family Office award at the International Investment Awards, London, and was also nominated Best International Discretionary Fund Manager. Per was additionally nominated as Personality of the Year. In 2018, Per also took an ownership stake in what is now Wimmer Horizon, an award-winning quantitative hedge fund, where Per achieved a significant turnaround from loss-making to substantial profit, and with more than 50 percent net performance to investors by the time he exited at the end of 2022. In October 2022, Per launched his latest venture, Wimmer Accounting.

Over the years, Per's WimmerSpace organization has supported many charities through long-term school programs in the UK and Denmark and on an ad hoc basis. Every new adventure Per undertakes must involve a local or other relevant charity to achieve the WimmerSpace mission of supporting charitable needs and inspiring children to live out their dreams. His 2008 skydive over Everest, for example, raised money for orphanages in Nepal via UNICEF and the Global Angels Foundation. In 2007, Per was bowling for charity with Natalie Imbruglia against Kylie Minogue and Sir Richard Branson in London. The activities of WimmerSpace also include motivational speaking for schools, charities and corporates based on the Seven Wimmer Fundamental Values.

Per has published three books to date under his own name. These include his book, written in French, about the future of European integration, *Vers une Europe à la Carte après Maastricht*; a book about bubbles in financial markets, *Wall Street*; and another about the future of green energy, *The Green Bubble*, published in Swedish, Danish and English. Per has also contributed to a number of books, including *Realizing Tomorrow: The Path to Private Spaceflight*.

Per is a regular commentator on space travel on Sky News TV and was previously a newspaper reviewer for BBC World. In July 2019, Per Wimmer featured on BBC World's "The Travel Show" in a broadcast marking the 50th anniversary of Apollo 11 and exploring the future of space travel. He has been the subject of episodes of the TV documentaries, "The Secret Millionaire" and "Undercover Angel", going incognito in poor communities and choosing the most effective and deserving charitable causes before revealing his identity and giving financial support. He contributed to the documentary film

"Elon Musk: The Real Life Iron Man". In 2018, Per featured on the front page of the *Financial Times* with the headline, "The Ultimate High Flyers."

Prior to founding Wimmer Financial, Per advised on equities at the MAN Group/Man Securities. Before that, he worked at Collins Stewart (now Canaccord) in a similar capacity, having previously worked for Goldman Sachs in New York and London, leaving the company as Executive Director for Institutional Sales of European Equity, advising Scandinavian-based financial institutions on investments.

In 1998, Per graduated with an MPA-2 (Master in Public Administration) from Harvard University, Kennedy School, with classes in business, finance and international relations. He received the Don K. Price Award for academic excellence, community contributions and potential leadership. Per also has an MA in European political science from the College of Europe in Bruges; an LLM Master of Law degree from the University of London, and a BA and MA in Law from the University of Copenhagen, where he was awarded the Academic Silver Medal, presented by HM Queen Margaret II of Denmark, for "an outstanding legal and political analysis of the protection of fundamental rights in the European Union." Following his degree at the College of Europe, Per worked in the cabinet of the Vice-President of the European Union.

Per's sporting activities include scuba diving, tennis, squash, badminton, handball, swimming and jogging. He is fluent in French, English and Danish and can get by in Spanish and German.

Top: Moving from Harvard to New York, August 1998.

Second row left: Arriving in stretched limo for interview at Goldman Sachs, New York, 1998.

Third row left: In my apartment at Battery Park, Manhattan Island, New York.

Bottom left: First day at Goldman Sachs: security registration and fingerprints, August 1998.

Bottom right: On Wall Street, day one, August 1998.

With Goldman Sachs on a visit to the New York Mercantile Exchange (NYMEX) trading floor, September 1998.

Flying Concorde London to New York – 3 hr 20m.

Bottom right: On the Goldman Sachs trading floor in London, 1999.

In 2001, after buying a ticket to space with Space Adventures, I was invited by them to Baikonur Cosmodrome in Kazakhstan to take part in space training sessions and witness the launch of the Soyuz rocket taking Dennis Tito, the world's first private astronaut, to the International Space Station.

Top left: In front of a Russian Ilyushin IL-76 freighter ahead of a zero-G space training session.

Top right: At Baikonur Cosmodrome in Kazakhstan, 2001, to see the first private astronaut, Dennis Tito, make his historic flight into space (see following pages).

Middle: With the Russian space shuttle Buran, which made one unmanned flight in 1988 and was destroyed in 2002 when its storage hangar collapsed.

Bottom: Ready to experience zero-G in the Ilyushin IL-76.

Top: Boarding the Ilyushin IL-76 for the zero-G training session.

Second from top: On the launchpad of the Soyuz TM-32 mission with Dennis Tito's family before his flight into space on April 28 2001.

Bottom left: The Buran space shuttle in its current hangar.

Bottom right: Tito with his fellow astronauts before launch.

Above: Lift off!

As part of my space training, I travelled to Zhukovsky Air Base, a major aircraft testing site for the Soviet Union during the Cold War. I flew in a MiG-25 fighter jet at 80,000 feet and Mach 3 (three times the speed of sound) and experienced high speed acrobatic manoeuvres in an L-39 Albatros jet trainer.

This page: Getting ready to fly in the MiG-25.

Opposite top left: At the edge of space in the MiG-25. At 80,000 feet, the curvature of the earth is visible. The sky above turns to the black of space.

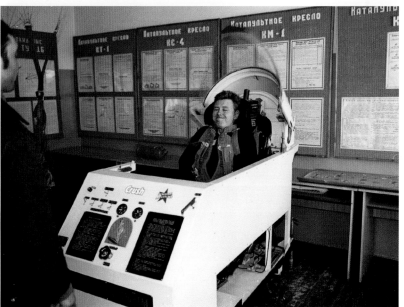

Top left: I signed up as the first European for a private ticket to space with Space Adventures in March 2001. Seen here in my flight suit with a model of the MiG-25 fighter jet I was about to fly in as part of my space training program (see previous pages).

Top right: MiG-25 cockpit.

Middle and above: Ejection training before flying MiG-25.

Mojave Air and Space Port October 4 2004: SpaceShipOne wins the Ansari X Prize for the first commercial manned spacecraft to enter space twice within a period of two weeks. I commented live for BBC World TV on the award-winning second flight.

Middle right: SpaceShipOne with its mother ship, WhiteKnightOne, in the background.

Travelling in Cambodia and China, 2005.

Top left: Arriving at Phnom Penh airport, Cambodia.

Top right and second row left: The Angkor Wat temple complex in north-western Cambodia.

Third row right: With Michel Ghigo, my flatmate from my high school days in Menton, France, who settled in Cambodia with his family and set up a successful Cambodian version of 'Yellow Pages', the business telephone directory.

Bottom right: On the Great Wall of China.

Recording 'Wimmersvej' ('Wimmer's Way'), sung to the tune of 'The Lion Sleeps Tonight' at PUK Studios with the Danish band, Bamses Venner, 2006.

Below: Presenting cheques to the chosen recipients as part of Denmark's TV 2 Den hemmelige millionær (The Secret Millionaire), 2007 .

Top left: Wimmer Financial was launched on 4 October 2007, the 50th anniversary of the launch of Sputnik, the world's first artificial satellite.

Top right: Outside the Science Museum, New York. I am a Fellow of the prestigious New York Explorers' Club, which is dedicated to advancing exploration and scientific inquiry.

Second row left: Second row left: Me in front of the mothership "Eve", named after Richard Branson's mother, at the launch at the Mojave Air and Space Port in 2009.

Second row right: Me with model of mother ship WhiteKnightTwo (VMS Eve) and SpaceShipTwo (VSS Unity) at a Virgin Galactic presentation in New York. Jan 28 2008, New York.

Third row: With Richard Branson, founder of the Virgin Group.

Bottom: Photo with Buzz Aldrin from my interview of him in Paris in June 2007.

Top row: Trekking in the Himalayas on the way to Syangboche (altitude 3,764 metres), the departure point and the drop zone for my record-breaking skydive over Everest.

Second row left: With the monks at the monastery of Tengboche.

At Syangboche preparing for the skydive.

Bottom right: The flight path for the jump.

Above: On board and ready to go!

Opposite page
On 6 October 2008, Ralph Mitchell and I completed the world's first tandem skydive from above Mount Everest, jumping from an altitude of around 9,000 metres at a temperature of around -50°c.

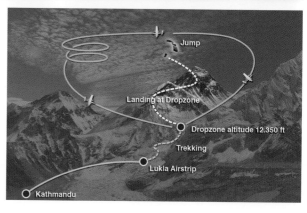

Jump

Landing at Dropzone

Dropzone altitude 12,350 ft

Trekking

Lukla Airstrip

Kathmandu

Top: At NASA

Second row. (Left) Signing autographs for excited school children. A core mission of WimmerSpace is to inspire today's children to live out their dreams, whatever they may be. (Right) Delivering a WimmerSpace inspirational corporate presentation for senior European executives of Sony in Barcelona, Spain.

Third row. With aerospace engineer Burt Rutan (left), designer of SpaceShipOne, and Greg Olsen (right) entrepreneur and third ever private astronaut.

Bottom row. With Buzz Aldrin, pilot of the lunar Module Eagle for the 1969 Apollo 11 mission and, with Neil Armstrong, one of the first two people on the Moon. I'm proud to be a friend of Buzz and one of the initial supporters of his ShareSpace educational foundation.

Test driving the North American Eagle jet-powered car at Black Rock Desert, Nevada, in preparation for an attempt on the world land speed record.

The North American Eagle was constructed from the remains of an old Lockheed F-104 Starfighter jet found in a junkyard in Massachusetts by Ed Shadle, team leader of the world record attempt.

After my involvement in the project, another attempt on the world record was made with driver Jessi Combs. The North American Eagle crashed during this attempt, killing Combs. She set a new world record for a woman driver during the fatal attempt, reaching over 522 mph.

Top row: Vicky on a modelling assignment; Vicky and me.

Second row: With Richard Branson and VMS Eve, the mothership of SpaceShipTwo, at the unveiling at the Mojave Air and Space Port, 2009.

Third row: Training for my coming journey to space.

Bottom left: My third ticket to space as First Astronaut for XCOR Aerospace's Lynx Suborbital programme, December 2008. XCOR filed for bankruptcy in 2017 without completing their space programme.

Bottom right: With astronaut Richard Searfoss, pilot of the US Space Shuttle Colombia and the XCOR Lynx.